The
NORTH BERWICK
AND
GULLANE BRANCH LINES

by
Andrew M. Hajducki

THE OAKWOOD PRESS

ISBN 0 85361 427 X

To my wife Gayle and to our children Catherine, Kenneth and David, to all of whom the North Berwick line often meant a day at the seaside.

Typeset by Gem Publishing Company, Brightwell, Wallingford, Oxfordshire.

Printed by Alpha Print (Oxon) Ltd, Crawley, Witney, Oxfordshire.

North Berwick Harbour and the Law.

Published by
The OAKWOOD PRESS
P.O.Box 122, Headington, Oxford.

Contents

The Dandy Car seen in action on the Port Carlisle line – this quaint vehicle operated the North Berwick branch passenger service during the winter of 1856–7; those unfortunate enough to be travelling third-class were seated on the outside of the car and exposed to the harsh realities of the East Lothian climate.

Introduction

Edinburgh is, indeed, a fortunate city for it possesses both virtues of its own in abundance as well as having on its very doorstep, a stretch of largely unspoiled and picturesque coastline with sandy beaches, rocky and romantic islands and an ever-changing panorama of the sea and sky against the backdrop of the beautiful East Lothian countryside. Views of this entrancing land can be had from the busy A1 road and from the Kings Cross main line both of which pass only a few miles to the South and, for rail travellers, there is a bonus of a brief glimpse of the single track branch line which sweeps away from the junction at Drem to the coast at the pleasant little seaside town of North Berwick.

This present book is an attempt, for the first time, to recount the history of that line together with its near neighbour, the Aberlady and Gullane branch. Although at first sight these two lines may appear to be little more than insignificant rural outposts of the mighty North British Railway, there is much of interest in the story of one of these branches which survived against the odds to become, uniquely, the only line in Britain to have had its normal passenger service worked, at different times, by steam, horse, diesel and electric power. The other line which was independent, was born out of high hopes and yet arrived too late to compete with the motor vehicle and changing fashions.

Much of this story will, the author hopes, be of interest not only to those who enjoy the history of the once vast network of minor railways which covered the map of Britain like a spider's web, but also to those who live in or like this favoured part of Scotland. The account of how these two railways came to be built and operated, the goods which they carried, and the countless commuters, golfers, holidaymakers and countryfolk who enjoyed, to a greater or lesser extent, their facilities reveals an important but hitherto neglected part of the story of the local communities which these lines faithfully but unspectacularly served. To many, aspects of the tale are already familiar and indeed there are still those who remember the slow steam trains which meandered to Aberlady and Gullane along a winding course, the busy Bank Holidays at North Berwick Station when every siding was full of 'specials' and the town was host for the day to numerous families, the sight of the majestic Lothian Coast Express which conveyed through coaches and even a restaurant car from North Berwick and Gullane to Glasgow and perhaps even the obscure and now almost forgotten narrow gauge line to West Fenton which enjoyed a brief and undocumented existence. To others the lines may mean little other than country roads crossing an abandoned trackbed or, more positively, a convenient hourly means of getting to Edinburgh which is seldom noticed and rarely commented upon other than to expose its imagined deficiencies.

To all of these readers the author hopes that this book will answer questions, provide enlightenment and, perhaps, open up the rich vein of nostalgia which the seaside branch line occupies in the popular imagination. Lastly, there may well be those to whom East Lothian is unfamiliar

The station master at Gullane waits personally on two gentlemen golfers returning home. It is August 1914 and the newspapers on sale at the 'cubbyhole' are no doubt assuring the villagers that the War will be over by Christmas.

W.F. Jackson, Glasgow University Archives

A post-war postcard view of the beach at North Berwick with holidaymakers who may well have arrived on the train. Behind the yacht is the harbour entrance and grain warehouse and had the branch been built to its original plans the railway would have formed a sea wall following the shore, in a wide sweep towards a harbour terminus.

Oakwood Collection

and its railways even less so, and for these fortunate persons (for they still have a pleasant discovery to make), the author can only wish that his efforts may inspire them to refer to what is currently Table 238 of the British Rail timetable and to make their own plans for a journey on the still flourishing branch line from Drem to the Biarritz of the North.

Edinburgh,
March 1992.   Andrew M. Hajducki

A Cautionary Note

For the unwary there are perhaps a number of caveats which should be given. Haddingtonshire is the old name, and East Lothian the new name of the former County and local government District in which the two branch lines are situated and for many years these names were virtually interchangeable. Secondly, the pronunciation of Gullane is variable and (to some) a matter of controversy and although those who arrived in third class carriages would have referred to the village in much the same way as it is spelt, i.e. 'Gullan', the more affected first class passenger would no doubt have booked to 'Gillan'; the author offers no guidance here! Finally, a warning against the logic which dictates that in the Lothians one would normally think of travelling 'up' to Edinburgh and 'down' to the coast; the railways, like the telegraph poles, always lead to London. To avoid confusion the General Manager of the North British Railway issued a Circular in the following terms:

> The staff is informed that, on and after 1st January, 1868, all Trains on the North British system going *Southwards* will be designated *Up Trains* and all those proceeding *Northwards* will be called *Down Trains*. The timetables will be prepared accordingly.

All the reader has to remember, therefore, is that although the trains to Gullane and North Berwick ran in a northwards direction from their respective junctions, they were, of course deemed to be *Southbound* and therefore *Up* Trains (and vice versa)!

Seabathers at Gullane beach at the turn of the century.   *Oakwood Collection*

The *raison d'etre* of the Aberlady and Gullane branch – golf! – a scene at Goose Green, Gullane, c.1900.

Oakwood Collection

The Post Office at Drem, 1991. This building, in the typical East Lothian vernacular style, replaced the original post office, the opening of which coincided with that of the North Berwick branch line. *Author*

A view over North Berwick and the Bass Rock from the station in 1900 – the harbour extension would have run straight across the middle of this scene. *Author*

Chapter One

The Links of Gold

THE NORTH HADDINGTONSHIRE COAST BEFORE THE COMING OF THE RAILWAY

'The firth, the rocky isles, the low trap hills to landward . . . comprise enough of scenery to give very pleasing exercise to the imagination.'

The Scotsman, 9th October, 1902

As the Forth majestically completes its sweep into the cold German Ocean, its southern shore, fringed by a series of sand dunes, grassy links and marram-backed beaches, is dominated by the oddly-shaped conical hill of the North Berwick Law which rises to a height of 613 feet and from whose summit wide views over the flat coastal plain of East Lothian are provided. Beyond this coastline lies the rich and fertile farmlands of the Vales of Tyne and Peffer, which once gave the area the reputation of being both the 'Garden of Scotland' and the 'Granary of the Lothians'. Through these favoured fields the sluggish and meandering Peffer Burn makes its way to the sea at Aberlady, a small village bearing a Celtic name, a venerable church and a collection of pantiled cottages which form a backdrop to the seemingly endless mudflats of the bay that takes its name. Once the port for the county town of Haddington, some five miles distant, Aberlady had by the middle of the nineteenth century sunk into such a picturesque and peaceful obscurity that it could be described by a contemporary source as being 'one long street of good appearance . . . [the] occasional resort of sea-bathers from Haddington'.

To the east of Aberlady lay the parish of Dirleton and the first habitation to be encountered was the small village of Gullane, nestling beside the strange and imposing sandhills which rise up there to form, in effect, a miniature mountain range. Like Aberlady, Gullane too was a quiet place where little appeared to be happening and it showed few signs of the dramatic re-awakening which it would undergo at the end of the century. Beyond Gullane the coastline became wilder, and offshore were rocks, skerries and the islands of Fidra and Craigleith, while inland lay the village of Dirlington or, more commonly, Dirleton where a small group of houses was prettily arranged around a green overshadowed by a romantic ruined castle and, in all, having rather more of an English than a Scots aspect. Past the village, the coastline provided the setting for several of Robert Louis Stevenson's tales and indeed the small hill at Yellow Craig was reputed to have been the original of Spyglass Hill in 'Treasure Island'; the surrounding area features in 'The Pavilion on the Links' and 'The Lantern Bearers', and in 'Catriona' his hero, David Balfour, describes the scene thus

> From North Berwick West to Gillane Ness there runs a string of four small islets . . . The shore in face of these islets is altogether waste. Here is no dwelling of man, and scarce any passage, or at most of vagabond children running at their play. Gillane is a small place on the far side of the Ness, the folk of Dirleton go to their business in the inland fields, and those of North Berwick straight to the sea-fishing from their haven; so that few parts of the coast are lonelier.

9

Virtually the whole of this coastal plain had been lived on since ancient times as several remains, including the Iron Age hill fort on the Law, testified and more than a thousand years ago a settlement existed on the northern point of the plain close to where a sandstone promontory reached out to form a natural harbour. This place was subsequently known as 'Norberwic' – the 'barley village', having the prefix to distinguish it from its more southerly namesake the Scots Burgh of Berwick-upon-Tweed. As time went on, a town grew up here and attained some prominence as an ecclesiastical centre at the southern landfall of the crossing from Earlsferry in Fife on the pilgrims' route to the shrine at St Andrews and in 1373, King Robert II bestowed upon North Berwick the honour of a Royal Burgh charter. Following the Reformation, the town achieved great notoriety as the scene of alleged witchcraft, sorcery and a plot against the King and in the words of the late William Roughead 'North Berwick was deemed a name of fear, and its ancient sea-beaten kirk and graveyard, long the dormitories of the dead, became for the time a very synagogue of Satan and suffered the unquiet walk of devils.'* By the dawn of the nineteenth century, such excitements had been left far behind and North Berwick had become something of a backwater, the whole parish boasting a population of just over fifteen hundred souls and the Burgh consisting of little more than two streets meriting the description given to it a little earlier – 'a small ill-built town on a strand'.

A vivid picture of North Berwick in the era immediately prior to the coming of the railway was provided by the contribution of the then Minister of the Parish to that encyclopaedic and invaluable work *The New Statistical Account of Scotland* who, in 1839, observed that the town had

> . . . a stagecoach to Edinburgh every lawful day which leaves North Berwick at half-past seven in the morning and reaches Edinburgh in three hours and leaves Edinburgh in the afternoon at four. It is conducted with great propriety. Four carriages go to Edinburgh on their respective days, in the course of the week. The turnpike roads, and bridges, and fences, are all in excellent condition; no canal or railroad . . . The harbour is secure and commodious; large sums from time to time having been expended on its enlargement and improvement: and though dry at low water, and somewhat difficult of access, it is considered very safe in consequence of its being a boomed harbour. There has been a considerable decrease of late years in the grain and lime trade but there has been increased traffic in the export of turnips and potatoes, chiefly to the Newcastle and London markets, with imports or rape and oil-cake, crushed bone manure and coal.

After commenting on the very limited extent of the local fishing industry, there is a further mention of coal 'from Bo'ness, the coast of Fife and Newcastle, principally for the use of the inhabitants of the town, at an average price of 14s. [£0.70] per ton for Scotch great coals and 17s. [£0.85] for English.' The landward part of the parish was supplied by road from the East Lothian pits at Pencaitland and Tranent and it was remarked that 'The coals are very costly, and form here a very heavy burden on the industry of the poor man'. A small foundry in the town employed 20 men 'in the manufacturing of steam engines and machines for making tiles according to the patent of the Marquis of Tweeddale', but otherwise the economy was almost entirely agriculturally based.

---

* 'The Witches of North Berwick' in *The Riddle of the Ruthvens and Other Studies*, Edinburgh 1919.

This period was, however, the beginning of a more leisurely age when the rich, at least, were beginning to discover the pleasures of the seaside and North Berwick was in some respects, ideally suited to this purpose being only 22 miles from Edinburgh and possessing a climate where,

> The winter is generally clear and mild; in spring, however, from the prevalence of the Easterly and North-Easterly winds, it is often keenly cold. The geniality of summer and autumn is amply attested in the crowded influx of strangers for the enjoyment of sea-bathing and perambulations among the beautiful scenery around.

Golf, a pursuit which became inexorably linked with the fortunes of the railway lines, was also in its infancy here; in 1832 the North Berwick Golf Club, with its course upon the East Links, was founded, although its principal purpose was little more than to provide recreational facilities for the well-to-do families of East Lothian whose country seats were all within easy driving distance. Of some significance were the contemporary proposals to feu [i.e. to divide into building plots] the southern and elevated portion of the Eastern Links where previously cows had grazed and linen was dried and bleached. These lands, belonging to Sir Hew Dalrymple of Leuchie, were admirably suitable for the building of large villas, 'being well-drained and commanding fine sea views', although the absence of any more efficient means of communication with the capital was to hold back any real development of these lands and the town as a whole, for many years.

This, then, was the country which the North Berwick and Gullane branch line railways would one day serve.

The Links of Gold – Canty Bay North Berwick with the islands of Craigleith and Fidra in the background.   *Author's Collection*

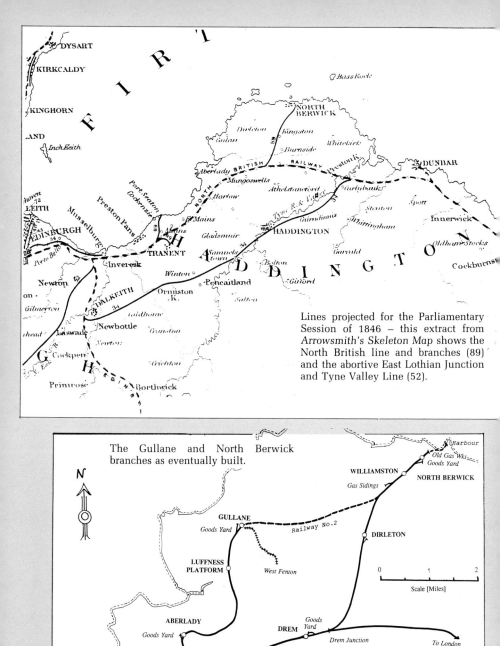

Lines projected for the Parliamentary Session of 1846 – this extract from *Arrowsmith's Skeleton Map* shows the North British line and branches (89) and the abortive East Lothian Junction and Tyne Valley Line (52).

The Gullane and North Berwick branches as eventually built.

THE RAILWAYS OF

NORTH HADDINGTONSHIRE

Chapter Two

James Gowans' Contract

THE PLANNING AND CONSTRUCTION OF THE NORTH BERWICK BRANCH LINE, 1846–1850

'The Committee regret that the Directors should ever have undertaken the formation of the North Berwick branch . . .'

NBR Minutes, 26th July, 1849

The genesis of what was to become the northern section of the main East Coast line from Edinburgh to London occurred in January 1842 when a small group of businessmen met in the former city and put forward proposals for a railway from there to Dunbar, later amending this to extend their line on and across the border to Berwick-upon-Tweed, making a total projected mileage of 57½. They chose as the name of their scheme 'The North British Railway' and in later years this title was to become famous as the company spread its network through a large part of the country and became the largest and possibly the greatest of Scotland's railways in the pre-grouping era.

The promoters of the North British, under the able leadership of an Edinburgh businessman John Learmonth, initially found it difficult to raise the necessary capital for their line, despite the apparent success of the newly opened Edinburgh and Glasgow Railway. But given the contemporary surfeit of railway investment proposals in Scotland, this reluctance to invest was perhaps not surprising and the fact that in the previous year a Royal Commission set up to report on Anglo-Scottish railway proposals had come out in favour of a single grand trunk route via the West Coast would not have added to the attractions of a potential rival. A prospectus was issued by the North British in September 1843 and, in this, Learmonth made it quite clear that it was his intention that the line was to serve as a link in a great East Coast main line between the capitals. Eventually the money was found, partly as a result of much lobbying in England and elsewhere by the company's supporters including George Hudson of York, the ruthless financier and so-called 'Railway King', and the scheme was ready to proceed.

On 8th July, 1844, the North British Railway Company held its first Board Meeting in Edinburgh and John Learmonth was elected as Chairman; four days previously, parliamentary authorisation had been given to the construction of a line by that company from Edinburgh to Berwick, with a short branch line from Longniddry to Haddington. Construction work got off to an early start (on 12th August, 1844) notwithstanding the somewhat haphazard arrangements caused by having 12 separate contractors engaged on the various sections and within two years the scheme had been completed.

The new line followed a course close to that of the Great North Road or London Turnpike (the present A1) and left Edinburgh at a terminus close to the North Bridge, the site of which later formed part of the present Waverley Station. From here the line passed under Calton Hill and then, falling on a 1 in 78 gradient, to St Margarets, (where the locomotive sheds were situated), before following a fairly level course to Portobello (2¼ miles), Joppa (3¼ miles), Musselburgh (later called Inveresk – 6½ miles), Tranent (later called Prestonpans – 9½ miles), Longniddry (otherwise Longniddrey – 13 miles), Ballencrieff (16 miles), Drem (17¾ miles) and from there onwards to East Fortune, East Linton, Dunbar and Berwick-upon-Tweed. From Longniddry a branch line some 4¾ miles long led to Haddington. The line was opened throughout on 22nd June, 1846 and was modestly described by the Directors as such 'that there is not a railway in Great Britain smoother and more comfortable to the passenger', although whether the latter might have agreed is another matter! Disaster struck almost immediately with a series of land-slips in the Drem to Berwick section closing the line between those points and causing havoc to the already depleted funds of the company.

Local passengers were well served; from the 8.15 am, and 5 pm up trains from Edinburgh, coach connections were provided at Drem for Dirleton and North Berwick and from Ballencrieff for Aberlady and Gullane. These are mentioned in a guide book published to coincide with the opening of the line – *Thompson's Account of the North British Railway* – and the tourist potential of the area was already apparently recognised for a somewhat partisan statement is included that, 'the village of Dirleton and its locality is by far the finest in Scotland and there are few in England that can surpass it in picturesque beauty'. In the down direction, the coaches left North Berwick at 7.50 am and 4.30 pm, and Gullane at 8.10 am and 4.50 pm. Ballencrieff Station, situated close to the crossroads there, was however somewhat short-lived and it closed permanently, through lack of custom, on 1st November, 1847; from that date the coach to Aberlady and Gullane left from Longniddry Station.

Apart from Haddington and Dunbar the only other town of any signifi-cance at all in the county was North Berwick, a place of comparatively little interest in a conventional sense to a railway company, having but a small population which had remained virtually stagnant in the previous half-century. By the spring of 1845, however, there was talk of building a branch line off the North British to serve the town and this prompted a local man, John Hope, to write to his father in May of that year that:

> I am surprised about the railway to North Berwick. The inhabitants of that city [sic] have a good idea of themselves. They should try an omnibus in the first place. A railway to North Berwick seems a most chimerical idea. What traffic can the 'bodies' expect? I should like to see their prospectus.*

The North British, however, had already formed the view that North Berwick had a potential for attracting first class season ticket traffic from Edinburgh as middle class professionals could be persuaded to live there by a combination of a good train service and suitable sites for building. In addition there was another and less obvious reason to build a branch, namely the threat of competition from an independent East Lothian and Tyne Valley Railway which had, in 1846, been authorised to run from East

---

* Quoted in *A sketch of the life of George Hope by His Daughter* (Edinburgh, 1878). This memoir of the radical farmer of Fenton Barns whose 'vigorous advocacy of free-trade contributed essentially to the abolition of the obnoxious cornlaws' contains several passages detailing his travels in Britain, Ireland and Europe by rail and forms a vivid picture of a least one aspect of East Lothian life in the last century.

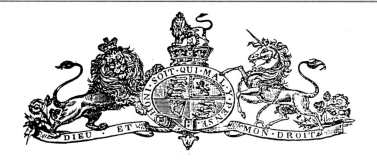

ANNO NONO & DECIMO

VICTORIÆ REGINÆ.

* *

Cap. lxxiv.

An Act to authorize the Construction of several Branch Railways and other Works in connexion with the *North British* Railway.

[26th *June* 1846.]

XI. And be it enacted, That it shall be lawful for the said Company to make and maintain the following Branch Railways, as, defined on the Plans deposited as aforesaid, from and out of the Main Line of the *North British* Railway, with all proper Works, Approaches, and Conveniences connected therewith; (that is to say,) a Branch Railway, commencing at a Point near *Bankton* in the Parish of *Tranent* and County of *Haddington*, and passing through and terminating in the same Parish at or near to the Village of *Tranent ;* a Branch Railway diverging from and out of the said Railway also at a Point near *Bankton*, and terminating at or near the Harbour of *Cockenzie* in the said Parish of *Tranent ;* a Branch Railway diverging from and out of the *North British* Railway at or near *Drem* in the Parish of *Athelstanford* and County of *Haddington*, and terminating at or near the Burgh of *North Berwick ;* a Branch Railway diverging from and out of the Main Line of the *North British* Railway at or near to *West Reston* in the Parish of *Coldingham* and County of *Berwick*, and terminating at or near the Town of *Dunse*.

Powers to make Branch Railways.

Extract from the North Berwick Railway Act of 1846 which authorised the construction of the North Berwick line.

Linton to Dalkeith via Haddington and Ormiston. This, as well as a dispute with George Hudson, caused the North British to fear that they might soon be facing unfriendly opponents within the heartland of their operations. The results were two-fold – the unnecessary provision of a second running line on the Haddington branch and the building of the railway to North Berwick, the latter alone eventually costing the company in excess of £75,000 and bringing the caustic comment from John Learmonth that 'when it [i.e. the North Berwick line] was entered into we were under very pressing circumstances and the shareholders were not aware of the causes which induced the directors to seize hold of the branch to protect intrusion.'

By the early part of 1846, several months before the opening of the main line, the North British had formulated proposals for no less than seven branch railways – these were to run to Cockenzie, Duns, Jedburgh, Kelso, North Berwick, Selkirk and Tranent and, on 11th May, a Special Meeting of the company's shareholders approved these plans and the draft Bill to authorise the construction of the branches; on 16th June, the North British Railway Act 1846, received the Royal Assent.

The plans which were drawn up for the North Berwick branch show the line almost exactly, with the exception of the northern part, as it was eventually built. Leaving the main line at Drem Junction, on the down side some 600 yards to the east of the passenger station there, the branch began on a slight decline of 1 in 320 for a distance of 150 yards before crossing, on the level, the Drem to East Fortune turnpike road (the present B1337); before construction, a bridge was substituted for the level crossing and the turnpike road was banked up accordingly. The line then swung round on a 40-chain radius curve to face a north-north-easterly direction and continued to descend, on a steeper decline of 1 in 110, for half a mile until the Peffer Burn was crossed. Close to milepost 19, the line began to climb at 1 in 93 for just over one mile, entering an impressive cutting through a ridge of hard igneous rock; in places this cutting was almost 40 feet deep. There then followed a bridge carrying the farm road to East Fenton over the railway and another level crossing where the Kingston to Fenton by-road crossed the line. This planned level crossing was also replaced by a bridge and there was some subsequent controversy between the company and the owners of Kingston farm relating to the gradients up which the road had to run in order to cross the bridge. The line then ran up an almost imperceptible incline, reaching the site of Dirleton Station within 500 yards before bridging the road leading to the village of that name. The railway then turned eastwards to face North Berwick and, passing milepost 22, it reached Williamston (otherwise Williamtown or Williamstone) a farm which lay just outside the Burgh boundaries and some 3¾ miles from Drem Junction. By now the line was again entering a cutting through igneous rock and the gradient suddenly changed to a steep decline of 1 in 66½. Half a mile from Williamston and close to the site of the medieval Priory at North Berwick, the line was crossed by what later became Ware Road and then passed where the present passenger station is situated before running on to a high embankment and, still dropping on the same gradient, it then crossed the Edinburgh turnpike road (the A198) before swinging almost due east to reach the sea. The line then ran along the foreshore on an embankment which would form a new sea wall some 20 feet high in front of (and blocking the views from) Forth Street before turning north-east on a 10-chain radius curve to a planned terminus at the harbour itself. It is, perhaps, surprising that the inhabitants of North Berwick did not raise an objection to the embankment which would certainly have disfigured this part of the town but, in an age which tolerated a gas works and iron foundry in prominent positions close to the beaches, the railway to the harbour was presumably seen as merely a necessary, if unaesthetic, evil.

At the Half-Yearly Shareholders' Meeting of the North British held at Edinburgh on 27th August, 1846, the Directors were pleased to report that 'the working plans for all seven branches are in a forward state and so that even as they are completed, the works will be gone on with'. The branches were to be 'financed by means of Quarter or Branch shares similar to those used to finance the Hawick line.' On 2nd November, 1846 the Board ordered that the contracts for the construction of the line were to be put out to tender in two separate contracts, namely the Drem contract and the North Berwick contract. On 20th January, 1847 the tenders of James Gowans of Edinburgh for, respectively, £29,095 13s. 3d. and £21,751 2s. 2d. were accepted, giving a total cost for the construction of the line from Drem Junction to North Berwick Harbour of £50,846 15s. 5d.

James Gowans was one of the more colourful of the Victorian railway contractors and was, in his own right, an interesting and talented man in several spheres. Born in 1821, of humble birth in Blackness, West Lothian, Gowans trained as both a mason (his father's profession) and an architect before becoming a railway contractor in 1846. He was responsible for many difficult stretches of line throughout Scotland, including parts of the Edinburgh and Bathgate Railway, the Caledonian Railway branch to Crieff and two long sections of the Highland Railway main line between Dunkeld and Ballinluig, and Dalwhinnie and Boat of Garten, as well as other projects such as Lochee Station on the Dundee and Newtyle Railway. His quarrying interests included Redhall Quarry near Edinburgh and it was from his practical knowledge of stone and the theories that he had evolved over many years, that he invented a scheme of architectural construction using a two foot modular sandstone grid with a rubble infill, giving a polychromatic effect, and being a form of early prefabricated system building. Putting this into practice, he designed a number of highly individualistic and sometimes bizarre houses including two which survive in Edinburgh – the tenements at Castle Terrace and the house named 'Lammerburn' (10 Napier Road) although, sadly, his masterpiece, 'Rockville' (its near neighbour) is no more. Described as a 'romantic rationalist', Gowans was interested in improving the welfare of the working classes and he built some of the earliest of the 'colonies' (a form of model main door housing with gardens originally for artisans and now largely 'gentrified'!) in the city. In 1885, Gowans was elected Lord Dean of the Guild of Edinburgh (i.e. the president of the court having jurisdiction over the city's buildings) and in the following year his career was crowned when, in recognition of his invaluable contribution to the Edinburgh International Exhibition, he was knighted by the Queen.

Sadly he did not prosper and in a typical example of Victorian understatement, he died 'in reduced circumstances' in 1890.

At the North British Railway Half-Yearly Meeting held on 26th February, 1847 the Directors announced that the North Berwick line and three other of the new branches had now been contracted for and that they would be proceeded with 'as fast as possible' and it would appear that Gowans began work shortly thereafter. A week later, on 3rd March, the Directors were beginning to have doubts as to continuing the line as far as the harbour and they resolved that 'in the meantime this line should not be carried into the town but should stop at the west end of it'. On 23rd March Learmonth and George Turnbull, another Director, were instructed to 'visit North Berwick and report as to the proper place for a station there'. This they did and on 24th April it was minuted at a Special Meeting of the Directors that as a result of their visit the Board resolved,

> . . . that the railway ought not to go in to the Harbour but should be formed on the south side of the west part of the town and that all works to the east of the road to the Abbey farm should be stopped in the meantime and that the engineer should be instructed to prepare a plan of the proposed alterations.

The reason for this was made obvious the next month when the company's Engineer was ordered to prepare a report showing the estimated savings to be effected by stopping the line at this point.

The matter of the terminus was still far from settled when, following yet another inspection by an *ad hoc* Committee at the beginning of June 1847, the Directors agreed to carry on with the line, but only as far as the Free Church (the present Blackadder Church) at the eastern end of Forth Street and a hundred yards short of the harbour. Even this was only on the condition that 'the Town Council will give their ground here for £200 and agree to limit their charge for town dues [i.e. rates] to £20 per annum or such other reasonable sum'. This view was not unanimous and two Directors dissented on the grounds that, not only had insufficient data been laid before the Board with regard to the question of expense, but also that they considered that the massive sea wall embankment would be too much exposed to the winter seas, particularly when the north-easterly wind would drive the waves upon it. Nevertheless, negotiations with the Town Council continued and the company increased their offer for the land to £500, which the Council rejected.

Negotiations with other landowners continued and on 4th January, 1848 the company Secretary was instructed to settle the most pressing of the claims of parties in North Berwick, presumably with the aim of demonstrating the company's good faith. On 6th March it was reported that James Gowans had applied for leave to commence building the bridge over the Edinburgh turnpike road at North Berwick and the Secretary was instructed to tell him not to proceed further with the bridge works pending further instructions. The North British was still having acute financial problems and at the Half-Yearly Meeting held in August 1848, the shareholders were informed that,

> The Dunse [sic] and Tranent branches are being proceeded with as fast as the funds at the Directors' disposal will allow; the Kelso and North Berwick branches are not

in so forward a state although they are also well advanced. They will be pushed on as soon as the Directors are put in possession of funds for the purpose.

The terminus question was finally resolved at the end of November 1848, when, after a query from the company's Engineer, the Directors decided that the line should not be carried beyond and west of the Edinburgh turnpike road (the A198) and that the passenger station should be constructed close to the Abbey Farm. This decision had an interesting consequence in that it led to the discovery of some Iron Age antiquities while excavating the station site. These were:

> ... two stone cists ... measuring a little more than 4 feet in length and each containing a human skeleton. In one of them an iron sword and dagger lay together, but so much corroded as to crumble to pieces in the careless hands of the railway navvies. At the sides of the skeletons, in both cists, were urns of rough grey ware, ornamented externally with parallel grooves running round them, and internally covered with a green glaze.*

In February 1849 the NBR company Engineer informed the shareholders that, in relation to the branch lines then being constructed:

> Beginning with the North Berwick branch which separates from the main line near to the Drem Station, and which was originally intended to terminate at the harbour at North Berwick; under your direction it now terminates outside the town of North Berwick and extends to 4¼ miles in length. The branch was contracted for by Mr Gowans and the quantity of the earth work upon it as now to be executed extended to about 30,000 cubic yards and of this about 21,200 yards have now been executed. Almost all of the masonry is completed and a considerable portion of the permanent way laid. The works are in such a state as would admit of the Branch being opened, were they pushed forward, within three or four months.

The financial problems continued and on 29th May, 1849 the Board once again resolved to complete and open the North Berwick branch as soon as possible, 'the reason for [it] not having been proceeded with more rapidly resting solely on the difficulty of providing the necessary funds for doing so'. It was now clear that further economies would have to be made and on 3rd July, the Directors agreed to a recommendation from the Secretary that 'the North Berwick branch be laid with a single line of rails and that so far as a double line is already laid the rails should be lifted'. The immediate result of this was that where it existed, the up branch line was lifted, leaving the down line in situ to serve as the sole running line. No attempt was made to realign it then, or in subsequent relayings, until eventually alterations had to be made in connection with the electrification of the line. What is perhaps surprising is that the Board had made the decision to single the line when the works were in such an advanced state; a great deal of unnecessary expenditure had already been incurred by providing double track clearances in the bridges, cuttings and embankments.

---

* Daniel Wilson, *Prehistoric Annals of Scotland*, 2nd ed. (1863), Vol. II, 119; cf. Nigel Tranter *Portrait of the Lothians*, (1979) where there is a description of the workmen coming across the tomb of a medieval nun which was opened and 'there lay a good-looking young fair-haired woman, her features and body preserved intact, until the fresh air turned all swiftly to dust.'

On 26th July, 1849 a specially appointed Committee of Investigation reported to the North British shareholders at a Special Meeting held in Edinburgh in the following terms:

> The Committee regret that the Directors should ever have undertaken the formation of the North Berwick branch and have recommended that it best could be laid with a single line of rails (to which the Directors concur), the length being only about 4½ miles and it may be worked as a single line without the least risk of an accident . . . The weight of the rail used is 75 lbs. per yard and the sums expended on the line have been £63,874 0s. 10d. up to 4th August, 1848 and £5,411 10s. 7d. since then making a total of £69,283 11s. 5d. with £47,483 0s. 6d. remaining to be expended. With regard to the cost of the land acquired, the original estimate was for £7,083 15s. 0d. and the actual cost will in fact be £18,949 7s. 0d., being £9,937 already expended and £9,011 13s. 10d. to be still spent . . .

By this time the line was virtually complete as far as Williamston, about half a mile short of the terminus, and the contractor was now engaged upon making the deep cutting here which was 30 feet deep in places. On 6th August, 1849 the Directors considered a proposal 'to make the cutting between Williamston and North Berwick to single line clearance only but to make the bridges suitable for double track in case it should ultimately be made necessary'. Having approved of this proposal, they instructed the Engineer and contractor accordingly, adding that 'There is a sudden and unexpected demand on the income of the [company]' and that 'proper economy should be made in the erection of the stations on the branch railway'. Subsequently there was further correspondence between James Gowans and the company as to the width of this cutting, the contractor pointing out that 'it would be preferable to make the cutting for double track, even though the rails need not be laid . . .' The Secretary was then instructed to investigate the difference in costs between a single and double width cutting but the outcome is unclear as the cutting was eventually built partly to single and partly to double track clearances!

Presumably in an attempt to recoup the heavy construction costs the company now resolved to open at least part of the line and, in July 1849, Mr Scott of East Fortune was appointed the company's agent (a post equivalent to station master) at North Berwick at a salary of £55 per annum and a porter from Heriot Station was transferred to North Berwick. In the same month, a table of goods rates was approved for the branch and a draft timetable of four mixed trains per day was approved. On 4th August, 1849 the line between Drem and Williamston was officially inspected by the Board of Trade and on 13th August, 1849 the line was opened to the public with no apparent ceremony.

The initial service of four branch trains per day from Drem ran to a temporary wooden platform at Williamston where a service of 'horse conveyances' connected with the town, access being gained over the farm road belonging to Sir Hew Dalrymple for which right the company later paid the sum of £30. No service was, however, run on Sundays although whether this was a commercial decision or related to the substantial body of Scottish opinion which felt that trains on the sabbath were an undue concession to Mammon, is unclear. From the same date, Drem became a post-town and no longer was mail for the Drem district sent via Berwick-on-Tweed, taking three days in the process.

Work was now in progress to build the permanent terminus of the branch on a site next to the old Priory and on 28th August, tenders were accepted from various trades for the main buildings. Part of the former goods shed at Portobello was taken down and re-erected at North Berwick for the same purpose, the company Secretary being authorised 'to make arrangements for the execution of a lime loading bank and a small coal drop for the accommodation of the lime works belonging to Mr Crawford'.

At the Half-Yearly meeting of September 1849, the shareholders were told that:

> The part opened is all but finished, the contractor requiring to dress up some of the slopes and other small finishing. The portion not yet opened, consisting mainly of a cutting, which the contractor is proceeding with, and he now has only about 54,000 cubic yards to remove and the stuff taken from the cutting is being used for the station at North Berwick. The station at North Berwick has been constructed and will be complete by the time that the line is completely opened which may be, if the line is finished, in January next.

This estimate was undoubtedly optimistic, for six months later the shareholders were being told that 18,000 cubic yards of earth were still to be moved and the expected opening date had been put back to May 1850. The small intermediate station at Dirleton was finished, the last building apparently being a small goods shed mentioned in the company Minutes of 21st February, 1850 when it was recorded that 'the tender therefor by Farquharson of Haddington is accepted for £87'. On 6th June, 1850, estimates for gas fittings at North Berwick station and a water tank for locomotives were accepted and on 11th June it was announced that, the line having been satisfactorily completed and officially inspected, the new stations at Dirleton and North Berwick would be opened to the public on the 17th of that month and the temporary station at Williamston closed with the passage of the last train the preceding day. The contractor was formally thanked for his efforts but, as late as 1857, James Gowans and the North British were still in dispute as to the sums outstanding as a result of the Drem and North Berwick contracts!

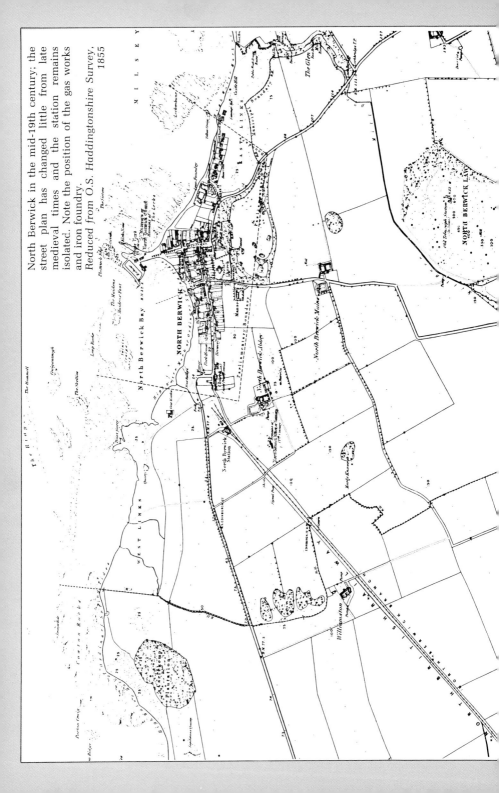

North Berwick in the mid-19th century; the street plan has changed little from late medieval times and the station remains isolated. Note the position of the gas works and iron foundry.
Reduced from O.S. Haddingtonshire Survey, 1855

Chapter Three

Trains, Trials and Tribulations

THE FIRST DECADE OF OPERATION, 1850–1859

'By the discontinuance by the defenders . . . of steam power on the branch line in question and the substitution of the slower and less convenient and agreeable mode of conveyance by horse power, they have committed a breach of contract with the pursuer. . .'

Pursuer's pleadings in Scott v North British Rly

In its early days the North Berwick line had a somewhat chequered history culminating in the suspension of passenger steam trains and an acrimonious legal dispute. The beginning was unexceptional, the first train to leave the new terminus being the 7.55 am to Drem on 17th June, 1850, calling at Dirleton at 8.05 and arriving at the junction at 8.15 where it connected with the 6.30 from Berwick giving an arrival in Edinburgh at 9 o'clock. The initial service consisted of a total of four mixed trains per day conveying both passengers and goods, three of them having connections for Edinburgh and all trains stopping at Dirleton. Four classes of passenger accommodation were provided and the single fare to Edinburgh (where, then as now, the majority of the travellers were bound) varied between 4s. 3d. [21p] for first class and 1s. 11d. [9½p] for fourth class.

Trains were hauled by a selection from the somewhat motley North British collection of locomotives and the passenger carriages were the company's usual wooden four-wheeled and claret painted stock of the day. Perhaps the coaches were not the most luxurious in Britain but they were reckoned to be solid, workmanlike and admirably suited to the dour Scots temperament! The furnishings, particularly in the third and fourth classes, were sparse and the provision of lighting, meagre and inadequate. Smoking was allowed only in designated compartments, and not at all at stations, and gaming and games of chance were strictly prohibited. 'Dogs will not be suffered to accompany passengers in the carriages, but will be conveyed separately and charged for'.

The terminus of the branch possessed a single passenger platform, on virtually the same site as the present North Berwick station, and rudimentary goods facilities including a private siding for the lime works; a small single track engine shed was situated beyond the passenger platform. Goods accommodation was gradually added to and improved and, two years after the opening, alterations were made to the cattle loading bank so as to render it suitable for handling the conveyance of private horse-drawn carriages. Inward traffic handled included general merchandise, manure, coal, livestock and agricultural necessities and outward traffic included fish, grain, potatoes, lime and even guano from the Bass Rock.

The fish traffic was especially important and a contemporary account noted that North Berwick

> . . . has been, to some extent, a fishing port from time immemorial, probably from the first existence of the town. But this branch of industry here, as in many other places on the coasts of Britain, has received a prodigious impulse from the opening up of a vastly extended market by railways; and the fishermen of North Berwick are now twelve times as many as when the branch railway to it was opened . . .

23

David Runciman

'Bus Proprietor

28 QUALITY STREET

NORTH BERWICK

'Bus meets arrival and departure of all Trains; also Coach to several places of interest in neighbourhood.

All Orders punctually attended to, and every information given at above Address.

THE HANDBOOK

OF THE TRIP

TO DIRLETON AND NORTH BERWICK

BY THE

NORTH BRITISH RAILWAY:

[On Saturdays at 2.30—Returning from North Berwick at 8 P. M.]

CONTAINING

TOPOGRAPHICAL AND HISTORICAL NOTICES OF ALL THE PLACES AND SCENES ON BOTH SIDES OF THE LINE,

WITH FULL DESCRIPTIONS OF

Dirleton Castle, The Bass, Tantallan,

&c. &c. &c.

EDINBURGH:

PUBLISHED BY ROBERT HARDIE & CO., FREDERICK STREET;

AND SOLD ALSO BY JAMES BRYDONE, 29 PRINCE'S STREET; AT THE BOX, NORTH BRIDGE; AND AT THE RAILWAY STATION.

Title page from the first guide book to the branch, published shortly after its opening. *Edinburgh Central Library*

In the years before the herring shoals suddenly deserted the ports of the Forth, North Berwick normally took in some 12,000 barrels of the fish each season (including fish from the East Fife ports which, at that time, had no other convenient railhead) and, in one memorable week, 7,000 barrels of herring were landed there. The merchants of the town began to despatch large quantities of herring by rail to London, Leeds, Birmingham and Manchester and this busy traffic continued until the mid-1860s; thereafter much smaller quantities of lobster, crab and fish from in-shore fisheries was handled by rail but the herring trade never returned in force.

Parcels were conveyed by train and delivered locally by the company and, after the Post Office contract for the North British mail from the town was secured in 1855, letters were carried in the guard's van. There was a staff of three employed at the station, namely William Scott the agent (station master) at an annual salary of £54 12s., John Doughty, part-time clerk paid £10 per annum and William Webster, the porter, who was paid 14s. [70p] per week.

The duties of the station agent were varied and comprehensive and, in the words of the North British Rule Book, he was to be 'responsible for the Company's property there and for the faithful and efficient discharge of the duties devolving upon himself and the servants under him'. Other relevant rules included Rule 157 which stated that 'The Stations and Offices must be put in a thoroughly clean and orderly condition every morning and kept so during the day – the station master must make a special inspection of every room, water closet and urinal every morning. He must also inspect the whole sidings, points and crossings and satisfy himself that everything is in proper order.' Rule 175 provided that 'The Station agent shall, on the arrival of every passenger train, cause the name of the station to be called out in a loud voice along all parts of the train, so that every passenger may hear it. At Junctions where it is necessary for the passengers to change carriages, the Agent must see that the passengers are properly warned'. A rule of even more general application and import was No. 6 – 'The servants are cautioned against rudeness or the use of improper language and are enjoined to be civil and polite to passengers.'

Occasionally the staff used their own initiative, not always to good effect. In one of the earliest mentions of train working on the branch the company Secretary, Charles Davidson, issued the following notice to staff on 12th December, 1849:

> The goods train from North Berwick has just arrived with two passengers on the engine, neither of whom have any right to be there. McCullock, the engine driver, must pay first-class fare, four shillings, for each of them. And I know that several persons are allowed to travel on the engine upon the North Berwick branch who have no right to do so, I now warn him that the next offence he commits in that way will cause his dismissal from the Company's service. Such proceedings are neither more nor less than fraud upon the Company and must be put a stop to instantly.

Presumably the penalty had the desired effect on the unfortunate McCullock but this was certainly not the last time that comment was to be passed on the subject of unauthorised footplate passengers on the branch.

Sometimes goods were not handled with the care which they deserved: shortly after the opening on the line, a claim was made against the company for silk mercery goods which were invoiced to North Berwick and damaged by rain as a result of being kept in the truck all night and not delivered. The claim was met but the station agent was fined £1 out of his wages 'for his inattention in not delivering the goods in time'. Another person who fell foul of the company was a Mr Eddington of North Berwick whose tender for the killing of rabbits on the line was accepted in 1854, 'on the distinct understanding that he is not to use a gun or trespass on other property'. Within a few weeks complaints were being received that Mr Eddington was adding to his income by openly poaching game from lands neighbouring the line.

Dirleton Station was a small wooden structure on a single platform with a goods siding, and was situated in the midst of delightful rural scenery a good mile and a quarter from the village of that name and some distance from the nearest houses in the hamlet of Kingston. In November 1850 the Board approved a tender in the sum of £96 9s. 9d. for the construction of a house for the station agent by J. Dorward of Haddington; the station house here remains inhabited to this day, long after the demise of the station. For many years Dirleton enjoyed considerable traffic in agricultural goods but an irregularity seems to have occurred in 1852 when, after a traffic return was ordered by the company, the station agent, Anderson by name, resigned and his place was taken by a Mr Bertram, a train guard on the line whose place was in turn taken by Weir, the Haddington branch guard. There appears to have been a quick turnover of staff here for in January 1856 the agent was John Roberts, at an annual salary of £45, and the only other employee was George Howden, porter, who earned 14s. [70p] per week. The station was apparently still lacking in accommodation, for in 1855 requests were made for additional goods storage facilities and also for a house for the porter there. The remoteness of the station meant that the inhabitants of Dirleton were faced with problems in getting to and from their railhead, particularly in bad weather. In the 1880s, when the village baker, George Oliver, acted as the carrier of mail and merchandise between station and village, he had to susbstitute a sledge for the usual horse and cart when the roads were icy.

At Drem Junction the branch trains joined the main line and ran to the two-platform passenger station where they terminated, although no bay platform was provided. A small goods yard for local and transfer freight and a holding siding were provided and there was a staff of five, namely Robert Lambert, the agent, who was paid £60 per annum, William Brown, clerk, at £10, two porters, R. Breckie and John Charles, who earned respectively 14s. [70p] and 13s. [65p] per week and John Fowler pointsman, at a weekly wage of 13s. The junction was, however, beginning to cause problems and in 1854 the company gave serious consideration to a proposal to build an additional line between Drem Junction and the station so that branch trains could run independently of the main line and could wait for a clear passage. The estimated cost of the works was only £330 17s. 2d. but the Board resolved to delay a decision on the matter 'because of the heavy expense involved' even though part of the cost was to be defrayed by the sale of surplus land at

Drem. Eventually the work to move the physical junction to the east end of the station was carried out and the additional line for the North Berwick branch trains remains in use today.

One other local railway facility worthy of mention, although actually situated on the main line, was the siding at Ballencrieff. In 1853 the North British agreed with Mr George Reid, the tenant of the farm of Ballencrieff, 'to have a siding constructed on the said farm for the use of an accommodation thereof' and his landlord, Lord Elibank, gave the necessary land while Mr Reid contributed 'towards the expense of constructing said siding the sum of fifty pounds'. A siding, some 235 yards long, joining the down main line in a trailing junction 1.7 miles west of Drem, was accordingly laid and catch points, a loading bank and access road were all provided. The siding was 'to be used in daylight hours only'.

Special trains were run on the branch when required. Apart from seaside excursions to North Berwick from Edinburgh and elsewhere in the summer, excursions were also run from the town to a variety of destinations, especially in the early years when railway travel was something of a novelty. Indeed, shortly after the line was opened, a special was run from North Berwick to Perth and Dundee. What would now be termed leisure traffic was also encouraged by the issue of reduced price tickets including 'Special Return Tickets', in effect weekend returns for outward travel to North Berwick on a Saturday and returning on Mondays at a fare of 4s. 1d. [20½p] first class, 3s. 4d. [16½p] second class and 3s. 0d. [15p] third. A more unusual form of ticket was that provided for 'Pic-nic parties of not less than 10 persons conveyed on the application of two respectable householders on the ordinary trains of the North British . . . in first-class carriages with return the same day at a fare of 4s. [20p] each, 48 hours notice of the same being required.' In 1855 a proposal to run special services to North Berwick on summer Saturdays at return fares of only 2s. 6d. [12½p] first class and 1s. 6d. [7½p] 'covered carriage' (i.e. third class) was approved and this would undoubtedly have made day trips to the town ever more popular.

For several years the branch had an uneventful existence with four trains a day making their way along the branch at a sedate average speed of less than 20 miles per hour, in timings virtually unchanged since the opening. Apart from a few minor accidents, including one at Drem caused by a wagon being blown out of a siding, and a collision there arising out of the porter neglecting to put the brake of a van on (for which he was subsequently fined 5s. [25p] and the station agent, who was held to be vicariously liable, 10s. [50p]), little else happened.

In order to encourage suburban traffic, and especially lucrative season-ticket traffic to Edinburgh, the North British published the following announcement in May 1854:

NORTH BRITISH RAILWAY

New Residences upon the Line of Railway

With the object of inducing parties to erect dwellings contiguous to the line of railway, the directors will issue a contract ticket, in the terms stated below, to each party whose avocation may require his daily attendance in Edinburgh, and who may not at the time of such issue reside on the line of railway, on his becoming the first occupant of a house hereafter to be built within one mile of the railway, and not nearer than eight miles from Edinburgh, such ticket to be available between Edinburgh and the station most convenient for such house, but to be forfeited on the party ceasing to occupy the house or to follow the occupation in question. The ticket will not be available at intermediate stations.

Scale of Charges, &c., for Railway Residents' Tickets

Rental or assessed Value of House per annum	Period during which Tickets will be gtd.	Class of Tickets	Charges
Above & under			
£20 £25	6 years	2nd	
£25 £35	9 years	1st	£5 per
£35 £50	12 years	1st	annum
£50	15 years	1st	

At this time North Berwick was beginning slowly to expand and a number of people took up the company's offer of the Line of Residence Tickets (which were attractive indeed given that the normal first class annual season between North Berwick and Edinburgh was, at that time, £21). These included one John Scott, Writer to the Signet*, of whom more was to be heard subsequently. Other applications were refused 'as not falling within the requirements of the advertisement', while a Mr Campbell of Drem applied for a free pass 'in respect of his large trade in potatoes, etc. on the line' but his application was declined 'with an expression of regret that it cannot be complied with without opening the door to abuse'. A further, but less generous, concession was the school tickets issued to children attending schools in Edinburgh – a reduction of 10 per cent was granted when there were four children travelling from one family, 15 per cent for five and 20 per cent for six and one would imagine that these reductions would be welcomed by the hard-pressed paterfamilias of Victorian times.

Despite these developments the North Berwick branch was still running at a loss, particularly in winter when traffic was extremely light, and in consequence various options for reducing costs were considered – as far back as October 1849 the company Secretary was requested to get estimates for the cost of running the branch by horse power as opposed to steam. In January 1853 William Smith, the North British locomotive superintendent, was asked to prepare drawings and estimates for a tank engine suitable for working the branch. He was also asked to state his opinion on the savings which would be effected if such an engine was used, but whether the request was ever complied with is unclear. Then, in December 1855 the Board instructed their Manager, Rowbotham, 'to test the practicability of working the branch by horse power'. Two days after Christmas he reported the results of his experiments with horse working 'from which it appears impossible to do as regards goods and very inexpedient as regards passengers'. The loco-

---

* *Writer to the Signet* – a member of an exclusive and ancient society of solicitors in Scotland which survives to this day – W.S. for short.

motive superintendent was then requested to make calculations for the saving in working the branch by 'light branch engine' of his own design in comparison with the present engine, and at the same time a full return of the branch traffic for the previous half-year was ordered.

The matter was still under consideration in March 1856 when the question of building a stable at Drem was raised and a decision on this was delayed until the matter of the motive power to work the branch had been resolved. At about the same time, a new horse-drawn carriage was being constructed at the North British works at St Margarets' works for use on the company's Portobello to Leith branch; on 17th April, 1856 the Locomotive Committee reported that they had inspected the same and 'were much pleased with it, thinking it well adapted and carrying forty two [sic] passengers on very little weight*.'

On 1st May the Locomotive Committee recommended 'that the carriage for Horse Trackage be tried on the North Berwick branch before being placed on the Leith line' and the trial was scheduled to take place in June. On the 13th of that month the new carriage was attached to the 2 pm Berwick mail train and conveyed to Drem. At the Board meeting of 11th July, one of the Directors, Mr Kinloch, moved 'that the experiment with the omnibus coach drawn by a horse on the 26th last month having proved satisfactory, detailed estimates shall be procured of the expense of making the road fit for horse trackage with a view to working the passenger traffic by horses after the 15th October' and this resolution was unanimously approved. Two weeks later the Locomotive Committee reported that 'as a result of an experiment made by breaking a small proportion of the ballast on the North Berwick line for the purpose of making the line fit for horse trackage' (i.e. making a path in the centre of the track upon which a horse could walk), the estimated cost of converting the whole line would be £65. The directors approved this sum with the object of having passenger traffic on the branch drawn by a horse from 1st November.

On 1st August, 1856 the Leith branch was closed to passenger traffic for the purpose of reconstruction and, accordingly, the horse carriage was now available for use on the North Berwick line, although the Locomotive Committee minuted on 8th August that 'if necessary another horse carriage can be built at St Margarets in three months without interfering with other works'. On 9th October, 1856 the same committee proceeded to St Margarets, where they inspected the horse carriage and agreed to recommend that an angular partition be put in, so as to separate first and second class passengers.

The minutes of the next Board Meeting contain this entry:

> The following scheme for working the North Berwick branch prepared by Mr Hardie was approved on the distinct understanding that the Tranent Branch is not to be worked in the dark.
> Proposed scheme for working the goods traffic on the North Berwick branch in November 1856 – this may be done by the coal train leaving Edinburgh at 10.40 am and timed to reach Drem at 12.20 pm.

---

* This figure may well be incorrect and a result of double counting of the first and second class passengers since it would have been an almost impossible load for a horse to manage on the branch and in any event does not coincide with later accounts of the same carriage.

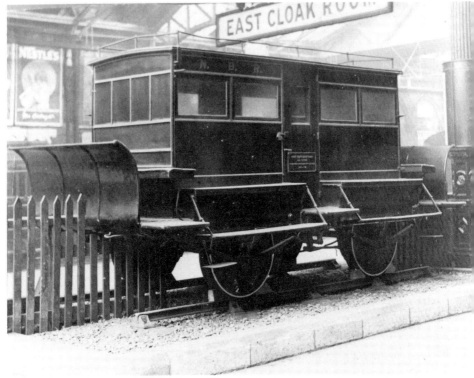

The Dandy Car seen on display at Waverley Station between the wars; it now forms part of the National Railway Museum at York. *SRO Collection*

Line drawing of the Dandy Car showing its cramped dimensions. *NBRSG*

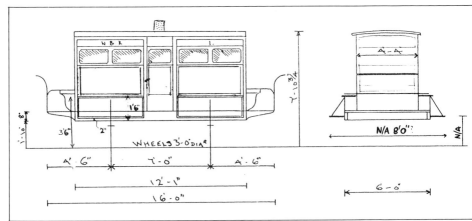

On its arrival at Drem it may proceed to North Berwick and Dirleton, clearing up these stations of all trucks loaded by that hour. These loaded trucks to be left at Drem for the 12.1 pm from Berwick and the 2.8 pm from Edinburgh to remove the former to take forward the trucks coming to the West and the latter to take all trucks going to the East and South. It is calculated that one hour and 15 to 20 minutes will be required to complete the branch work, so that this train will then reach Edinburgh at about 5.30 pm instead of 4.10 pm as at present. This arrangement will in some cases render it necessary for the coal train to work the Tranent Branch in the dark, a thing that should be avoided if possible as the incline is very steep.

The effect of this method will be that the branch goods will not arrive in Edinburgh until 6 pm, too late for delivery that evening, and any goods coming from stations south of Drem for stations on the branch after the 7.40 am train has passed must remain at Drem until 12.20 pm next day and any goods from Edinburgh and stations between and Drem for stations on the branch after the 5.30 am train has passed must remain at Drem until 12.20 pm of the following day. Further there will not be any transmission or reception of goods from or at the branch stations after 12.20 pm daily, so that grain, potatoes, or other goods loaded at that hour must remain overnight at these stations.

I have seen Mr Jamieson, fishmonger, who has ten boats engaged in the deep sea fishings at North Berwick, and he thinks that by allowing him to send forward by passenger train in the morning two small kits of white fish weighing about 50 or 56 lbs. each for his Edinburgh forenoon's sale. This arrangement of bringing in the bulk of his fish by 6 pm might work, except for the Manchester fish. He would not however state positively that he would continue to send by rail to Edinburgh and further mentioned that he contemplated putting on two sprung vans if he found upon calculation that the difference of expense was not great.

It appears to me that this arrangement would not answer the cattle traffic coming off the branch but that they would probably be loaded at East Fortune or Drem.'

The passenger service adopted was as follows:

		am	pm
Edinburgh	d.	8.00	5.55
DREM	d.	8.52	6.57
DIRLETON	d.	9.10	7.13
NORTH BERWICK	a.	9.32	7.37
NORTH BERWICK	d.	7.45	5.54
DIRLETON	d.	8.03	6.16
DREM	a.	8.25	6.34
Edinburgh	a.	9.23	7.50

Handbills were then displayed in the locality giving notice that as from 1st November, 1856 all passenger services on the branch apart from the first and last trains in each direction would be discontinued, but no mention at all was made of the fact that those remaining services were to be horse-drawn. The horse carriage itself was a curious small vehicle some sixteen feet in length in total and was known as 'The Dandy' after a contemporary smart form of road vehicle. Built at St Margarets (to Diagram No. 117), the Dandy

had a total weight of 2 tons 13 cwt and 3 qts and had internal accommodation for 12 first and second class passengers in a saloon which was lit
by a single oil lamp. Third class passengers were seated around the outside
of the carriage and exposed to the harsh realities of the East Lothian winter.

The horse service did not prove to be an unqualified success, despite the
apparent savings in running costs. The passenger accommodation was
cramped, the journey time on the branch was doubled, and reservations
were expressed as to the possible dangers of snow and ice causing the rails
to become slippery, especially on the steep gradient leading to the terminus.
At the North British Board meeting of 28th November, it was noted that a
deputation from North Berwick had been met in order to discuss demands
for an extra train each way and, more ominously, that a summons from John
Scott had been remitted to agents to be defended.

This summons was the beginning of the celebrated Court of Session case
of *Scott v The North British Railway*. Scott was an Edinburgh solicitor (a
partner in the firm of Scott Moncrieff & Dalgetty, W.S.) who, in his own
words,

> . . . was induced by the advantages of easy access to and from Edinburgh, and the
> comfortable and expeditious means of conveyance thus afforded by the Railway
> . . . in the summer of 1852, rented a house in the town of North Berwick where he
> resided with his family during the summer and autumn months of that year,
> coming up to Edinburgh as frequently during the week as his business avocations
> required, breakfasting and dining at North Berwick every day, except on rare
> occasions, and always returning there at night. Relying on a continuance of the
> same advantages, and particularly that of Railway conveyance by means of steam
> or locomotive power, . . . in the month of November of the same year, [he] entered
> into a lease of another house upon the East Links of North Berwick for five years
> from and after Whitsunday 1853, and throughout the four summers which have
> since elapsed he has, with his family, continued to reside in the said house and to
> make the same constant use of the Railway during the same periods of each year,
> and he has also occasionally, at intervals of a few weeks, gone down to North
> Berwick for the day during the Winter and Spring months. Having thus experi-
> enced the advantages of the locality, and trusting that the same were of a per-
> manent nature [he] being desirous of having a country residence possessing such
> advantages, resolved to fix it at North Berwick in preference to any other place . . .

He accordingly entered into missives with Sir Hew Dalrymple agreeing to
build a large dwelling house on a piece of ground adjoining the West Links
and, prior to commencing any building works, purchased a first class Line
of Residence ticket for £5. Following the publication of the handbill in
October 1856, Scott contacted the North British and learnt of the plan to run
a horse-drawn service whereby

> In consequence of the notice and the loss and inconvenience which would be
> sustained by the proposed change, the pursuer was obliged to remove himself his
> family and servants from North Berwick on 31st October, 1856 which he would
> not have otherwise have done.

Scott's claim was for specific implement* of the contract which he
entered into with the company by the issue of the Line of Residence ticket to

---

* Scottish legal terminology meaning 'full performance'.

him and he required them to continue to convey him 'between Edinburgh and North Berwick by means of steam power, and a locomotive engine or engines impelled thereby' for a period of 14 years, which failing and in any event for damages of £5,000. The company vigorously defended the action on the basis that, firstly, the pursuer (Scott) did not fall within the category of persons properly entitled to a Line of Residence ticket, notwithstanding the fact that they had issued him with one since, by his own admission, his house at North Berwick was still being built and he had not taken up his residence there for the winter and accordingly was not the first occupant of a house built after May 1854. Secondly, that in any event it was no part of their contract with him that trains on the branch would be hauled by steam engines and that there was no statutory obligation on them to do so. The case reached the Procedure Roll (a legal debate) where the judge, Lord Mackenzie, upheld the company's first argument and ruled that the pursuer's pleadings did not disclose a relevant case. He therefore dismissed the action, finding Scott liable to the North British for their legal expenses and added that:

> ... even supposing the action had been raised in a different form, it is far from clear that in the absence of a special undertaking, the pursuer could have compelled the Railway Company to work the branch line with locomotive power, or to pay damages on their failing to do so. But as the defence of irrelevancy has been sustained, it is unnecessary to consider that question here.

Scott promptly reclaimed (appealed) to the Inner House of the Court of Session, but his motion was unsuccessful and in February 1860 the case reached the end of the line, the horse-drawn service having done the same some three years previously.

Returning to the winter of 1856, it would appear that the savings made by withdrawing the steam service were not as great as had originally been anticipated; on 12th December the Directors resolved that 'with effect from 9th January, 1857, the clerk at North Berwick is to be dispensed with, the boy to remain meantime till the driver can manage to dispense with a guard and so free the porter of his attendance as guard' – obviously job demarcation was somewhat fluid in those days! On 9th January, 1857 a return of traffic from the horse service was ordered by the Board, and as a result of this it was decided to resume the normal steam service on 1st May, as had been originally intended, and this was duly done.

The service now operated with four mixed trains per day running as follows:

May 1857

Up trains		am	am	pm	pm	Down trains		am	am	pm	pm
DREM	d.	8.50	11.01	4.45	6.36	N. BERWICK	d.	8.00	9.45	2.20	6.11
Dirleton	d.	9.00	11.11	4.55	6.46	Dirleton	d.	8.13	9.55	2.30	6.24
N. BERWICK	a.	9.08	11.20	5.04	6.55	DREM	a.	8.21	10.04	2.55	6.33

The Dandy Car never ran again on the North Berwick branch and became surplus to the requirements of the North British. In about June 1859 it was sold to the Silloth Railway in England who used it on their branch line between Drumburgh and Port Carlisle and passed back into the ownership of the North British when they took over the smaller company. Finally withdrawn from service shortly before the First War, the Dandy Car returned to Scotland and was exhibited for many years at Waverley Station; it survives to this day as part of the National Railway Collection at York.

Once more the North Berwick branch settled down to a humdrum existence. Soon the motive power on the line was to be provided by a small single-framed 0−4−2 well tank engine, No. 20, which had been designed by the North British locomotive superintendent, William Hurst, and built at St Margarets at a cost of £952 14s. 4½d. This locomotive, one of a pair of the company's own design intended especially for branch line use, was allocated to work the North Berwick line in December 1857 and it did work the line for a short period – the subsequent fate of the locomotive is, however, something of a mystery. Passenger traffic on the branch was slowly improving and, although mainly seasonal in nature, there were a handful of what would now be called commuters who made the daily journey to Edinburgh.

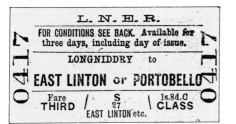

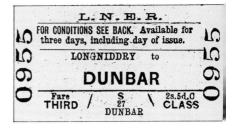

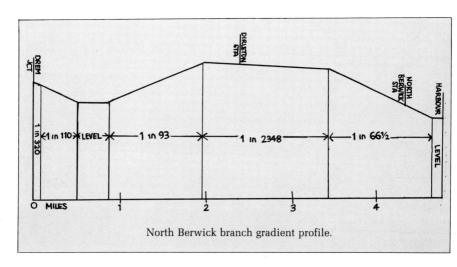

North Berwick branch gradient profile.

Main street, Aberlady, *c.*1900 – by this time the village had assumed much of its present appearance.   *Author's Collection*

Gullane High Street looking east, shortly after the opening of the Aberlady and Gullane railway – the shops, then relatively new, still survive but the coast road, along which the NBR pioneer buses ran, now forms the busy A198 and present-day villagers would be unlikely to pose for a photographer in the same way!   *Author's Collection*

Chapter Four

A Genteel Watering-Place

THE VICTORIAN HEYDAY OF THE NORTH BERWICK LINE, 1859–1899

'The visitors, belong almost entirely to the better classes of society, and North Berwick
has the great advantage of being entirely free from invasions of cheap day-trippers'
George Ferrier: North Berwick and its Vicinity (1875)

When on 20th August, 1859 Albert Edward, Prince of Wales (the future
King Edward VII), paid a visit to North Berwick, he arrived by rail and found
that the entire way from the station to the centre of the town had been
garlanded with flowers, and that the whole town had been gaily decorated
in his honour. At this time the town was still in its infancy as a 'watering
place' or resort and although it had always been a fashionable place in
which to spend the day, it was only now, as the railway age was getting
underway, that the idea of a holiday by the sea at North Berwick was gaining
popularity; the visit of His Royal Highness helped this process in no small
way. One serious deficiency, however, was the lack of suitable accommodation for tourists in the town, and it was generally felt that the pro-
sperity of North Berwick would be enhanced by the building of a hotel next
to, and convenient for, the station.

A hotel had, in fact, been first proposed as far back as 1853 and two years
later the Secretary of the North British had reported to the Board that 'efforts
were being made by some private parties to set up a good hotel at North
Berwick' and 'that he would keep them advised of the progress of the move
since such a building would be of an advantage to the company'. The
venture became associated with a proposal to build a new gas works,
somewhat incongruously next door to the hotel, and in 1859 it was agreed
that stockholders in the new North Berwick Hotel and Gas Company would
be granted a special Edinburgh season ticket at a rate of £5 per annum for
each £100 of paid-up shares for a maximum of three years. In October of that
year the company sold 1.12 acres of surplus land to the Hotel Company for
£250 and agreed to widen the approach road (the present Station Road) at
their own expense; subsequently the North British refused to donate the cost
of the furniture in the hotel after the new venture ran into financial difficulties, but they did agree to make a loan for that purpose. The hotel was
duly opened and, in honour of the Prince, was named the Royal Hotel and it
was said to be

> . . . the principal hotel, which is now one of the largest in Scotland. The view from
> this hotel, as from most parts of North Berwick, is splendid, and passengers by the
> steamboats on the Firth say that, when lighted up by gas, being on an eminence, it
> looks from the sea perfectly fairy-like.

At a later date the North British entered into a contract of co-partnership
with the proprietors of the Royal and this existed until 1923 when their
successors, the London and North Eastern Railway, sold the railway's share
to the then tenant of the hotel for £8,500.

The new gas works also became a reality when the small works on the
West Links was closed in 1860 and replaced by a larger and more modern

High Street, North Berwick at the turn of the century with a very early motor car and a very unconcerned dog.   *Author's Collection*

Quality Street, North Berwick with the distinctive Town House and the now-demolished corner shop opposite; the cart on the left is making a delivery of Crawford's biscuits.   *Author's Collection*

establishment, situated on the section of the turnpike road now known as
Station Hill. This works was served by a siding which extended from the
goods yard and on to the embankment next to the hotel, and from there
wagons were unloaded by gravity down to the store adjoining the retorts
below. The North British Works Committee minutes of 14th September,
1860 record that they 'recommend that the Board find the rails and sleepers
and lay the road of the new siding at North Berwick for minerals if the Gas
Company will do all the other work and pledge themselves to use no coal
except they that come over the North British line' – an agreement which no
doubt suited both parties admirably.

During the three decades which followed the coming of the railway the
permanent population of the burgh and its parish increased by over a
thousand (from 1,643 in 1851 to 2,686 in 1881) and the town underwent
several radical changes. Many new houses were built, including a number of
large stone villas, and the town acquired a library, bowling green, curling
club, waterworks and many of the other trimmings of a typical prosperous
Victorian town in Scotland. It was, however, the tourist trade which made,
or at least contributed to, some of the most notable additions to the town –
by 1880 there were three golf clubs in the town, the Bass Rock and Tantallon
joining the original North Berwick and the latter boasting a fine new club-
house erected in that very year. The Royal had been joined by a number of
other hotels including the Commercial, the Dalrymple Arms and the
massive Marine Hotel described as being 'a splendid hotel on an extensive
scale, with cold and hot water baths, the want of which is much felt.'
Visitors were attracted from a wide area and through train fares were

Rival establishments, 1885.

advertised from a great variety of destinations, both in Scotland and England – indeed the visitors from the latter country were so prominent that an Episcopalian (Anglican) church was established in the town. The fact that North Berwick was a select resort was not in dispute and George Ferrier, commented in his book *North Berwick and its Vicinity*, published in 1875, that 'The society at North Berwick is exceedingly good, and pleasant withal, being entirely free from the display of an ultra-fashionable watering-place.'

Golf was gaining in popularity and, following upon the opening of the Muirfield course at Gullane in 1882, the North British capitalised on their trade by issuing the members of the Honourable Company, who leased the course, special first class return tickets from Edinburgh to Drem at a fare of 3s. 6d. [17½p] (as opposed to the ordinary return of 5s. 6d. [27½p]). By the 1890s this traffic alone was worth some £600 to £700 annually to the company. When the Muirfield Golf Championships were being held, it was said that many thousands of working people came by train to see them and this too, would have generated valuable revenue for the North British.

The timetable of this period indicates the amount of traffic on the branch and its seasonal nature. The basic winter pattern of eight daily trains was as follows:

March 1881

		Mixed Pass.	Mixed Pass. AB	Mixed Pass. B	Mixed Pass.		Mixed Pass.	Pass.	Pass. B	Mixed Pass.
		am	am	am	pm		pm	pm	pm	pm
DREM JUNCTION	d.	8.00	10.05	10.45	12.35	...	2.48	4.53	5.51	7.33
Dirleton	d.	8.08	10.13	10.53	12.43	...	2.56	5.01	5.58	7.41
NORTH BERWICK	a.	8.17	10.22	11.02	12.52	...	3.05	5.10	6.07	7.50

		Mixed Pass.	Mixed Pass.	Lt Eng.	Mixed Pass. C	Mixed Pass. C	Mixed Pass. CDE	Mixed Pass. F	Pass.	Mixed Pass. G
		am	am	am	Noon	pm	pm	pm	pm	pm
NORTH BERWICK	d.	7.10	9.30	10.27	12.00	2.00	3.45	4.10	5.25	6.50
Dirleton	d.	7.20	9.40	...	12.10	2.10	3.51	4.18	5.35	7.00
DREM JUNCTION	a.	7.30	9.50	10.39	12.20	2.20	3.57	4.25	5.45	7.10

Notes:

A – Does not carry goods wagons to or from Dirleton, but takes three from Drem to North Berwick.
B – Through carriages from Edinburgh.
C – Through carriages to Edinburgh.
D – Saturdays only.
E – Works no goods traffic. Runs through to Longniddry.
F – Saturdays Excepted.
G – Through carriages to Edinburgh, except on Saturdays.

The summer service was more complicated:

August 1881

		Mixed Pass.	Mixed Pass. A	Pass. BCDE	Mixed Pass.	Mixed Pass. FGH	Pass. BM	Fast Pass. B	Fast Pass. BE	Mixed Pass.
		am	am	am	pm		pm	pm	pm	pm
DREM JUNCTION	d.	8.00	10.05	...	12.35	2.42	2.48	5.09	...	7.33
Dirleton	d.	8.08	10.13	...	12.43	2.49	2.56	5.17	...	7.41
NORTH BERWICK	a.	8.17	10.22	11.30	12.52	2.57	3.05	5.25	6.35	7.50

		Mixed Pass.	Fast Pass. IL	Mixed Pass.	Mixed Pass. J	Mixed Pass. K	Pass. IL	Pass. I	Mixed Pass. J	Pass. IM
		am	am	am	Noon	pm	pm	pm	pm	pm
NORTH BERWICK	d.	7.10	8.50	9.15	12.00	2.00	3.15	4.25	6.50	9.00
Dirleton	d.	7.20	...	9.25	12.10	2.10	...	4.33	7.00	9.07
DREM JUNCTION	d.	7.30	...	9.35	12.20	2.20	...	4.40	7.10	9.13

Notes:

A –Through carriages from Ediburgh.
B –Through train from Edinburgh.
C –Through carriages from Glasgow.
D –On Saturdays the Engine of this train will make a light run from North
    Berwick to Edinburgh about midday in order to work the 2.20 pm Saturday
    train from Edinburgh to North Berwick, arriving at 3.05 pm.
E –The speed of this train to be reduced to 3 mph while passing Drem to enable
    drivers to receive train staff or train ticket.
F –Through carriages from Edinburgh except on Saturdays.
G –Goods wagons for Dirleton not to be sent by these trains.
H –On Saturdays does not wait at Drem for the arrival of the 12.45 pm train from
    Berwick-upon-Tweed.
I –Through train to Edinburgh.
J –Through carriages to Edinburgh.
K –Through carriages to Glasgow.
L –The speed of these trains must be reduced to 3 mph when passing Drem to
    enable the drivers to deliver the train staff or train ticket.
M –Saturdays Only.

Most passenger trains were required to stop at a small wooden ticket
platform, situated just short of the main passenger station, so that incoming
passengers' tickets could be checked before arrival at the terminus. There is
an interesting footnote to the working timetable:

Six wagons Police Manure are loaded at South Leith every Wednesday and
Saturday for North Berwick. These wagons must not be taken further than Dirleton
station on Wednesdays and Saturdays, and they will be worked forward from
Dirleton to North Berwick as follows: Every Monday and Thursday morning the
North Berwick branch engine with Guard and Van only, will follow the 8.50 am

NORTH BRITISH RAILWAY COMPANY

TIME TABLE

OF

EXPRESS AND FAST TRAINS

BETWEEN THE

PRINCIPAL STATIONS

IN

ENGLAND AND SCOTLAND

AND

NORTH BERWICK.

INDEX.

RETURN FARES TO NORTH BERWICK.

Tickets available for Two Months, except where otherwise specified.

From	1 (s. d.)	2 (s. d.)	3 (s. d.)
Aberdeen	36 0	27 0	18 0
Airdrie (South)	14 3	...	7 6
Alexandria	12 6	9 6	6 6
Alloa	19 6	16 6	10 0
Alnwick	12 6	9 6	6 6
Alva	19 9	14 6	9 6
Arbroath	19 9	14 6	9 7
Balloch	14 3	...	7 6
Bathgate (Upper)	9 0	7 0	...
Berwick	12 0	8 0	5 0
Bothwell	12 6	9 6	6 6
Broughty	16 6	11 6	8 0
Canobie	25 6	19 0	10 11 6
Carlisle	28 6	21 0	14 3
Coatbridge (Sunnyside)	12 6	9 6	6 6
Cupar	15 3	11 0	6 7
Darlington	38 0	31 0	20 9
Dollar	13 0	10 0	7 0
Dunbarton	14 3	11 0	7 6
Dundee (Tay Bridge Stn.)	16 0	11 6	9 0
Dunfermline	10 9	8 6	6 0
Durham	32 6	26 6	18 10

From	1 (s. d.)	2 (s. d.)	3 (s. d.)
Edinburgh	5 6	4 6	3 0
Do.	5 *6	4 *6	3 *0
Do.	3 6	3 *1	3 +1
Falkirk	3 0	2 0	...
Glasgow	12 0	9 0	6 6
Grahamston	12 0	9 0	6 6
Greenock	17 6	...	6 *3
Hamilton	12 6	9 6	6 6
Holensburgh	14 0	11 0	7 6
Hexham	32 0	25 0	16 8
Kirkcaldy	9 0	7 0	4 3
Leven	11 0	8 0	5 0
Linlithgow	9 0	7 0	4 0
London	107 *4	85 *0	62 *8
Montrose	24 0	17 0	9 12
Morpeth	23 6	19 2	13
Newcastle	27 0	22 0	15
Northallerton	42 0	34 0	23 *0
Paisley	16 6	11 6	9 0
Perth	16 0	11 0	8 8
Polmont	16 0	9 0	5 6
St Andrews	16 0	11 0	6 8
Stirling	12 0	9 0	6 3
Thirsk	44 0	36 0	24 0
Tillicoultry	13 0	10 0	7 0
Uddingston	12 0	9 0	6 6
York	50 0	41 0	27 0

* Available for one month.

NBR local timetable, Summer 1875 — the Fares List is interesting in that it presumably gives the more popular starting points for

One of William Hurst's 0−4−2 well tanks at St Margarets shed, Edinburgh − No. 20, built in 1857 at a cost of £952 14s. 1½d., was designed specifically for North Berwick branch line duties. *Author's Collection*

Wheatley 0−6−0ST No. 39 at Waverley − for many years a North Berwick branch stalwart, this was the locomotive involved in the accident at the terminus on 9th August, 1884. *A.G. Ellis Collection*

The eponymous *North Berwick* at North Berwick, *c.*1875 – this Drummond 0–6–0T was later renamed *Meadowbank* before becoming the anonymous LNER No. 10331; she was withdrawn in 1925. *Author's Collection*

LNER 'D51' class 4–4–0T No. 10462 – originally NBR No. 52 *Dirleton* and used on the North Berwick branch between about 1883 and 1890; after the grouping it was transferred up to the GNoSR Fraserburgh to St Combs line and fitted with cowcatchers before being withdrawn in August 1933. *A.G. Ellis Collection*

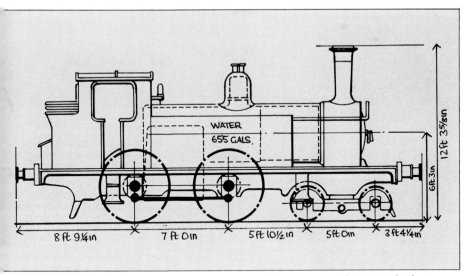

LNER official line drawing of class 'J82' 0−6−0T; these Drummond 'Terriers' built at Cowlairs in 1875 owed much to Stroudley's LBSCR famous tank engines with the same nickname and No. 158 was named *North-Berwick*.   *SRO Collection*

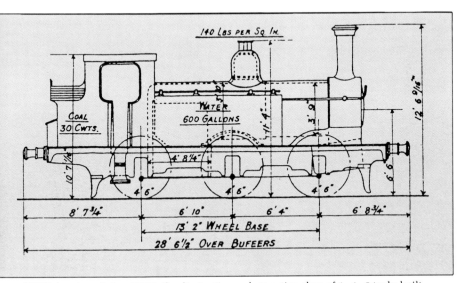

LNER drawing of class 'D51', the diminutive and attractive class of 4−4−0 tanks built by the North British for branch-line work in 1883 and which included No. 52 *Dirleton*.   *SRO Collection*

fast train from North Berwick to Dirleton and will at once convey to North Berwick the manure wagons which have been left at Dirleton as above mentioned. The manure wagons must be placed in position for the Farmers' Carts unloading them at North Berwick not later than 9.15 am.

Locomotives working the branch were still a mixed lot but in the early 1870s purpose-built 0–6–0 saddle tank engines, designed by Thomas Wheatley, began to make an appearance. Shortly thereafter the branch engine was an attractive 0–6–0 tank engine numbered 158 and named North-Berwick, the hyphenated name being painted in large letters on the side of the tanks. This locomotive had been built at the North British works at Cowlairs, Glasgow in 1877 and was one of a class designed by the new locomotive superintendent, Dugald Drummond, specifically for branch line work. Drummond had formerly been employed under William Stroudley at the London Brighton and South Coast Railway and his design was closely derived from the famous Brighton 'Terriers' of Stroudley. Indeed the livery of the engines, and the practice of naming them after the places served by the railway, had also come from the Brighton company. When this locomotive was finally moved elsewhere, it acquired the name of Meadowbank before becoming an anonymous No. 1331 and ending its days as a member of LNER class 'J82' before withdrawal in 1925.

North-Berwick was followed by No. 52 Dirleton, a Drummond 4–4–0 tank built at Cowlairs in 1883 and which, appropriately, worked the North Berwick branch for many years. Described as being one of a class of extremely neat engines which 'blended perfectly with the branch lines which they were designed to serve', No. 52 had a long life, eventually becoming No. 10462 of LNER class 'D51' and ending its life with a sister far from home on the Fraserburgh to St Combs line of the former Great North of Scotland Railway. There, in the words of railway historian Hamilton Ellis 'they were given cowcatchers against such unwary sheep as they might encounter in the windy deserts of Buchan'. Dirleton was finally withdrawn from service in August 1933.

A serious accident occurred on the branch line on 9th August, 1884 when the 10.25 pm passenger train from Edinburgh, which had started out from there 32 minutes late, overran the ticket platform at North Berwick a quarter of an hour before midnight, ran into a siding and collided with some empty carriages. The locomotive, Wheatley 0–6–0 saddle tank No. 39, and one pair of wheels of the leading carriage left the rails. None of the passengers riding in the carriages were hurt but one of two passengers riding on the engine had his arm severed and the driver and fireman were both injured, the driver severely. The engine and leading carriages were severely damaged and six other carriages were slightly damaged; one rail and 12 chairs were broken.

The Board of Trade report revealed that the Westinghouse brake pump on No. 39 had failed in the afternoon and, as there had been insufficient time to repair it, the train had made its last two journeys of the day with only the hand brakes functioning. The driver, being aware of this, had experienced no difficulty in drawing up his train at Prestonpans and Drem but said that he was unable to pull up at North Berwick on account of the rails being slippery. Major Marindin, who conducted the Board of Trade inquiry, noted that the driver had made up five minutes of his lost time between Drem and North Berwick and concluded that he had entirely miscalculated his speed and neglected to get his train under proper control. The two footplate passengers had persuaded the driver to let them travel on the engine from Edinburgh. Major Marindin considered that the driver was very much to blame for allowing them to do so as he could not but think that their presence on the engine had contributed to the accident, despite the driver's assertion to the contrary. The Major added that 'I think that they [the passengers] were themselves still more to blame for pressing the driver to break a rule which they must have known to exist, and the fact that they were of superior position in life to the driver makes their conduct all the worse.'

The points had been left set for the siding because the porter whose duty it was to hold them, had gone away to Edinburgh without leave and was actually a passenger on the train! Major Marindin added, however, that 'His absence probably did not much affect the accident, for the train would have overrun the station platform and dashed through the shed beyond it if it had been on the proper line, but such points should certainly be interlocked and bolted, and worked from a proper signal-cabin.'

The station master, Adam Hogg, blamed a second porter, Andrew Black, stating that it was his duty to hold the points, and that he did not know that Black had gone home. But porter Black was able to prove to Major Marindin's satisfaction that the station master knew perfectly well that he had gone home and of an arrangement by which all three porters worked the late duty in turn; accordingly the Major did not consider that Black was in any way at fault. 'It has been stated', he concluded, 'that unauthorised persons are in the habit of riding upon the engines of this branch, but this is denied by the driver, and I have not been able to obtain any evidence that it is so.'

In the last decade of the century, the station at North Berwick was extensively rebuilt to cope with both the increasing traffic resulting from the growth in the town's tourist trade and in anticipation of additional trains arriving over the proposed line from Aberlady and Gullane*. A new platform was added and waiting rooms, station offices, a concourse and new frontage to Station Hill built, together with a goods shed, weigh house, stables, engine shed and signal box. By the end of March 1894 the new facilities had been completed and the *Haddingtonshire Courier* of 22nd April, 1894 commented that:

> There was a crowded influx of visitors on Monday, owing to the Edinburgh Spring Holiday, about one thousand persons arriving in the forenoon by special and ordinary trains.

In the same year *Baddeley's Thorough Guide to Scotland* stated that:

> North Berwick shares with St Andrews the premiership of the watering-places on the East Coast of Scotland and is in special favour with the business-men of Edinburgh, many of whom deposit their families there for one or more months during the summer season, and themselves travel to and from the capital daily.

* See Chapter 5.

The journey by fast evening train takes from 40 to 45 minutes and the distance is just great enough to secure the habitues of the town from the annoyance of a constant excursion traffic and little enough to be accomplished twice a day without undue wear and tear.

The same guide commented on the relative unsophistication of the town saying that:

There is no stately row of sea-fronting apartments, or marine promenade; no regular band, good bad or indifferent; visitors regulate their goings out and comings in according to their own caprice, and etiquette is at a discount. The spirit of free and easiness extends even to the dustman, who seldom goes his round before 10 am. In this, and one or two kindred matters, affecting neatness and propriety, we may, perhaps, without prejudice to the dustman, suggest to the authorities a little wholesome reform.

Consequent upon the station alterations, the goods yard was extended and remodelled and enhanced facilities for general merchandise, minerals and livestock were provided. Coal was in great demand not only for the gas works via the connecting line but also for domestic use through the several coal merchants in the town although one producer, the Arniston Coal Company, had their own depot at the station. Further down the branch several alterations of a more minor nature to those at North Berwick were made to Dirleton Station where both the passenger and goods accommodation was augmented.

On 20th August, 1898 the North British carried out a goods train survey of all freight movements throughout their system on that day in order to facilitate a more efficient use of locomotives and stock. It was recorded that the 12.35 pm North Berwick to Drem goods was hauled by 'P' class 0–4–4T No. 91 and its load was 11 empty wagons while the return working, the 1.10 pm ex-Drem, conveyed nine loaded wagons in contrast to its usual load of six; the types of wagon and the goods conveyed in them were not, however, specified. The locomotive, one of a class of 12 designed by Matthew Holmes and built between 1886 and 1888, served the branch for many years and became the last survivor of what was then LNER Class 'G7' on its eventual withdrawal in 1932.

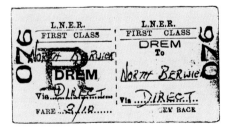

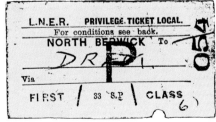

Two views of Holmes class 'P' 0−4−4T No. 91, the motive power for the North Berwick branch goods train on 20th August, 1898, the day of the NBR system-wide survey.   *Both A.G. Ellis Collection*

CHAPTER cxcix.

An Act for incorporating the Aberlady Gullane and North
Berwick Railway Company and authorising the construction of railways in the county of Haddington
and for other purposes.   [24th August 1893.]

A.D. 1893

WHEREAS the construction of the railways in the county of
Haddington herein-after described would be of public and
local advantage :

And whereas the persons herein-after named with others are
willing to carry the undertaking into execution and it is expedient
that they be incorporated into a company (herein-after called "the
Company") with all proper and necessary powers for the purpose :

And whereas it is expedient that the Company and the North
British Railway Company (herein-after in this Act called "the
North British Company") be empowered to enter into and carry
into effect working and other agreements as herein-after provided :

And whereas by the agreement between the promoters of the
Company of the first part and the North British Company of the
second part confirmed by and set forth in the Second Schedule to
this Act it is inter alia provided that in the event of the net
revenues accruing to the Company in any year being insufficient
after defraying certain payments to yield a dividend at the rate of
four and a half per centum per annum to the holders of the share
capital of the Company from time to time issued so far as paid up
the North British Company shall out of fifty per centum of the mileage
proportion of receipts accruing to them on their own railway in
respect of through traffic advance and pay to the Company such
a sum as shall be sufficient to make up the said dividend and it will
facilitate the raising of the capital required for the execution of the
undertaking if the Company are authorised to raise part of their
share capital as preference capital and it is expedient that such
power should be conferred on the Company :

[*Price* 1s. 6d.]   A   1

Chapter Five
The Golfers' Line

THE ABERLADY, GULLANE AND NORTH BERWICK RAILWAY
COMPANY, 1892–1899

'It is the policy of the North British to encourage little lines like these . . .
Evidence of Benjamin Blyth at AG&NBR Bill hearing, (1893)

While North Berwick continued to prosper as a holiday resort and residential town, the villages to the west did not. Aberlady was especially quiet, its harbour ceasing to do much business once Haddington had been connected to the railway network and the populations of both that parish and the neighbouring Dirleton parish were virtually static. A local writer commented that:

> When the main line of the North British Railway was opened, the station of Longniddry was the nearest to [Aberlady], and a Gullane 'bus was started by the hotel proprietor there (Mr Stevens), which also served Aberlady, picking up and letting down passengers as it passed. Through time Aberlady initiated a service of its own, and for many years the two ran regularly twice a day to Longniddry. Passengers were not always plentiful, but the means of travel was there if wanted, and it was a convenience long appreciated. No doubt in stormy weather some hardships had to be endured, but in decent weather the drive was a real pleasure. Many, of course, of the younger people especially, were in the habit of walking the distance, which, after all, was only three miles, and walking was a commoner accomplishment then.*

The answer to the problem of encouraging the growth of the villages was seen to be a railway and a scheme was promoted in 1892 to build a line from Longniddry to North Berwick via Aberlady, Luffness and Gullane. It was envisaged that an independent company, provisionally named the Aberlady, Gullane and North Berwick Railway, would construct the line. Although the North British officially remained aloof, the promoters of the scheme included two of their Directors, Henry Grierson and George B. Wieland (who had for many years been the NBR Company Secretary); the other promoters were an Edinburgh banker, David Kemp, and Peter Brodie, sometime Provost of North Berwick. A prospectus was issued and, in due course, a Bill was promoted.

The Consulting Engineer for the scheme was Benjamin Hall Blyth, who acted in a similar capacity to the North British and Great North of Scotland Railway, and he proposed that there should be two lines, joined end on and referred to as 'Railway No. 1' and 'Railway No. 2'. Railway No. 1 was to be 4 miles, 3 furlongs and 3.8 chains [about 4.5 miles] in length, running from a junction with the North British main line near Longniddry to a site at Gullane, and Railway No. 2 was to run from there to Williamston, where it would join the North Berwick branch line. There were to be running powers over the North British between Longniddry and the junction and between Williamston and North Berwick and stations were to be provided at Aber-

---

* J.P. Reid, *A Historical Guide to Aberlady* (Haddington, 1926).

51

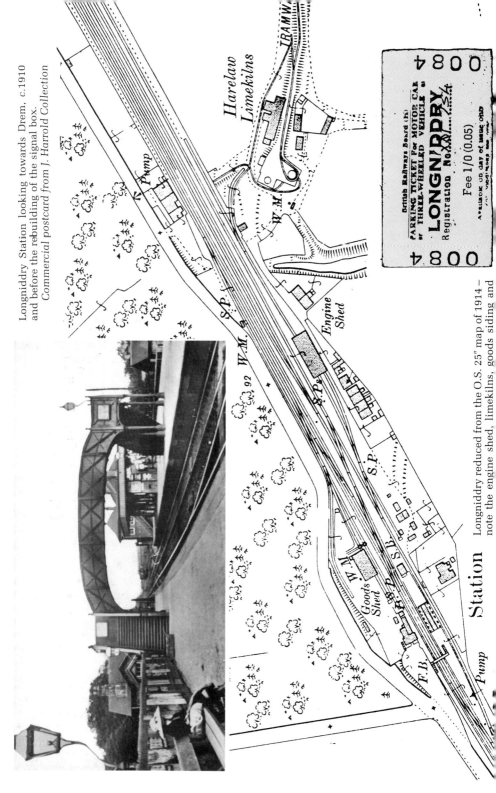

Longniddry Station looking towards Drem, c.1910 and before the rebuilding of the signal box.
Commercial postcard from J. Harrold Collection

Harelaw Limekilns

Engine Shed

Goods Shed

Station

Pump

Longniddry reduced from the O.S. 25" map of 1914 – note the engine shed, limekilns, goods siding and

British Railways Board (h)
PARKING TICKET for MOTOR CAR
or THREE-WHEELED VEHICLE
LONGNIDDRY
Registration No.XXXX7¾
Fee 1/0 (0.05)
AVAILABLE ON DAY OF ISSUE ONLY
4 800

A little girl watches an up train pull into Longniddry on a hot day in July 1911 – next to the parasol a poster extolls the virtues of emigration to Canada.
W.F. Jackson, Glasgow University Archives

Longniddry looking eastwards on 9th July, 1952 with the Haddington branch on the right. *A.G. Ellis*

The engine shed at Longniddry, 8th September, 1959; the cottages in the background survive as a reference point. *J. Harrold Collection*

Reid 'J35' 0−6−0 at the Haddington branch platform of Longniddry on the day of the SLS railtour, 11th June, 1960 − the footplate seems to be rather overcrowded! Again, the cottage in the background survives. *H.C. Casserley*

The Longniddry West or Manure Siding.

Reproduced from the 1912, 25″ Ordnance Survey map

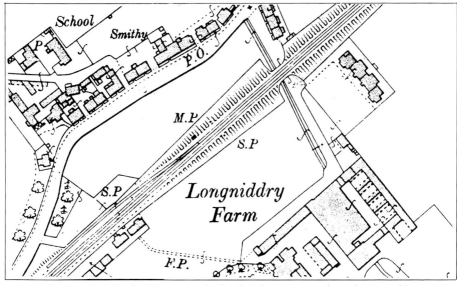

Peppercorn 'A1' Pacific *Bonnie Dundee* heads a down express through Longniddry on 11th June, 1960 − compare the rebuilt signal box with that shown on page 52. *H.C. Casserley*

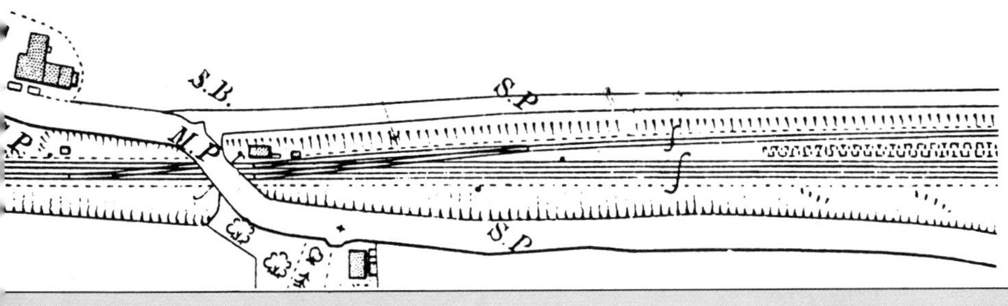

Aberlady Junction, 1914, showing the signal box, the Spittal road bridge.

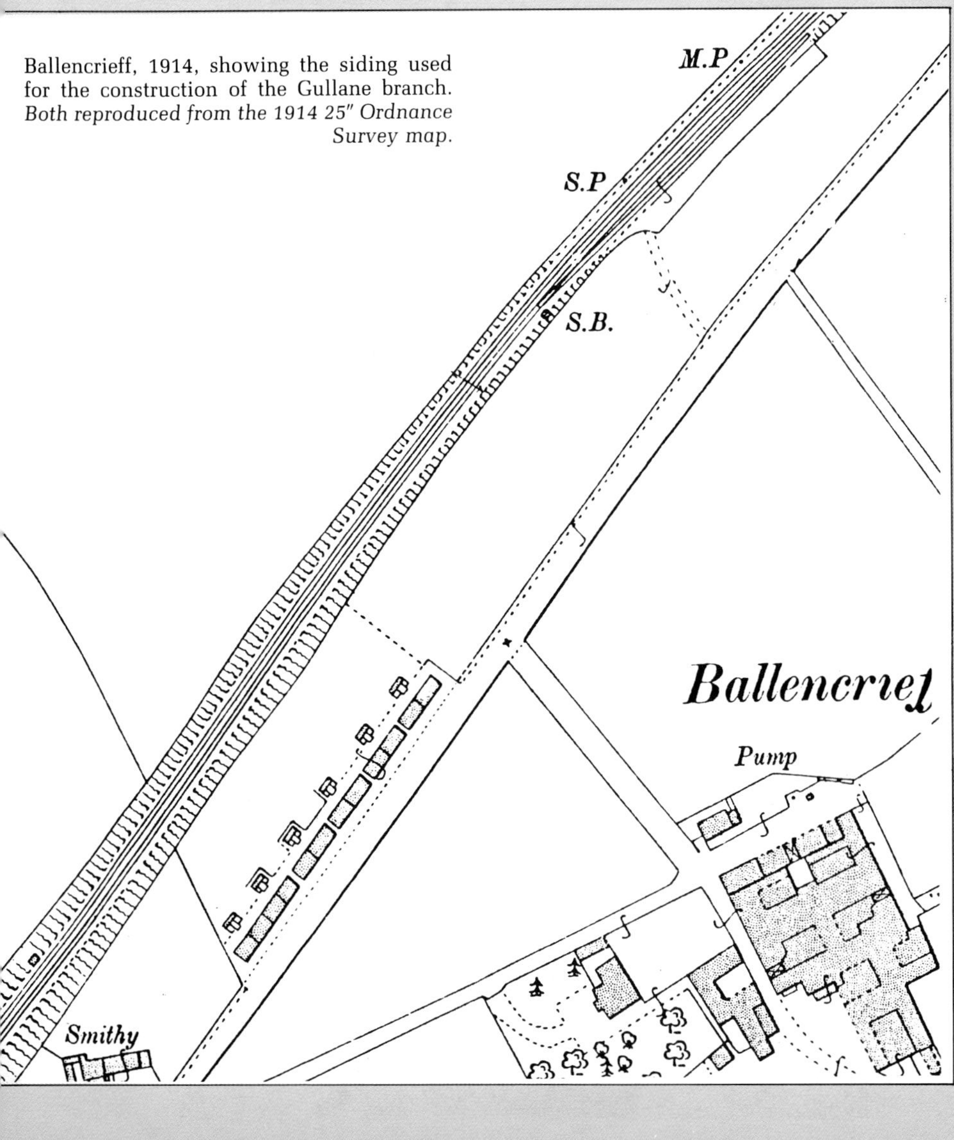

Ballencrieff, 1914, showing the siding used for the construction of the Gullane branch. *Both reproduced from the 1914 25″ Ordnance Survey map.*

M.P

S.P

S.B.

Ballencrie[

Pump

Smithy

The first of a set of photographs taken on 3rd March, 1898 for the benefit of the shareholders of the Aberlady, Gullane and North Berwick Railway – the Spittal bridge and Aberlady Junction signal box.   *D. Neilson/P. Marshall Collection.*

The 'Sunday Brig' over the main line and Gullane branch – originally built to facilitate those attending the kirk at Aberlady the bridge was rebuilt in the 1920s and demolished in 1989 – BR have now 'temporarily' diverted the footpath via the Spittal road bridge.   *D. Neilson/P. Marshall Collection.*

Aberlady Station as the contractors add the finishing touches – their iron shed was removed prior to the opening of the line the following month.

D. Neilson/P. Marshall Collection.

Aberlady Station, March 1898 – the loop and signal box were removed in the 1920s; the bridge survives to the present day. *D. Neilson/P. Marshall Collection.*

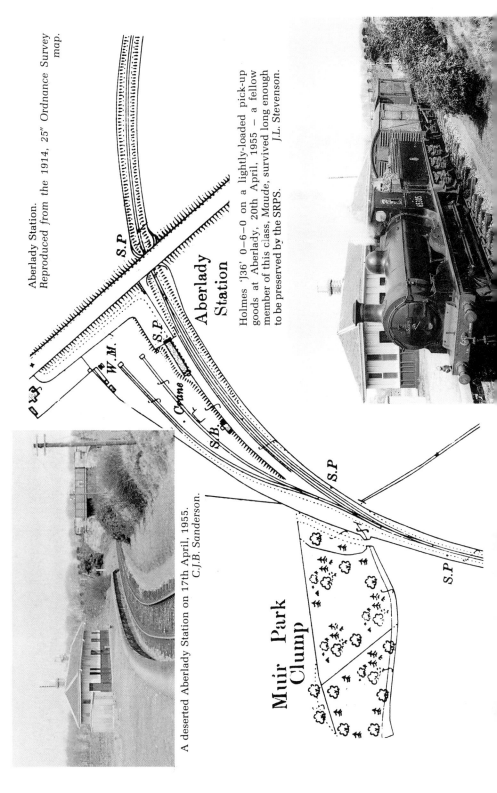

Aberlady Station.
Reproduced from the 1914, 25" Ordnance Survey map.

Holmes 'J36' 0–6–0 on a lightly-loaded pick-up goods at Aberlady, 20th April, 1955 – a fellow member of this class, Maude, survived long enough to be preserved by the SRPS. *J.L. Stevenson.*

A deserted Aberlady Station on 17th April, 1955. *C.J.B. Sanderson.*

Aberlady Station

Muir Park Clump

Holmes 'J36' class No. 65267 runs tender first through Aberlady with the branch goods – a typical load well illustrating why the line was already an anachronism by the 1950s. *RCAHMS, Rokeby Collection.*

A Reid class 'J37' at Aberlady in the final week of traffic, June 1964 – despite the imminent closure the trackwork and station buildings are in excellent condition!
G.N. Turnbull

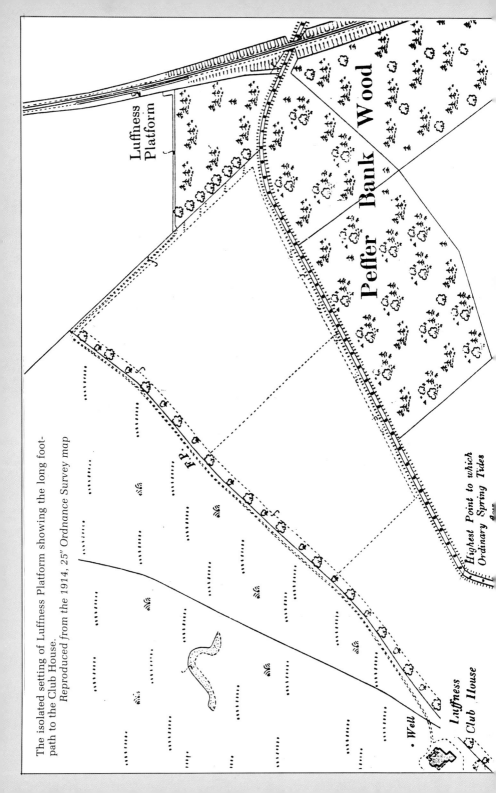

The isolated setting of Luffness Platform showing the long foot-path to the Club House.
Reproduced from the 1914, 25" Ordnance Survey map

Luffness Platform

Peffer Bank Wood

Highest Point to which Ordinary Spring Tides

Well

Luffness Club House

The only known photograph of the small timber structure at Luffness Platfrom; only members of the Luffness New Golf Club were permitted to use the station (April 1913). *W.F. Jackson, Glasgow University Archives*

The 4.18 pm train from Gullane to Longniddry passes Saltcoats Farm behind an unidentified Holmes 4−4−0 on a day in August 1911.
W.F. Jackson, Glasgow University Archives

Bridge No. 4 at Luffness Mains – a month to go and the road banking has barely been
started.   D. Neilson/P. Marshall Collection

The bridge carrying the Luffness to West Fenton Road across the line – the original
course of the road and the considerable earthworks needed to avoid a level crossing
are both clearly visible.   D. Neilson/P. Marshall Collection

Bridge No. 6, the skew bridge over the Peffer Burn at Luffness – the plans of this bridge are reproduced on page 72. *D. Neilson/P. Marshall Collection*

Gullane Station, March 1894 – the contractor's locomotive peeps out from behind the signal box. *D. Neilson/P. Marshall Collection*

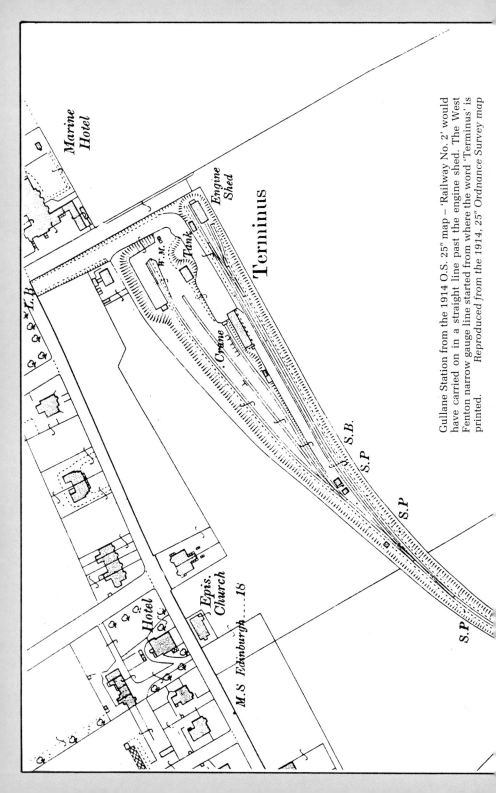

Gullane Station from the 1914 O.S. 25" map – 'Railway No. 2' would have carried on in a straight line past the engine shed. The West Fenton narrow gauge line started from where the word 'Terminus' is printed.　　Reproduced from the 1914, 25" Ordnance Survey map

Marine Hotel

Engine Shed

Terminus

Tank

W.M.

Crane

Hotel

Epis. Church

M.S Edinburgh ...18

S.P

S.B.

S.P

S.P

S.P

lady, Gullane and Dirleton village. The estimated costs were:

Railway No. 1	£39,245 12s. 0d.
Railway No. 2	£20,844 13s. 10d.
	£60,090 5s. 10d.
Sum for contingencies	£ 2.909 14s. 2d.
	£63,000 0s. 0d.

The capital to build the line was to be raised by way of an issue of 6,600 £10 shares, half of which were to be Ordinary shares and the other half Preference shares, and powers were sought to borrow on mortgage a further sum not exceeding £22,000. The new railway was not designed to be a cheaply built or sub-standard line (which was, perhaps, somewhat surprising given the contemporary moves towards Light Railways throughout Britain), and it was apparently never envisaged that the line would be doubled at a later stage.

The proposed route of Railway No. 1 was that it would leave the main line about 1 mile and 40 chains east of Longniddry Station, close to the hamlet of Spittal – 'the point of divergence', as the *Haddingtonshire Courier* reported, 'bearing the imposing title of "Aberlady Junction", a dignity to which the village [Spittal] will no doubt have to live up to'. Here the branch diverged and ran for 450 yards parallel to the down main line before swinging abruptly to the north-west on a sharp curve, the radius of which was 18 chains, before running in a straight line for half a mile over land belonging to Lord Elibank. At the junction the land belonged to Lord Wemyss, and it was necessary both to divert a private road belonging to him (since the new railway was to occupy its solum), and to construct an additional span on the existing footbridge carrying a path over the line at the junction. This path formed part of a route favoured by country people wishing to attend the kirk at Aberlady and in consequence the railway crossing was known locally as 'the Sunday Brig'. The first 1,100 yards of the branch were on a steeply falling incline of 1 in 60; this gradient was to prove a serious problem in later years when trains, which had drawn up at the signal short of the junction, often found themselves unable to start again until, after a few attempts, the drivers managed to coax the slipping wheels up towards the signal box.

The second mile was over a largely flat course as the line turned due north passing close to Aberlady Mains and having a station immediately behind Aberlady village. From here the line was to swing north-west close to the shore, passing directly in front of Luffness House, the seat of Walter Henry Hope, and bridging the Peffer Burn close to its mouth. The line then crossed the links to Saltcoats Farm before terminating in a field belonging to Mrs Hamilton Ogilvy, close to both the east end of Gullane village and the gates of the Muirfield Golf couse.

From here Railway No. 2 commenced and ran due east for one mile to the farm of Queenstonbank, where it then swung towards Dirleton, passing within half a mile of the village, before joining the North Berwick branch a couple of hundred yards south of Williamston. This line was generally undulating and rose on a gradient of 1 in 100 towards Queenstonbank, before falling back on the same gradient towards Williamston.

Two Petitions were now presented in opposition to the Bill. The first of these was from the North British who protested, *inter alia*, that the new railway would abstract traffic from the North Berwick branch; that it was insufficiently funded and that the estimates were too low; that it was objectionable from an engineering point of view and that the proposed junctions were unsatisfactory; that 'there are other provisions in the Bill to which your Petitioners object as prejudicial to their property, rights and interests' and, in a general 'sweeping-up' omnibus objection 'The preamble to the Bill [i.e. the statement that the railway would be of public and local advantage] was untrue and incapable of proof'.

The second Petition was from Walter Henry Hope of Luffness who objected to the railway on the grounds that it would traverse his valuable farm at Aberlady Mains, destroy the farm house as a residence and ruin some of the best fields on the farm. Further Luffness House 'has been in the possession of Your Petitioner and his forefathers for many generations and large sums of money have from time to time been expended in improving and embellishing the mansion beauties of the estate'. In particular, the proposed embankment running 250 yards in front of the house would have the result that 'The amenity of the House and estate will thereby be most prejudicially affected if not entirely destroyed and no money compensation can recompense Your Petitioner for such injury to his old and cherished home'. Mr Hope went on to say that the area was already well served by the North British, and that 'greater facilities of locomotion are not required and are not likely to be required for many years to come'. Then, in perhaps the most extraordinary attack of all (especially so since Mr Hope had already leased certain of his lands for the very purpose he was now to castigate) he said that:

> Your Petitioner believes that the Bill is primarily, if not solely, promoted in the interests of the Edinburgh members of a private club for golfers who have recently rented on a lease for 19 years as a golfing green of 100 acres at Muirfield opposite the termination of Railway No. 1 and in order to provide these Edinburgh members of this private club with better facilities for reaching their private golf links. There has been no desire expressed by those residing in the district. Whether the golf club confers any real benefit on the locality is in the opinion of Your Petitioner very doubtful. The chance of casual employment at a remunerative wage which the pastime offers to the golfers' attendants fosters habits of idleness and a dislike to steady labour adverse to the interests of the agricultural community . . .

On 10th March, 1893 the promoters of the new company entered into an agreement with the North British whereby the new company would construct the lines and the North British would work them on their behalf. The first clause of the agreement provided that:

> The intended Company shall make, construct and complete as a first class single line of railway with rails, chairs and sleepers for the permanent way of the weight of the quality used and laid down in the manner observed in the North British Company's main line the proposed railways or such of them or such parts thereof

as shall be authorised by Parliament and shall also before the proposed railways are opened for traffic construct or provide all necessary stations, station accesses, station masters' houses, gate-keepers' houses, goods sheds, sidings, loading banks, cranes at stations and weighing machines, signal cabins, signals, water tanks with water, supply speaking telegraphic apparatus [i.e. telephones] and Tyer's train tablet system of working (unless otherwise agreed) and all other furnishings and conveniences required for the efficient and economical working and carrying on of the said railway . . .

The agreement also provided for the maintenance, management and working of the lines by the North British in return for 50 per cent of the gross revenue, and for the payment of a dividend of £4½ per centum per annum to the Ordinary shareholders, with certain contingencies should the lines not produce a profit.

On the 14th of March of the same year the proposed line was considered by the Parliamentary Select Committee on Railway Bills. The proceedings were opened by Counsel for the company who began by saying that:

I daresay some of the Honourable Members know North Berwick which has a great reputation as being the place which has, I think, more than any other caused the introduction of one of the national games of Scotland into England . . . The number of people who go to North Berwick has been growing larger every year and in point North Berwick is full to overflowing . . . there is much land ripe for feuing . . .

Evidence was then given by Mr Blyth who gave the Committee an outline of the works which would be required, and also the benefit of his personal knowledge of North Berwick where he himself resided for six months of the year. He ended by stating that (notwithstanding their Petition) 'it is the policy of the North British to encourage little lines like these'.

A robust exchange then took place with regard to Mr Hope and the averments in his Petition and it became obvious that there was a difference in opinion between Lord Wemyss and the Ogilvy family, who both supported the line, and Mr Hope, who did not. Farmers gave evidence to the effect that they would use the line for the produce from their farms and evidence was also given by travellers who used the Longniddry to Aberlady horse bus service that they would patronise passenger trains between these points. The Parish Minister of Dirleton spoke of the benefits in general of the proposed line while a Mr Thompson said that he thought the new railway would be of great benefit both for the carriage of potatoes and school-children. John Lees, a rope maker from Aberlady, said that he was a daily commuter to Edinburgh and he reckoned that the new railway would save him between £15 and £20 per annum. Favourable comments came even from John Pincott, despite the fact that he owned the competing bus service. George Dalziel, Writer to the Signet, was asked 'If he thought that the present inhabitants of Gullane and Aberlady . . . would be gratified by the discharge of train loads of excursionists from Edinburgh?' and pragmatically replied that they would, by reason of the railway giving them better facilities and higher rents.

The hearing was then adjourned to enable the promoters to come to an arrangement with Mr Hope. The following month, new proposals were drawn up for a substantial deviation of Railway No. 1, starting at a point 500 yards south of Aberlady Mains and taking a great sweep south of Luffness Mains and Aberlady village before joining the original formation at Saltcoats Farm. This was acceptable to Mr Hope and formed the route of the line as eventually built – unfortunately it extended the line by over half a mile, caused a number of severe curves and resulted in the station at Aberlady being somewhat remote from and inconvenient to the village.

The promoters of the Aberlady Gullane and North Berwick met formally on 7th July, 1893 and Messrs Weiland, Grierson, Kemp and Brodie were appointed as Directors, along with Ralph Dundas, a solicitor who occupied the prestigious and ancient legal post of Clerk to the Signet. John Campbell, another Edinburgh solicitor, was appointed as Company Secretary at an annual salary of £52 10s. and the new company was informed that 'there was a very favourable disposition towards shares, £1,500 being subscribed by Members of the Honourable Company [i.e. Muirfield] alone . . .' Messrs Cunningham, Blyth and Westland, consulting engineers of Edinburgh, agreed to take 300 shares at 10s. each 'as payment to account of their fees and outlays as engineers'. The meeting was informed that 'Railway No. 2 will not be constructed without the consent of the North British and that a formal agreement to that effect would be entered into along with a perpetual working agreement.'

On 24th August, 1893 the Aberlady, Gullane and North Berwick Railway Act 1893 received the Royal Assent. The Act ratified the agreement between the new company and the North British and contained many of the usual clauses to be found in contemporary railway legislation with regard to fares, rates for goods and miscellaneous traffic, financial arrangements and other diverse matters. One curiosity was, however, Section 28 which, considering the nature of the land through which the line was to pass and the fact that it took great steps to avoid human habitation *en route*, provided that:

> The Company shall not under the powers of this Act purchase or acquire in any district within the meaning of the Public Health (Scotland) Act 1867 ten or more houses which on the fifteenth day of December last were occupied wholly or partially by persons belonging to the labouring class as tenants or lodgers or except with the consent of the Secretary of State for Scotland ten or more houses which were not so occupied on the fifteenth day of December last but have been or shall be subsequently so occupied.
>
> For the purpose of this section the expression 'labouring class' means and includes mechanics, artisans, labourers and others working for wages, hawkers, costermongers, persons not working for wages but working at some trade or handicraft without employing others except members of their own family and persons other than domestic servants whose income does not exceed an average of thirty shillings a week and the families of any of such persons who may be residing with them.

Progress was now slow and the take up of the shares was not as rapid as had been hoped. On 10th March, 1897 the Directors of the new company were informed by the Secretary that some of the accounts for expenses due to witnesses at the Select Committee hearings some four years before had still not been paid. He was instructed 'that payment of these be delayed so that the Secretary may negotiate for their withdrawal or very material reduction'. More importantly, there were still shares which had not yet been allocated or taken up and the final 790 shares were now allocated – these final shareholders were a mixed lot and included four iron merchants from Kirkcaldy and Glasgow, an Edinburgh merchant, a Glasgow contractor and, not unsurprisingly, George Bradley Weiland (who received 300 shares) and Ralph Dundas (100 shares). At the end of the day the line was financed with £33,000 of Ordinary shares, £33,000 of Preference shares and £11,000 of Debentures. All of these were fully paid up by September 1898 with the exception of £10 – the Directors appear to have chased up this reluctant single shareholder but without success!

The contractor chosen for the line was John Howard of Victoria Street, Westminster and on 18th November, 1896 a draft contract was entered into with him for the construction of Railway No. 1. The actual work was begun in February 1897 and Howard agreed with the North British that he could use the existing main line siding at Ballencrieff for the delivery of construction materials. In May 1897 the NBR agreed to loan Howard 50 yards of old permanent way materials for the purpose of extending the siding and 150 old sleepers for a new loading bank, both of which were to be built at his own expense. The construction of the new line was fairly rapid since the earthworks were minimal, except for the heavy banking required to carry the public roads over the railway and the only difficulties were when hard boulder clay was encountered at the Gullane Station site. The bridges were faced with freestone ashlar brought from Fife and the superstructures were metal. Of the stations, the *Haddingtonshire Courier* commented that:

> The station houses, both Aberlady and Gullane, are neatly furnished with the usual modern equipments and each has a passenger platform 140 yards long, while ample siding accommodation has also been provided for goods traffic.

Two standard gauge tank locomotives were used by the contractor in connection with the construction works namely *Rose*, which had been previously employed on the building of the East of Fife Central Railway (the Lochty branch) and was probably built by Andrew Barclay, and (although this has not been definitely confirmed) *Falcon* 0–4–0ST No. 45 of 1884 – this latter locomotive was sold by Howard to the Summerlee Iron and Steel Co. Ltd at Prestongrange Colliery in about 1898.

On 15th September, 1897 the Directors approved of calling the junction at Spittal 'Aberlady Junction' and the signal box there was opened in the following week. Two key members of staff were now appointed by the North British (who, in terms of their Agreement were responsible for staffing the new line). At Aberlady, the first station master was to be William Yorkston, formerly employed in the Lost Property Office at Edinburgh, and John Seth was transferred from Uddingston West to occupy that position at Gullane. In March 1893 the official Board of Trade inspection of the line was carried out by Colonel Addison accompanied by Mr Blyth, Mr Westland, Mr Howard, Mr James Bell (Chief Engineer) and Mr Deuchars, superintendent of the North British.

On Friday 1st April, 1898 the line opened to the public and the *Hadding-tonshire Courier* commented that:

> The day was favoured with pleasant sunny weather and the first train, which started at Longniddry at 7.10 am, carried a fair number of passengers. This, however, was rather early in the day for even enthusiastic railway 'openers' and it was by the later forenoon trains that passengers, mostly curious to see what the new railway was like, travelled. Several people left the county town [Haddington] by the 9.30 train to perform the journey to Gullane. There was the suspicion of a smile here and there as the enterprising voyagers called for 'Gullane – return' while they looked doubtfully at the clerk as if the novel order could not be met after all. However the tickets were forthcoming and in the usual leisurely process of time Longniddry was reached.
>
> The Longniddry platform was busier than usual and a certain suppressed excitement proved that things were a little out of the traditional. Away down the siding to the west lay the new train, newly painted gilt and lettered, nay even ribboned, for an artistic bandeau of white relieved the sable complexion of the very wheels. Dull crimson, gold, black, white, polished brass, glittering windows, it looked like a train on a honeymoon bashfully waiting for travelling orders. The passengers moved about the platform discussing the exciting situation and marvelling at the splendour just lavished upon the new line. 'New carriages – a new train out and out' was the general verdict but the cautious ones half-closed their eyes, smiled and slowly delivered 'Nae fears, they are the auld ones peinted', which was the case!
>
> Just before ten o'clock the Edinburgh train appeared and the passengers transferring into our train with its vermilion tickets bearing the legend 'LONGNIDDRY, ABERLADY & GULLANE' and we set out . . . Sweeping north from the junction, the men at the harrows stopped to gaze, and far up the fields there were shaded eyes and figures that came quickly into sight to get a clear view . . .
>
> Decorations had been put in the tasteful hands of Mr Jardine of Haddington and as we twined up to Aberlady station strings of the gayest bunting waived a welcome over the newly varnished woodwork and children hung over the bridge . . .

The reporter for the rival *Haddingtonshire Advertiser* was obviously an earlier bird for he travelled on the very first train, the 7.57 am to Gullane in the company of Mr Deuchars, the general superintendent of the NBR, John Howard the contractor, chief inspector Hogg and, on the engine itself, Mr Brown, locomotive inspector. Clearly he was less suspicious than the *Courier* man for he describes the train of three third class and one first as being 'new'. He then went on to say that:

> The train departed promptly from Longniddry and its progress on the way to Aberlady and Gullane was noted with interest by cottagers, workers in the fields, and workmen employed about the new line. Aberlady was reached at 8.4 and some villagers were present to welcome the train. A string of flags was displayed, and the station house was also festooned. The train then steamed off to Gullane, which was reached on time at 8.11. The station-house was also festooned, a number of people from the village were on the platform, and cheers were raised as the new train arrived.

The railway had finally come to Gullane and even though men were still

CHAPTER ccix.

An Act to authorise the North British Railway Company to construct certain new railways widenings and other works to confer further powers upon the Company and upon other companies in connexion with their respective undertakings to amalgamate the Aberlady Gullane and North Berwick Railway Company the Newport Railway Company and the Eyemouth Railway Company with the Company to transfer to and vest in the Company the undertaking of · the Borrowstounness Harbour Commissioners to enable the Burntisland Harbour Commissioners to borrow and the Company to advance them further money to authorise the Company to enter into working and other agreements with the Invergarry and Fort Augustus Railway Company to raise additional capital and for other purposes.   [6th August 1900.]

A.D. 1900.

WHEREAS it is expedient that the North British Railway Company (in this Act called " the Company ") should be authorised as in this Act provided—

To make and maintain certain widenings of their Stirlingshire Midland Junction Railway and certain new railways in extension of and in connexion with that railway ;

To make and maintain a widening of their branch railway from South Leith to Portobello ;

To make and maintain a railway to form a junction between the railway authorised by the North British Railway (Waverley Station &c.) Act 1891 and the railway of the Company from Easter Road to Piershill ;

To make and maintain in connexion with their system certain new railways in Glasgow ;

The Act of Parliament that brought the short life of the independent Aberlady Gullane and North Berwick Railway company to a close.

at work finishing off the line and laying the sidings at the terminus, the enterprise was virtually complete.

The Aberlady, Gullane and North Berwick Railway Company was, however, destined to have but a short independent life. The line seems to have been a profitable venture in that the shareholders regularly received their 4½ per cent dividends and there were, apparently, no 'unforeseen circumstances'. There was, however, little logic in having such a small concern operated by the North British but remaining nominally independent of it, and on 14th October, 1899 the Secretary of that company wrote to the Aberlady, Gullane and North Berwick. He offered to purchase the smaller concern for a consideration of £29,333 6s. 8d. of North British 3 per cent Debenture Stock 1893 and £93,500 North British 3 per cent Consolidated Stock, 'to be allocated to the holders of stocks of the Aberlady, Gullane and North Berwick Company in such manner as that Company may determine'. The shareholders appear to have considered this a good enough offer, for at the Board Meeting of 8th November the Directors accepted the offer 'in principle'. On 6th August, 1900 the North British Railway (General Powers) Act was passed and, on that date, the Aberlady, Gullane and North Berwick Railway Company (together with the Newport Railway Company and the Eyemouth Railway Company) passed into the hands of the North British.

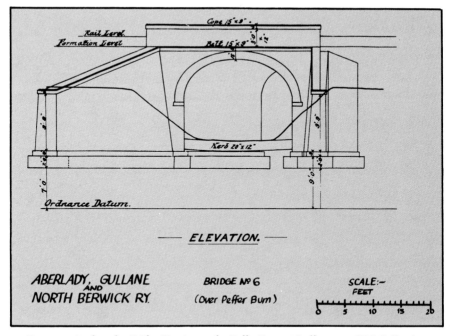

Contractor's plans for Bridge No. 6 over the Peffer Burn at Luffness.   *SRO Collection*

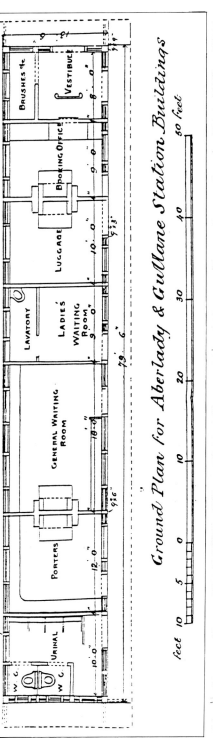

Ground Plan for Aberlady & Gullane Station Buildings

BRUSHES &c.

VESTIBULE

BOOKING OFFICE

LUGGAGE

LAVATORY

LADIES' WAITING ROOM
9' 0"

GENERAL WAITING ROOM
18' 0"

PORTERS
12' 0"

URINAL
10' 0"

W.C.   W.C.

8' 0"

6' 0"

10' 0"

9' 0"

9' 6"

79' 6"

7' 3"

Feet 10   5   0   10   20   30   40   50 Feet

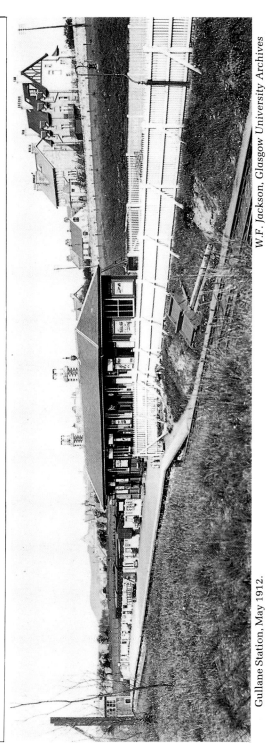

Gullane Station, May 1912.

Gullane – the passenger platform looking eastwards, 9th July, 1952. *A.G. Ellis*

Another view taken on the same day – note the council housing scheme under construction on the right. *A.G. Ellis*

Two views of Gullane Station buildings in June 1960 – their condition is surprising given that passenger trains last called there 28 years before. The train is an SLS special and includes a fine Gresley teak saloon coach.   *R.M. Casserley*

The engine shed, release road and water tower at Gullane, seen in May 1912.
W.F. Jackson, Glasgow University Collection

The engine shed on 18th June, 1936 after the withdrawal of the passenger service and the branch engine. *W.F. Jackson, Glasgow University Archives*

The goods yard at Gullane, May 1912.   *W.F. Jackson, Glasgow University Archives*

Holmes class 'D' 0−6−0 No. 269 with empty stock in the carriage siding at Gullane, June 1902.   *W.F. Jackson, Glasgow University Archives*

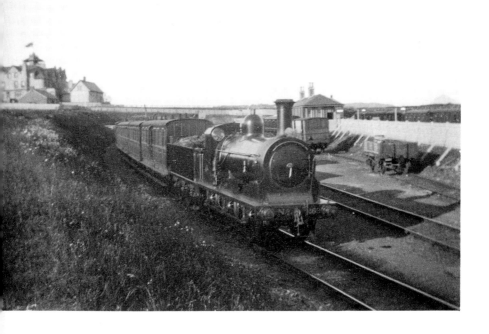

Chapter Six

From Aberlady to Biarritz

THE LATTER DAYS OF NORTH BRITISH OWNERSHIP, 1900–1922

'North Berwick is occasionally designated the "Scarborough of Scotland" but it is only so in so far as Scarborough might be called "The North Berwick of England".'

North British Railway Tourist Guide, 1914.

The Aberlady and Gullane Railway proved to be a success. The initial summer service provided for eight daily services with an additional five on Saturdays, including one express which omitted to stop at Longniddry, running fast to Aberlady. Now that it was much easier to reach the two villages, they proved to be even more popular with summer visitors and some 14,560 passengers used Aberlady Station in the year 1900 while at Gullane the total was 20,900 – among the latter was no less a person than William Fulton Jackson, the General Manager of the North British, who regularly spent his holidays in Gullane and, somewhat fortuitously for the present author, was a keen amateur photographer*. The effect on permanent residence was also clear – in the decade between 1891 and 1901 the population of the village virtually doubled from 243 to 575 persons.

Goods services were less spectacular in their success and there were no specific goods trips shown in the working timetable other than a Tuesdays Only cattle train to serve Gorgie Market in Edinburgh, but the crew of one of the branch passenger trains to Gullane were instructed to make a special return goods trip along the branch if required. At Aberlady Station, the Aberlady and Gullane Gas Light Company Limited built a new gas works and this small but successful enterprise was, by the time of its nationalisation in 1949, serving 722 consumers and producing four million cubic feet of gas per year. The rival horse buses from Longniddry ceased to run, the last being that run by John Pincott who, despite the challenge to his livelihood, had given evidence in favour of the new railway at the Parliamentary hearings; he was described as being 'a noted expert at packing a crowd into his two-horse brake'. Aberlady harbour now ceased to be used apart from occasional potato traffic and, if only for a brief period, the railway was to enjoy a complete and unchallenged monopoly.

In the early years of the new century there was a spate of accidents and incidents upon the branches. These included a collision between two wagons and a passenger train between Dirleton and Drem on the Halloween of 1901, causing the derailment of one carriage and injury to three passengers including two ladies who were subsequently paid £10 by the company as compensation 'for shock to the nervous system'. In the same year Alex McLean of Buccleuch Street, Edinburgh, jumped or fell out of a train at Gullane, rolling between the platform and footboards with fatal

---

* W.F. Jackson (1855–1931) was a clerk who rose up through the hierarchy of the North British Railway to become its General Manager between 1899 and 1918. Something of a stickler for discipline and order he was sometimes feared, but always respected, throughout the company and had the unique distinction of having walked all 1,240 miles of the NBR system. He lived in Edinburgh but was clearly fond of East Lothian and spent several summer holidays in Gullane; his fascinating photographic collection is now held in the Glasgow University Archives and is freely available for inspection.

results. Two years later the NBR accident books record that one G. Riddel was struck by a potato at North Berwick Station and that he sustained an eye injury but that no claim was being made against the company. A more spectacular incident occurred on 20th August, 1904 when a train of empty carriages broke away, ran down the gradient and collided with the buffer stops at North Berwick, before careering over the concourse and ending up in the public road. Much damage was done and four persons standing by were injured including Miss Gilholm, the station tobacco stall attendant, who was paid £15 damages for shock.

This was also the beginning of the period in which the town was to reach its zenith as a fashionable holiday resort and North Berwick was soon rather self-consciously to use the soubriquet of 'The Biarritz of the North' (perhaps only as pretentious as Edinburgh dubbing itself 'Modern Athens'!). The *North British Railway Official Tourist Guide* commented that:

> It has been said that in the season you may knock up against the original of a picture post-card at every turn; and at least one many has placed amongst his personal glories the memory that he once played the Right Hon A.J. Balfour's ball on the golf links by mistake.

(Balfour, of course, being the Prime Minister!) In *Through the Lothians*, a publication of the North British designed for potential holidaymakers to the area, the exclusive nature of the town was further extolled:

> There are times when the visitors' list reads like a page from Debrett, and a survey of the local newspapers suggests that the journalists detailed for duties at gatherings such as church bazaars, flower shows, golf tourneys &c., find that they have to devote the greater part of their attention to dealing with what follows the stock journalistic phrase 'Among those present . . .'.

Not all commentators, however, agreed that progress was necessarily desirable and in 1913 Ian Hannah was to write in *The Berwick and Lothian Coasts* that:

> Neither the endless motors, nor the strings of cycles, not the numerous lodging houses, nor even the human race represented by that kilted cockney over there can destroy North Berwick's charm. On the pier which protects the little harbour, or in the old part of the town, one may readily forget the dull, uninteresting line of brick and stone that has stretched its length along the sea-front, or at the sight of the blissful children who play all day on the broad smooth sands, perhaps in charge of a dark-skinned native of Madras in her flowing Eastern robe of yellow cloth, forgive the extremely indifferent style of villa architecture. There is indeed a cemented swimming-pool upon the very rocks, also close by an Esplanade where, on a little cabin with a tiny stage in front, it is advertised that certain entertainers will twice daily appear. But even these attractions fail to detract materially from the fascination of the place . . .

Some visitors made special arrangements with the company and in a 'Special Traffic Notice' for Thursday 2nd October, 1902 under the heading of 'Mr J.P. Morton's Party', the railway staff were informed that:

> A sleeping-car will work through with this party per 8.45 pm ex-London (Kings Cross) on 1st October and the 4.40 am ex-Berwick must call specially at Drem on

2nd October to detach the vehicle, which will then be worked forward to North Berwick by special Drem dep. 5.35 am, North Berwick 5.45 am.

A more distinguished visitor, however, was to arrive in the town in the following week when the newly-crowned King Edward VII (although the local press pointedly deleted the regal number) came to stay for a couple of nights with his relatives Prince and Princess Edward of Saxe-Weimar at the Knoll, Clifford Road. The King had been staying at Balmoral and a special Royal Train left from the nearest station to the castle, Ballater, on the Great North of Scotland Railway, at 1 pm on Thursday 9th October. It then ran fast to Dundee, where there was a brief stop to enable the engine to take water, followed by a second stop at Haymarket West Junction where, in order to accommodate members of the Royal Party, 'four carriages for London (Euston) were to be detached and handed over to the Caledonian Company'. At 6 pm the Royal Train reached North Berwick where, in accordance with the special instructions issued, a telegraph message in confirmation thereof was sent immediately to the Superintendent of the Line at Edinburgh. It was decreed that

> Engines must be in first-class order, and every possible precaution is to be taken to avoid failure in any part of the machinery. The drivers, both of the Pilot Engines and the Royal Train, must be selected from the most experienced hands, and must know the road well.

Extensive disruption throughout the North British system was caused and a large number of ordinary passengers and goods trains were

> . . . to be shunted into sidings or otherwise dealt with to ensure SAFETY and (as far as possible) ABSENCE OF NOISE on the passing of the Royal Train from ABERDEEN to NORTH BERWICK. All level crossings [were] to be secured across the road at least 30 minutes before the passing of the Royal Train. The stations are to be kept quite clear and private while the Royal Train is stopping at or passing them and none of the public are in any circumstances to be admitted to ANY of the stations. The servants of the Company are to perform the necessary work on the platform without noise and no cheering or other demonstrations are allowed, the object being that His Majesty shall be perfectly undisturbed during the journey.

At North Berwick, only invited guests in morning dress were permitted to attend the King's arrival and departure at the station and special permits were issued. On the Thursday afternoon a half-holiday for local schoolchildren was declared, and for two days the town was virtually en fête. The King departed in his Royal Train on Saturday morning at 10 o'clock, and after arriving at Drem the train was passed over to the care of the North Eastern Railway who provided an engine and guards.

Facilities for ordinary visitors to North Berwick multiplied and, following the construction of a new pier at the Platcock rocks, Galloway's pleasure steamers began to call there regularly – a special inclusive fare was quoted for a round journey by sea from Leith and Portobello to North Berwick and a return by train. A new golf course at the town appeared in 1894 and this was redesigned by James Braid in about 1906, when the resident professional was none other than the great Ben Sayers. Subsequently the Town Council, who owned the course, negotiated a special return fare from Edinburgh with

The driver of Holmes '633' class 4−4−0 No. 617 on a down express at North Berwick surveys the photographer with suspicion, *c*.1902.   *A.G. Ellis Collection*

Reid 'L' class (LNER 'C16') 4−4−2T No. 451 shortly after its violent collision with a pig and a cattle wagon between Drem and Dirleton on 21st September, 1921; the scars of battle are still evident!   *A.G. Ellis Collection*

the North British, of 3s. 6s. [17½p] first class and 2s. 5d. [12p] third class for the members of the North Berwick Corporation Golf Clubs. Much building went on in the town, and a series of solid and imposing stone villas were erected in the vicinity of Dirleton Avenue on feus from Sir Walter Dalrymple.

At Aberlady business was brisk, despite the remoteness of the station from the village, and the combined effects of the railway and golf created a boom in Gullane. According to the author of *Through the Lothians*:

> There is a glorious spaciousness about the place. The wee village is unspoiled. It is little more than a single street, although round and about it are the fine villas of those who, having paid a summer visit, have also paid something in homage to the charm of the district by building permanent residences. At Gullane there is room, and to spare, on the links for crowds of players, yet they never seem to be crowded. You may play on any course for one shilling [5p] or, at the most, one shilling and sixpence [7½p] per day . . .

Between Aberlady and Gullane lay the estate of Luffness owned by the same Walter Henry Hope who had so vociferously opposed the coming of both the railway and the game of golf to the locality. Notwithstanding his professed dislike of both these manifestations of a modern age, he proceeded to lease out a further portion of his land to a private club of gentleman golfers named the New Luffness Golf Club and provided them with both a well laid out links, situated between the main road and the railway, and a spacious club house and, realising that when the motor car was still in its infancy the railway could provide suitable access to the course for Edinburgh members, he proposed to the North British that a private halt be provided on the Gullane branch line. The NBR responded with alacrity and in August 1903 Hope entered into a Minute of Agreement with the company whereby they undertook to construct and maintain, at their own expense, a halt 'for the use and convenience of golfers playing over the golf course' in return for which Mr Hope obliged 'himself and his heirs and successors in the estate of Luffness to pay to the Company an annual rent of £15 and that by two equal instalments at Whitsunday and Martinmas'. Following upon this, a short wooden platform with a simple shelter was constructed on the down side of the line, a hundred yards north of the bridge over the Peffer Burn, and this was opened to traffic on 1st September, 1903 under the name of Luffness Platform – a cinder path connected the halt to the New Luffness Club house. Certain daylight hours passenger trains called at the halt as required and passengers from Edinburgh were charged a special fare, but there was no mention of Luffness in the public timetables. Those wishing to alight at the halt had to make their request to the staff at Longniddry prior to the departure of the branch train and in the down direction, according to the working timetable, 'These trains will only stop when passengers are on the Platform to be taken up. When a stop is made, trains will leave Aberlady one minute later than booked and run correspondingly later to arrive.' It was stressed that stops were to be made 'ONLY for the accommodation of members of Luffness Golf Club'. It was common practice for intending passengers to telephone the station master at Gullane from their Club House to make sure that the train would stop to pick them up, even when these

The myth: a contemporary postcard issued by the Cynicus Publishing Co. of Tayport.
J. Harrold Collection

The reality: NBR motor-bus No. 1 at Dirleton village, *c.*1907.   *Author's Collection*

were not scheduled to call at the halt. The facility was well used up to the late 1920s and some of the older villagers of Gullane can still recall the sight of the gentlemen golfers in their plus fours waiting on the platform on summer evenings.

About the time that Luffness Platform was constructed, serious thought was being given to the position of 'Railway No. 2', the extension from Gullane to North Berwick, particularly because of the lack of development east of Gullane and, according to the author of a local guidebook* in respect of Dirleton 'the want of proper railway facilities had seriously retarded its progress, otherwise its natural attractiveness might have brought about its development as a summer resort'. As an interim measure, the North British decided to start up an experimental motor bus service along the main coast road between Aberlady Station and North Berwick via Gullane and Dirleton village. This provided a connection between the branch line stations and the various golf courses *en route*. Accordingly, on 8th September, 1904, the North British Directors approved of the purchase of two Arrol-Johnston 'motor cars' for the service at a cost of £560 each from the Mo-car Company of Paisley. These motor cars were, in fact, 23-seater open-sided charabancs finished in a varnished walnut livery and carrying both the North British coat of arms and large fleet numbers (respectively 'No. 1' and 'No. 2'). A petrol store was built at North Berwick so that a supply of fuel would be always available and, on 23rd March, 1905, the Board approved the construction of a garage (rather quaintly referred to as a 'motor car house') next to the station there.

The bus service commenced on 14th June, 1905 with an ambitious number of 12 runs in each direction at regular hourly intervals. The through journey between Aberlady and North Berwick was scheduled to take 40 minutes at a fare of one shilling [5p]. Unfortunately these pioneer vehicles were bedevilled with mechanical problems and, on one occasion, by an altercation with a telegraph pole. The service ran until 31st October when it ceased for the winter, the buses being sent up to Fort William to work another experimental service from that town to North Ballachulish. In the following summer they returned to East Lothian and the service recommenced on 2nd July, 1906, although for some curious reason there was no mention of this in the NBR public timetables then or subsequently. In order to alleviate the disruptions caused by the all too frequent breakdowns, the service was recast so that only one bus at a time was needed and the other held as a spare.

In April 1907 the North British returned the vehicles to their makers and they were part-exchanged for two new models which cost £700 each, less a trade-in for the old ones of £250 apiece. The existing bodies were retained and mounted on the chassis of the new vehicles. The service continued, but not without incident – in the same year a bus from Aberlady parted company with the road near Luffness and ended up in the ditch. A steam wagon was summoned to pull it out, but a further difficulty was then encountered when the local constabulary arrested the driver on the not unreasonable suspicion that he was intoxicated. There was now no one

* Wilson's *Guide to North Berwick*, published in 1907.

present who knew how to drive the bus and so two horses had to be attached to drag it to the Marine Hotel at Gullane, where it lay until the following day when the other driver rescued it. In a sequel at Haddington Sheriff Court, the original driver faced a drunk driving charge.

On 30th September, 1910 the bus service was discontinued for the winter as usual, but the following year for reasons which were not announced at the time and are not at all obvious, it did not reappear and it was 20 years before another railway-owned bus was seen again on the country roads in the area.

Another example of Edwardian entrepreneurship was provided by the North Berwick Gas Company. Always a prolific user of railborne coal (using some 1,149 tons in the year 1894–5 alone and rising to more than double this in a decade), the original works next to the station were by now too cramped and were also considered by a more aesthetically-minded age to be something of an eyesore. In the autumn of 1903, construction commenced of a new works on a green field site at Ferrygate, adjacent to the railway some distance to the south of Williamston, and this was brought into use the following year.

Two trailing sidings (complete with wagon turntable and catch points) were laid into the new works on the up side of the line and they were known officially as Gas Works Siding. Served by special trip workings from North Berwick station, trains to Gas Works Siding were propelled there by the branch engines and the North British Rule Book permitted this unusual form of working on the condition that 'the guard or shunter must ride in the front vehicle, which must be a brake van'. The gas works flourished, being taken over by the North Berwick Town Council, and the original siding site was sold to the Marine Hotel where, to this day, it forms part of the hotel grounds.

In the years leading up to World War I, there were a series of labour disputes affecting Scottish industry and trade; one that had a particularly disastrous effect was the great Miners' Strike of 1912. This began on 4th March and the North British system was particularly hard hit. A reduced emergency service was brought into force, but by the following week this had to be drastically curtailed, and both the North Berwick and Gullane lines were served only by one branch shuttle return working in the morning and a similar service in the evening. Normal services were resumed at the end of the strike on 13th April, 1912, but not until a certain bitterness in labour relations had taken place and at least some regular commuters had been permanently alienated.

Ironically the North British were, at the very time of the strike, developing plans for what was to become the most prestigious train to serve the two branch lines. As a writer in the *Railway Magazine* commented:

The more important of the Haddingtonshire resorts are within easy travelling distance of Glasgow and are each year becoming more popular with the West Coast businessman, who travels daily to and from his summer residence. All along the North British have fostered this traffic, which has now assumed dimensions which warrant the putting on of a special through summer coastal express between Glasgow and East Lothian. Happily named, the 'Lothian Coast Express', the new train began to run on June 3rd and it has one of the best timings on the North

British system . . . This very credible effort on the part of the North British has already met keen appreciation on the part of the public, and as the new service becomes better known, there is little doubt that the summer population of Haddingtonshire will show a marked increase.

The 'Lothian Coast Express' was, indeed, a 'credible effort'. Made up of three separate sections of modern vestibuled stock (in contrast to the rather shabby stock used even on the Edinburgh 'residentials'), the train was hauled by one of the new 'Scott' class 4–4–0 locomotives from St Margarets (two particular favourites being No. 895 *Rob Roy* and No. 359 *Dirk Hatteraick*). Starting at Dunbar at 7.55 am, three carriages, namely a five-compartment Brake Third, Lavatory Composite and an eight-compartment Third, were taken non-stop to Drem where they arrived at 8.09. Here they were joined by the North Berwick portion, consisting of an Open First Dining car, a Brake Third Kitchen and a seven-compartment First, and these were taken by the branch engine to the junction and then propelled on to the rear of the Dunbar portion. Some four minutes later the combined portions departed for Longniddry where the Gullane portion, a Lavatory Composite carriage and a Brake Third were waiting. The complete train now left Longniddry at 8.25, arriving at Waverley at 8.42 and then running through to Glasgow Queen Street where it arrived at 9.49.

Both the Gullane and North Berwick portion guards travelled back on the footplate of the light engine workings to their respective termini – the timetable noting that, in respect of the Gullane engine, 'the engine working this train to Longniddry, after placing the vehicles on the down Lothian Express, must immediately return to Gullane to work out [the 8.37 Gullane to Longniddry local] and must on no account be delayed in order to ensure a punctual start to [that train]'. The return working of the 'Lothian Coast Express' left Glasgow at 3.50 arriving back in the coastal resorts just after half-past five. The train ran on weekdays only and on Saturdays the up working left Queen Street some three hours earlier, that day being, of course, a half-holiday for most businessmen. The original publicity stated that the train was to run until the end of August 1912 – its popularity, however, ensured that it was extended for another two weeks, the final down working running on the morning of Monday 16th September, 1912.

The most surprising feature was the fact that meals were served – in 1912 such facilities were still fairly rare in Britain especially on runs of such a length. A *Railway Magazine* contributor noted of the 'Refreshment Car' (also referred to by the NBR as the 'Tea Car') that 'this luxurious vehicle is certainly up-to-date in all its appointments, and the kitchen arrangements kept quite separate, are carried on in an adjoining vehicle specially fitted up for that purpose'. Another innovation was the fact that the train engine bore a headboard displaying its title and this was said to have been the first example of a British named train to do so. The 'Lothian Coast Express' was a smart train, its carriages being clean and well turned out; at least two Gullane schoolboys travelling daily to school in Haddington just after World War I were so impressed by the train that they made a special effort to catch it every schoolday, rather than the more prosaic following 'residential'. The

NBR official view of the 'Lothian Coast Express' with Reid 4–4–0 No. 359 *Dirk Hatteraick* posed at North Berwick in about 1912 – normally only three carriages of this train would be conveyed along the branch to Drem where it would meet up with the Dunbar portion. *A.G. Ellis Collection*

NORTH BRITISH RAILWAY.

NEW THROUGH

LOTHIAN COAST EXPRESS

BETWEEN

GLASGOW (QUEEN STREET)

AND

GULLANE, NORTH BERWICK, and DUNBAR.

The new Through Morning and Evening Lothian Coast Express now runs as follows :—

	Ex. Sat. p.m.			Ex. Sat. a.m.	
Glasgow (Queen Street) ... leave	3 50	During July and August only.	Dunbar leave	7 55	During July and August only.
Edinburgh (Wav.) ,,	4 55		North Berwick ,,	8 0	
Aberlady ... arrive	5 26		Gullane ... ,,	8 0	
Gullane ... ,,	5 32		Aberlady ... ,,	8 6	
North Berwick ,,	5 38		Edinburgh (Wav.) arrive	8 43	
Dunbar ... ... ,,	5 42		Glasgow (Queen Street) ... ,,	9 49	

Tea and Light Refreshments are served on these Trains.

Comfortable Vestibule Corridor Carriages.

Cheap Periodical Tickets.

Finest Golfing Centre in the World.

Bathing.   Boating.   Bracing Air.

THE SUMMER SEAS POSTER

NORTH BRITISH ROUTES ARE "AS THE CROW FLIES"—DIRECT.

"THE HEIGHT OF THE SEASON"
—NORTH BERWICK STATION.

Three examples of NBR publicity from the Company's *Official Tourist Guide* for 1914.

two of them still remembered the Express with affection when the author spoke to them almost 70 years later!

The 'Lothian Coast Express' was part of a peculiarly Scottish phenomenon – during the summer months it was common for middle-class families to take a house at the seaside for a whole month, during which the father of the family would travel to and from the resort to his business; it was particularly from Glasgow that this annual event was most pronounced. Other examples included the Clyde islands and resorts served by the Caledonian and Glasgow and South Western companies and, on the North British, the 'Fifeshire Coast Express', which ran to Anstruther, Crail and the East Neuk resorts. The whole family, including servants and pets, would travel out together, their luggage having been sent a day or two in advance at a greatly reduced rate, and on the North British special 'Additional Train Services in connection with Families Removing to and From Summer Quarters' were run. In 1912 a special from Queen Street and Lenzie was run to Aberlady, Gullane, North Berwick and Dunbar on 30th June and 1st July, the return workings leaving on 30th and 31st July. These trains were somewhat unusual in that they ran fast over the 54 miles between Lenzie and Longniddry, omitting Waverley altogether. Part of the promotion of these services consisted of the issuing, by the North British, of a large coloured 'birds-eye view' poster of the Forth resorts and several picture postcards of local views and the train itself. For many years the 'Lothian Coast Express' was a popular attraction for potential holidaymakers, in the days before cars and the lure of more exotic destinations.

As a resort, North Berwick was now enjoying some success in attracting families, particularly those where the fathers and sons wished to play golf while the younger children and their mothers were occupied with seaside pursuits and, in view of the popularity of the town with visitors from the South, the NBR instituted from July 1913, a summer service of two through carriages per day between London King's Cross and North Berwick, the branch line engine conveying the carriages to and from Drem. This experiment was short lived and for obvious reasons did not survive beyond the end of the following season.

When World War I was declared in August 1914, the government assumed overall control of Britain's railways, although they still remained in private ownership. At first little happened to affect directly the two branch lines and the holiday season was not cut short, but at the beginning of 1915 there was a great deal of renewed local agitation for the construction of 'Railway No. 2', the line between Gullane and North Berwick. A petition from the Provost and Magistrates of North Berwick, the Committee of the Gullane Golf Club and numerous private individuals in the locality was then sent to the Directors of the North British, who duly considered it at their Board Meeting on 11th February. The Petition stated that:

> The district through which the intended railway would be carried would be improved by increased travel facilities . . . and there would be great economy in the working of the railway. At present some expresses stop at Drem and some at Longniddry; a common stopping place would [be desirable] . . . There would be a great economy in the working of the branches and a reduction of locomotive and

labour costs would be assured. The traffic of summer visitors between Aberlady and Gullane and North Berwick would be much facilitated and the inducements to build in the vicinity of the railway would be increased. The railway, if gone on with at an early date, would furnish employment to many who might otherwise be out of employment due to the war . . . as a collorary of the extension of the line from Gullane to North Berwick, Your Petitioners understand that the service on the branch from Drem will be much curtailed without detriment to the existing conveniences for the transport of agricultural produce, etc. . . .

The petition was signed by 632 residents in Gullane alone (out of a possible total of 842 but 'owing to the war a large number of houses are closed') and the total number of signatures was 1,240. On 18th March, 1915 a deputation met the North British Directors and pointed out that amongst the benefits would be that of making Longniddry an important main line stopping-place serving a surrounding area containing over 27,000 people.

There are eight golf courses within the vicinity and Lord Wemyss has decided to develop his estate at Longniddry for residential building. There were no objections to the closing of the line from Drem because the new station at Dirleton would fill the purpose and there would be no problem in acquiring the land.

The times were not auspicious, however, and the Directors of the North British were, in any event, well aware that with the rise of the motor vehicle, it would be an act of folly to spend money on this project, despite its attractions from the operational point of view – for all practical purposes the age of rural railway building was over. Nothing more was heard of the scheme, and it is interesting to speculate on the likely history and fate of what would almost certainly have been the last ever country branch line in Scotland to be constructed.

During World War I, certain necessary economies were made. In 1915 the North British Estates Committee postponed the approval of expenditure on bathrooms for the station agents' houses at Aberlady and Gullane, and certain seasonal and excursion trains, including the Lothian Coast Express, were suspended for the duration. Additional military traffic was, however, run on the North Berwick branch and had a semi-serious suggestion that North Berwick should be made the temporary seat of Government while London was vulnerable to Zeppelin bombing raids been acted upon, the fortunes of the line might have been somewhat different. In the event, Edinburgh was also attacked by Zeppelins and the experiences of Hartlepool, Whitby and Scarborough ('The North Berwick of England') demonstrated the vulnerability of the Eastern seaside towns to enemy action. On the Gullane branch, construction materials were conveyed in connection with the airfield at West Fenton.* During 1917 passenger fares were increased throughout the country by 50 per cent and traffic on both branches showed a marked, if only temporary, fall off. After the war the economic climate did not greatly improve and on 31st August, 1920 the restaurant cars on the Fife and Lothian Coast Expresses were withdrawn, although in the case of the latter their absence was not greatly noticed, given the comparatively short journey times and the civilised hour of the morning departures. Another necessary economy was effected when, on 3rd October, 1921, Aber-

* see Appendix One.

lady Station signal box was closed. At the end of the 1922 season the through coaches from Dunbar and Gullane were deleted from the 'Lothian Coast Express' and thereafter it became a single through train from North Berwick to Glasgow with connections at Drem from Dunbar and at Longniddry from Gullane. The Express was drawn between North Berwick and Waverley by a 'C15' or 'C16' tank locomotive from North Berwick or (on occasions) St Margarets, and thereafter by a 'D34' or other NBR tender locomotive from Haymarket shed that took the train through to Glasgow and considerable savings were thereby made in the costs of operating this train, in contrast to the previous post-war habit of using a 'D34' on the North Berwick and Gullane portions.

The motive power of this period was varied. In late Victorian times the Drummond 0–6–0 and 4–4–0 tanks (both confusingly classified as class 'R' by the North British) continued in service and were joined by Holmes 0–4–4T locomotives Nos. 90 and 91 – the latter were normally shedded at St Margarets and used on the Edinburgh to North Berwick 'residentials'. Other regular workings on the branch were provided by Holmes 'M' or '633' class 4–4–0s (LNER Class 'D31') and Holmes 'C' class 0–6–0s (LNER class 'J33') and examples of these engines also appeared on the Gullane branch. From 1909 onwards, Reid 'M' class 0–4–4T locomotives (LNER 'G9') appeared on Edinburgh 'residentials' and in 1913 his 'M' class 4–4–2Ts (popularly known as 'Yorkies' by reason of their having been built by the Yorkshire Engine Company in Sheffield and later classified as 'C15' by the LNER) made their debut on the Gullane branch and in the following year, Glasgow-built 'L' class ('C16') locomotives of a similar but superheated design began working on the North Berwick line. In common with standard North British practice the engines of passenger trains carried boards with the appropriate destination painted in white letters against a dull red background.

In 1921 a most unusual accident occurred at Drem. The night of Tuesday 21st September was dark, overcast, with no moon, and a gusty wind was blowing from the west. At about 6.45 pm the up cattle train from Gorgie Market deposited two loaded cattle wagons in the siding at the east end of the cattle dock at Drem, the one nearest the buffer stops being destined for Drem and the other for Dirleton. The guard of the cattle train, Simpson, in accordance with his normal practice, pinned down the brakes of the outside wagon (i.e. the Dirleton wagon) but left the other unbraked. The siding led straight on to the North Berwick branch line but trap points, for the purpose of stopping any runaway wagons, were situated before the junction of the siding and branch. Shortly afterwards Wilson, the signalman on duty at Drem, telephoned Dirleton Station to inform them that he had a cattle wagon for a consignee there. Dirleton then telephoned North Berwick and arranged that a special trip would be made from North Berwick to pick up and deliver the wagon to Dirleton, and that this would follow after the passing of the 8.20 passenger train from North Berwick. Mr Renton, the station master at North Berwick, who retired shortly after the incident, then spoke to the NBR Southern Control on the telephone about this special working, adding that he did not have a guard but that he would work the trip himself. Although

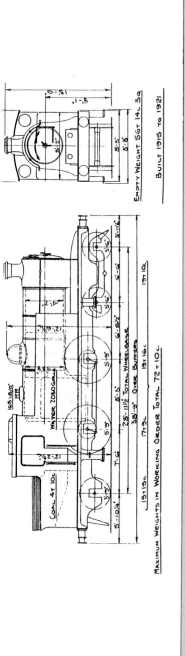

LNER drawing of NBR class 'L' 4–4–2T – the superheated version of the 'M' class 'Yorkies', these later formed LNER class 'C16' and were seen at North Berwick up until the end of steam in 1958.
SRO Collection

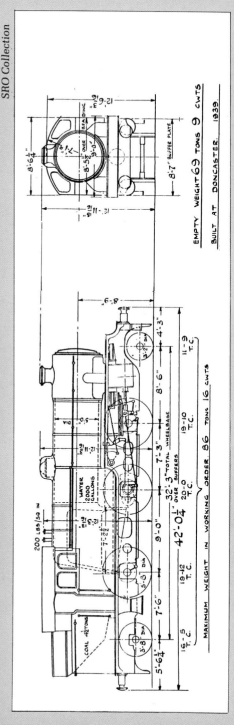

The impressive lines of Sir Nigel Gresley's 'V3' 2–6–2 tanks, used on the North Berwick branch and throughout the LNER system.
SRO Collection

Control stated that 'they did not think it was a very nice thing to do', they sanctioned this irregularity because the consignee of the wagon was pressing.

The special, driven by Driver Hooton with a crew consisting of porter McGurn and station master Renton then set out, and arrived at Drem a few minutes later. McGurn then coupled up the wagon for Dirleton but, other than by merely flashing his handlamp upon it, he ignored the Drem wagon and in particular failed to notice that it was unbraked. The special then set off at 8.44, the Drem signalman watching its tail light vanishing into the night. He then spent about half a minute writing up his train register, before pulling off lever No. 22 which set the trap points against the siding and thereby making sure that the branch line was properly protected. In that brief space of time between the departure of the train and the pulling of lever 22, the unlit and unbraked Drem cattle wagon set out on its unauthorised journey down the falling gradient and on to the branch line, helped on its travels by its well-oiled axle boxes and a strong tail wind. The truck then came to a halt just over a mile from Drem; no one noticed its absence. The 8.30 pm Edinburgh to North Berwick passenger train, hauled bunker-first by a class 'L' 4−4−0T No. 451 weighing 72½ tons and with a load of four 6-wheel passenger coaches weighing a total of 54 tons, left Drem at 9.37. As the train was accelerating down the branch line (the driver, Mitchell, afterwards estimated that the speed of the train was between 30 and 40 mph), it collided violently with the runaway wagon causing the locomotive and train to part company, with the result that the track was destroyed over a considerable distance. The truck was a write-off and the engine was considerably damaged. No passengers were injured, other than a pig, the hapless occupant of the cattle truck, which was killed.

At the subsequent Inquiry, Major Hall reported to the Ministry of Transport that he held Renton and the controller to blame, and he completely exonerated McGurn and Wilson, although he did comment that it was unfortunate that the latter had left the trap points open while making his entries. No blame attached to Simpson or Mitchell. He concluded that 'The case is one which might, in view of the speed of the passenger train, have had far more serious effects, and is another example of results which are likely to follow the assumption by untrained men of duties which they are not qualified or authorised to perform.'

In these last years of the North British, it is perhaps interesting to survey the railway facilities which existed in the area since it was at this time that they reached their maximum extent. Starting with the North Berwick branch, the station at Drem had two platforms on the main line bisected by an iron lattice footbridge manufactured by George Smith, Ironfounders. The main station building, a single-storey stone structure on the up side with low twin pitched gables, contained the booking hall and other station offices, and beside this stood the station master's house in a similar style. Adjoining the platform was a small goods shed and water tower, while to the north were three goods sidings and a cattle dock. On the down platform was situated a small waiting room and on both platforms were typical North British wall mounted cast-iron drinking fountains bearing the legend 'NBR

Drem looking westwards at 2.30 pm on Sunday 28th March, 1954.   *C.J.B. Sanderson*

Drem looking eastwards in March 1969 – the runaway cattle wagon which caused the 1921 accident was positioned in the siding behind the platform fence.   *N.D. Mundy*

Drem on 13th July, 1950 – the branch 'C16' waits in the up siding and the signals are set for the main-line; in the age of the HST and 225 one would hesitate to take a picture from this viewpoint today! *A.G. Ellis*

Class 40 locomotive No. 40123 seen here on the 17th June, 1976 passing Drem Junction signal box with an oil-train. Note the token exchange platform.

Tom Heavyside

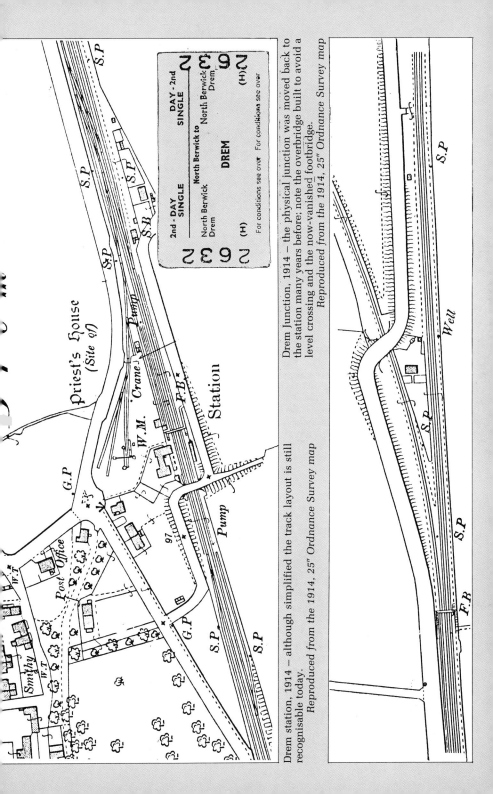

Drem station, 1914 – although simplified the track layout is still recognisable today.
Reproduced from the 1914, 25" Ordnance Survey map

Drem Junction, 1914 – the physical junction was moved back to the station many years before; note the overbridge built to avoid a level crossing and the now-vanished footbridge.
Reproduced from the 1914, 25" Ordnance Survey map

A Cravens/Metro-Cammell hybrid dmu gains the branch line at Drem on 10th June, 1976 – the signal relay room under construction behind the train will spell the end of the manual signal box in the background.   *Tom Heavyside*

A class '150' Sprinter on the 12.35 pm Haymarket–North Berwick service framed by the new footbridge at Drem on Saturday 13th April, 1991 – the connection to the up loop leading to the branch can be seen at the end of the platform.   *Author*

Keep the Platform Dry'.* Large sign boards proclaimed 'DREM JUNCTION FOR ATHELSTANEFORD CHANGE FOR NORTH BERWICK AND DIRLETON', Athelstaneford being a village a couple of miles south of Drem and giving its name to the parish in which the station was situated. Opposite the entrance to the goods yard was the signal box, an austere brick and wooden structure containing a newly-installed 45 lever frame. The track layout at Drem was complex and there were trailing and facing crossovers on the main line before the branch line started its 600 yards-long run along the up loop, parallel to the up line, before diverging in a north-easterly direction. Other facilities included shunting sidings on both lines, a down goods loop and a carriage siding.

Dirleton was a simple small country station of which only the projected down side was ever built. This consisted of a fairly short platform on which a substantial single-storey brick building was situated. At the north end was a wooden lamp hut while to the south was a small goods shed – latterly a grounded coach body of uncertain vintage also appeared on the platform. There were two goods sidings worked by a ground frame and a crane was provided. Opposite the main station building was the station agent's house with its distinctive tall chimneys. Access was via a short road leading in from the east.

North Berwick was a rather grander station. At the entry was situated a tall brick signal box and, immediately opposite, a two road brick-built engine shed. The two passenger platforms were on a curve and, to permit engine release, there was an ingenious double scissors crossover – a most complicated piece of trackwork, especially since it was built upon a curve Formerly the main buildings had been on the up side platform, but in 1893/4, new waiting rooms and offices were added on the down side and beyond the buffer stops, a concourse, waiting room and other facilities were built, greatly increasing the size of the passenger accommodation. The goods yard was extensive, having facilities for livestock, coal and, in the large goods shed, general merchandise. The trackwork was again ingenious here and, to save space, a three-way point was a prominent feature. Small stables were situated close to the road and the site of the level crossing which had originally carried the old gasworks siding; the stables were later demolished when 'mechanical horses' and, later, vans took over the carting duties. A refuge siding lay to the south of the station, and the bus petrol store and water tank were situated near to the engine shed.

Longniddry was a busy place, the main station buildings, dating from 1846, being situated on the up side and reached by a short approach road. The down platform was joined to the up by a lattice footbridge and it was an island serving the main line on its inner face and the Haddington branch on the outer; a waiting room and other offices faced the main up buildings. To the immediate north lay three sidings and a large goods shed, and there was a loading bank, crane, cattle dock, wagon turntables, weighbridge and, at the east end of the down platform, a tank and water column. Almost immediately opposite, at the east end of the down platform, was the signal box, a tall brick and wooden structure similar to that at Drem. South of this was the

* The drinking fountains were removed in March 1992.

station master's house, some cottages for railway employees and a two-road engine shed which, like that at North Berwick, was operated as a sub-shed of St Margarets. As the main lines left the station in the direction of Drem, the Haddington branch diverted and began to climb to the right and a short line ran down into a standard gauge tramway network serving the adjacent Harelaw Limekilns.

At the Prestonpans end of the station on the up side, was a loading bank served by a siding some 113 yards long. This siding, known alternatively as Longniddry West siding and, more graphically, as Longniddry Manure Siding, was, as the latter name suggested, for agricultural purposes and was to be used only during daylight hours. Longniddry Station could sometimes be busy and the signalman's job was particularly hectic when the various portions of the 'Lothian Coast Express' were being joined at the station. When the branch connections were awaiting a main line train, Longniddry was again a hive of activity and many of the older inhabitants of the village could recall hearing the loud cries from the station staff of 'Longniddry Junction for Aberlady, Gullane and Haddington'.

At Aberlady Junction the small signal box was situated on the down side to the immediate east of the Spittal roadbridge. A hundred yards or so down the line was a lattice footbridge carrying a footpath across both the main line and the branch. Aberlady Station was situated on a curve and had a single passenger platform on the up side with a long, low building, containing all the usual offices, situated at the east end. The small signal box was halfway along and behind the platform and opposite was a passing loop. Two goods sidings and the station master's house all lay to the north.

The layout at Gullane was quite complex. The station buildings, in the same cottage-like style as those at Aberlady, were placed at the end of the single passenger platform beyond which the line continued to a crossover and a short siding, which permitted the release of the locomotive. Here also was situated a water tower and a small single-road engine shed and coaling stage. Behind the station were three sidings, a coal staith, cattle dock, crane and small goods shed and the signal box was situated at the west end of the passenger platform.

The stations were great centres of local life and they provided a focus for people to meet on business, socially or even just to watch the trains pass. Among the facilities available were John Menzies bookstalls on both Gullane and North Berwick stations – the former was in a small shed known as 'the cubbyhole' and presided over by Chrissie Robertson, while the latter station had a much grander curved and varnished wooden edifice which sold a wide variety of goods. At Gullane, Mr Seth presided over an immaculately kept station and, in addition to being station master, also ran a coal business (a concession which the NBR readily granted). Originally from Dunbar, Mr Seth took an active part in local village life and was a member of the bowling club; his son, with an eye to the future, kept Foden lorries. When Mr Seth retired, he was replaced by a Mr Whytock and later, in the final years of the station, Tom Smith was the goods agent (there being no passenger service by then). In 1920, an 0–6–0 tender locomotive was stationed at Gullane shed

John Seth, Gullane's first station master, proudly in charge in August 1914; he regularly won prizes for his flower displays and for his efforts in keeping the station in a fine state.   *W.F. Jackson, Glasgow University Archives*

The General Manager and a companion cast their shadows on the platform as 'C' class 0–6–0 No. 292 prepares to leave Gullane on an afternoon in August 1914.
                                                                    W.F. Jackson, Glasgow University Archives

and there were two engine crews employed on the branch – George Dent and fireman Horwood and George Hume and his fireman 'Jerks' McKenzie. George Hume's son was employed as the cleaner at the shed (working a 10 pm to 6 am shift, the main purpose of which was to prepare the branch engine for the next day's duties). The staff also included two porters, John Thomson and Paddy Morin (whose wife took on similar duties during World War I) and a clerk, A. Scott. The signalman was John Emslie. The branch guards were named Fairgrieve and Davidson and, later on, a Mr Howden. Local deliveries were made by Archie Watt and Thomas Hogg, the two carters employed by the North British and their horse-drawn lorries were kept at Gullane Station. Mr Watt was something of a local character and the sight of his lorry drawn by 'Clinker' and followed by his faithful bull-terrier 'Bonzo' was a familiar sight in the village. According to local legend 'Clinker' would, of his own accord, come to a halt outside Bisset's Hotel and wait patiently until Mr Watt had partaken of his daily 'refreshment' there. At a time when virtually all the supplies for the village were brought in by rail, the two carters had a busy time delivering all variety of goods and these included passengers' luggage, tea-chests containing china for a local shop, fresh flowers, straw baskets in which salmon were packed and, when Lord Derby paid his annual summer visit to Gullane, His Lordship's household goods including silverware, china and fine linens were brought by rail.

In 1921 the government relinquished its control over the railways and almost immediately put forward a programme for the amalgamation of the 120 or so separate Railway Companies in Britain into four great combines. On 1st January, 1923, and despite some spirited opposition, the North British passed into the hands of a new conglomerate with its headquarters in England, the London & North Eastern Railway.

1926 advertisement; for many years the company were excellent customers of the railway.

Chapter Seven

Indian Summer

THE LNER YEARS, 1923–1947

'On a recent visit North Berwick station was a sight for sore eyes . . . all locomotives seen there being spotlessly clean'.

Railway Observer, September 1939

The new owners of the two branch lines brought little immediate change and although the initials 'LNER' or 'NE' appeared on publicity, the stations and the rolling stock, the same ex-North British locomotives, carriages and wagons continued to provide the same local service; the 'Lothian Coast Express' sped the morning commuters to their work, the holidaymakers still enjoyed the delights of the breezy coastal resorts. Outwardly it would have seemed to the casual onlooker that the railway was one of the few stable elements in the changed and changing post-war world. The reality, however, was different.

In 1923 there were few private cars or motor buses in rural Scotland and, in an area which the electric tramway had failed to reach and the steamship was unknown except for pleasure trips from North Berwick pier and some desultory coastal trade, there was no real competition with the railway as the universal common carrier of both passengers and goods. This near monopoly was, however, destined to vanish within a generation and the cause of this was the internal combustion engine. World War I had proved the catalyst; although the private motor car was still a comparative rarity (there were only 1,000 cars registered in East Lothian in 1928, but by 1938 this number had doubled), it was soon to deal a death blow to much of the first class off-peak train travel of golfers and other well-heeled day-trippers. The motor bus did the same for the less wealthy, and the steam, petrol and (later) diesel lorry provided efficient and cheap door to door transport in a way which the local railways could not.

The final chapter in the saga of 'Railway No. 2', the Gullane branch extension, took place when the powers to construct the line were finally allowed to lapse and in reply to a letter from solicitors acting for a Mr A.B. Stevens of Queenstonbank farm, who wanted to know if the company were intending to buy any of his land to construct the line, the LNER in February 1924, replied that they had no further proposals in respect of the scheme and that there was no likelihood of Mr Stevens being required to sell his land to them.

For the time being, however, there was optimism in the air and the LNER made some fairly immediate improvements. Several restaurant cars were transferred from England to the Southern Scottish area of the LNER and one of these was allocated to the 'Lothian Coast Express', thus reintroducing the facility removed in 1920. In 1924 a complaint was received from the Dunbar Town Council that their connection to the Express was composed of 'old carriages which were very dirty and this state of matters is rendered worse by contrast with the great comfort in which passengers can travel by the Express to North Berwick.' The LNER responded by providing a bogie brake composite coach 'of the old West Highland pattern' in place of the 6-wheel brake formerly used but noted that 'it was against our desires that a connection was afforded because it was well known that such would not pay.' Other improvements were made to local passenger train carriages and in the words of Hamilton Ellis, writing some years later:

> The first thing that struck the traveller by the North British Railway in the days previous to the amalgamation was, in my experience at any rate, the generally shabby condition of the passenger rolling stock. On the whole, however, the rolling stock on the present North British section has changed very much for the better. The new standard L.N.E. stock needs no introduction, while the renovated N.B. carriages look remarkably smart in many cases.*

Another innovation was the introduction of a through sleeper service to London from North Berwick. During the summer season, a single first class sleeping car was detached from the 10.35 pm night express from Kings Cross at Drem and conveyed forward from there to North Berwick by the branch engine, returning in the evening to be attached at Drem to the up sleeping car express. This service, which began in 1924, survived until 1939 although latterly it was 'conditional' and, for at least part of the season, the up train ran on Mondays only while the down service was on Fridays only. Presumably the sleeping cars were serviced at Edinburgh and conveyed to and from there as empty coaching stock since there would have been insufficient staff and supplies at North Berwick to permit this to have been done there. Until 1980, certain London sleepers made calls at Drem to pick up and set down local passengers and this facility (which was without North Berwick connections latterly) was thought to have survived for so long, partly to accommodate a former local member of Parliament who lived close to Drem; now the East Coast sleepers themselves are, of course, a thing of the past!

Passenger traffic remained buoyant until 1926 and indeed in the previous year, North Berwick Station had enjoyed its highest ever number of passengers – almost 94,000, or more than 30 times the population of the town. In the same period Aberlady had dealt with over 15,500 passengers, Gullane 28,000 and even the much quieter Dirleton had seen 6,500. Some measure of the importance of the railway in local life can be gleaned from a selection from contemporary Special Traffic Notices. At Hogmanay, North Berwick to Edinburgh trains were to be augmented by the addition of two or three third class carriages for the additional traffic. Throughout the summer additional trains were run, particularly 'Advertised One-Day Excursion Specials' from Edinburgh during the school and trades holidays. For the duration of the latter, the staff were instructed that 'The ordinary trains must be strengthened as required to meet the extra traffic during the holiday period, but no train may be strengthened beyond a single engine load'. It was the duty of the North Berwick station master to 'make application in good time to the depot for a supply of carriages'. At the end of the Trades, North Berwick to Edinburgh trains were 'to be made up to full strength and ample van accommodation to be provided'. Special trains to Glasgow were run 'for families and luggage' and on ordinary trains, a van was to be provided for carted luggage to Glasgow.

* 'A Scottish Retrospect' in January 1931 *Railway Magazine*.

There were numerous examples of special parties being catered for – a typical example was that of 24th July, 1926 when two extra third class carriages were provided on the 4.29 pm Drem to North Berwick local to accommodate 40 adults and 60 juveniles of the Third Edinburgh Company of the Boys' Brigade on an outing to Dirleton. Unlike more recent times it appeared that the railway was both able and willing to accommodate extra traffic and that efforts were made to retain sufficient coaching stock for this purpose.

Two events in 1926 radically affected the dominant position of the railway. The first of these was the nationwide General Strike in May – a sad climax to a series of railway strikes which proved to the travelling public in East Lothian and throughout Britain that the railway was not indispensable; the second factor was the arrival of competing bus services. In 1923 the Scottish Motor Traction Company began to run a Sunday bus service of five return journeys along the main road (now the A198) between Edinburgh and North Berwick, calling en route at Longniddry, Aberlady, Luffness and Gullane. Although this was not the first service of motor buses to serve the coastal resorts, it was the precursor of the modern through service from Edinburgh along that route. In November 1924 the Haddingtonshire Courier commented that, following the recasting of the LNER timetable so that eastbound connections from North Berwick via Drem were reduced, 'a private motor service might well be patronised'.* The Sunday service between Edinburgh and North Berwick now became daily and a second route, running via Drem rather than Gullane, ran between 1926 and 1929. It was later rerouted via Ballencrieff crossroads and Aberlady. In 1927, a 'limited stop' service over the principal route was run but this proved unsuccessful and was withdrawn after a few months. In 1928 the competition intensified when another company, the Edinburgh Omnibus Company 'White Line', operated along the same route and the rivals cut their fares and ran at 20 minute intervals on each other's tails in a vicious commercial war which ended in victory for the SMT Company.

The answer of the LNER to the bus competition was two-fold. In 1929 they, together with London, Midland & Scottish Railway, acquired a 50 per cent shareholding in the reconstituted SMT Company and thus obtained an indirect financial interest in their rival. The route prospered and has continued ever since, surviving changes of ownership including nationalisation and, more recently, the transformation from 'Eastern Scottish' to the revived and privately owned 'SMT' and 'Lowland' banners as Routes 124 and 125. The other response of the LNER was to attempt to cut costs and thereby improve the financial return from the two branch lines.

The most radical attempt to cut costs was the introduction of a steam railcar service on the North Berwick branch. The railcar concept was not a new one and worked on the principle of a single, self-contained, steam powered unit with limited passenger accommodation in a saloon and, if necessary, the capability to haul a trailer. This avoided the need to maintain

---

* A Dunbar to North Berwick service was, in fact, started by a local firm, Stark's of Dunbar, and this initially consisted of four daily return journeys. In addition Stark's also operated daily services from North Berwick to Haddington and the company was later taken over by the SMT concern, although it remained nominally independent for many years.

Down goods hauled by a 'C15' 4−4−2T passes Dirleton Station in April 1913 with the unmistakeable bulk of the North Berwick Law looming up in the background.

W.F. Jackson, Glasgow University Archives

A class 'V1' 2−6−2T running bunker-first with a local for Drem leaves Dirleton Station on 29th July, 1950.

D.L.G. Hunter

Dirleton Station in splendid isolation, April 1913 − the tall chimneys in the background belong to the still extant station master's house.

W.F. Jackson, Glasgow University Archives

Dirleton looking southwards, 9th July, 1952; the station was closed shortly afterwards.

A.G. Ellis

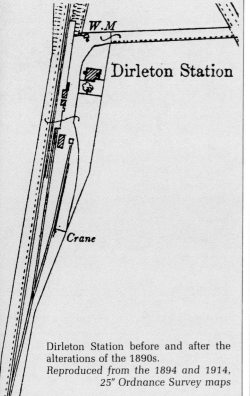

W.M

Dirleton Station

Crane

Dirleton Station before and after the alterations of the 1890s.
Reproduced from the 1894 and 1914, 25″ Ordnance Survey maps

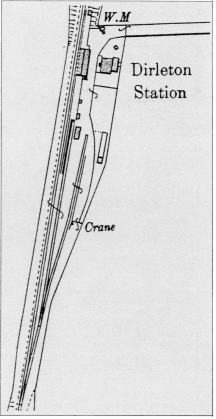

W.M

Dirleton Station

Crane

London and North Eastern Railway Company

(SCOTTISH AREA)

JOINT CIRCULAR.   *5th September* 1932.

To Station-masters, Goods Agents, Parcel Agents and Others concerned.

Withdrawal of Passenger Train Services on Gullane Branch.

With reference to General Manager's (Scotland) Circular G.M. 238, dated 2nd September 1932 : on and from 12th September 1932, passengers must not be booked to Aberlady and Gullane, and the station names and fares must be neatly struck out of the public fare lists. All series of printed tickets must be withdrawn and sent to the Divisional Accountant, Edinburgh, accompanied by the usual list.

Passengers to these places should be booked to Longniddry, from which point road services, operated by the Scottish Motor Traction Company, are available.

Parcels and Miscellaneous (Guard's Van) traffic should, however, still be accepted for Aberlady and Gullane, and charges raised thereon should be based on the throughout mileage to these stations. Such traffic will continue to be stamped or waybilled, as the case may be, but in dealing with "waybilled traffic," the following instructions should be carried out :—

Station.	Waybills to be Headed	Rates to be Applied.	Waybills to be Abstracted.	
			Local.	Foreign.
Aberlady	Longniddry for Aberlady	Aberlady	Longniddry	Longniddry for Aberlady
Gullane	Longniddry for Gullane	Gullane	Longniddry	Longniddry for Gullane

Traffic for these stations will be conveyed by Passenger train to Longniddry, from which point it will be taken forward to destination by L.N.E.R. road motor, and traffic forwarded from these stations will be conveyed by road motor to Longniddry for despatch by rail.

Transfer Vouchers should be declared to Longniddry, and all communications relating to traffic for, or from, the stations mentioned should be similarly addressed.

Goods, Coal, other Mineral and Live Stock traffic will continue to be dealt with as hitherto.

All concerned to give these instructions careful attention, and acknowledge receipt.

G. S. BEGG,	GEORGE MILLS,	W. PHILIP,	W. JOHNSTON,
Passenger Manager,	*Goods Manager,*	*Divisional Accountant,*	*Traffic Superintendent.*
Southern Scottish Area.	Southern Scottish Area.	Scottish Area.	Northern Scottish Area.
(G.C. 30/1728.)	(L. 1845/8.)	(D.A. 465.)	(P.R. 32/4328.)

The closure notice issued to staff a week before the end of passenger services.

separate locomotives and carriages, especially where these were becoming progressively older and more expensive to keep running. The company, intending to run a large fleet of railcars on branch lines throughout their network, chose the Sentinel-Cammell company of Shrewsbury as suppliers and adopted a smart green and cream livery for the cars. Each was named after a stagecoach (preferably one that had a connection with the locality in which the railcar was to operate).

In June 1928 No. 21 *Valiant* was used on a number of test trips from St Margarets and made at least one journey to North Berwick, in the course of which it came to a halt, having involuntarily shed its chains while running at speed. In due course, several railcars of an improved design were sent to St Margarets, and several of these were known to have operated services on the North Berwick branch from November 1930 onwards. One in particular, No. 36 *Royal Eagle*, was a stalwart of the line for many years; in July 1935 this car was noted as being used on both the North Berwick and North Leith lines. Not universally popular by reason of the hot, cramped and intolerable operating conditions imposed on the crews and the rather smoky atmosphere within the passenger saloons, the railcars ran for a number of years and the service varied. The basic pattern, however, involved return trips from Edinburgh to North Berwick after the morning and evening peak hours. The last working of the railcars in the area were in the late 1930s on the 7.23 am Longniddry to Edinburgh local service, but they survived until just after World War II on the North Leith branch line.

It was the Gullane branch which was hardest hit by bus competition, and there were several reasons for this: the comparative absence of large-scale commuting as at North Berwick; the isolation of Aberlady Station from the village; and the fact that passengers at Edinburgh had to climb the Waverley Steps whereas bus passengers were deposited directly in St Andrews Square. At Aberlady the annual number of passengers dropped to 1,168 in 1929, 652 in 1930 and in the six months between December 1931 and June 1932, the station managed to handle only 285 passengers – an average total of only 10 per week! At Gullane the figures were equally discouraging – the 1929 and 1930 totals were, respectively, 4,132 and 4,220 and in the first half of 1932, 2,071 – an average weekly total of 80!

A number of economy measures were taken and on 7th May, 1929, the signal box at Gullane was closed, the passing loop at Aberlady taken out of use and from then on the whole branch was worked on the 'one engine in steam' principle. Luffness Golf Platform was the next casualty. Little used in its latter years, and with the timber platform quietly decaying, the station was closed as from 1st June, 1931, the golfers having deserted the railway *en masse*. The stage was now set for the withdrawal of the whole passenger service on the branch. The disappointing passenger returns for the summer season of 1932, and the worsening financial crisis in which the LNER found itself, provided the impetus for the end of this little, and by now insignificant, country branch line.

On 2nd September, 1932, the Scottish General Manager of the LNER issued a circular to the effect that the passenger services on the Gullane and Lauder branches would be withdrawn on and after 12th September. This was followed up by a second circular, dated 5th September, which set out the alternative arrangements that were proposed for the Gullane branch passenger traffic; these arrangements included the booking of passengers only as far as Longniddry 'from which point road motor services operated by the SMT Company are available'. Items which had normally been carried in the guard's van (such as parcels and miscellaneous traffic) were now to be carried by LNER lorry from Longniddry to Aberlady and Gullane. In anticipation of this change, Thomas Hogg, the sole remaining railway carrier at Gullane, was sent to the company's training centre at Glasgow Cowlairs, where he was taught how to drive a motor lorry, and on his return was put in charge of a new Albion lorry. Goods services were to continue as before, but the mails were no longer handled by the company, the Post Office making their own alternative arrangements with their vans from Longniddry Station.

The falling of the axe on the passenger service was not, however, unexpected and initially, at least, this development appears to have attracted next to nothing in the way of local comment. September 12th was a Monday and, there being no Sunday service, the last passenger train to run was on Saturday the 10th; to the end the faithful NBR $4-4-2$ tanks ran the service and 'Yorkie' No. 9053 had the melancholic task of heading the 6.35 pm Gullane to Longniddry train on that date and thereby bringing to an end an era which had lasted a mere 34 years. On the same date the small engine shed at Gullane was closed, the necessity for having a separate branch engine having been done away with.

The cessation of the branch passenger service soon began to cause local controversy and, after a short while, the inhabitants of the two villages began to realise just what they had lost. The tourist season of 1933 was a quiet one and as many of the regular visitors to Aberlady and Gullane made alternative arrangements for their holidays, the effects on local hotel and house bookings were soon felt. A protest meeting was held in Gullane and arising out of this, a number of informal approaches were made to the LNER. These failed and accordingly a committee of local persons including Annie S. Swan, a popular romantic novelist of the era who lived in Gullane and whose novels have now been all but forgotten, and Lord Pitman, a Court of Session judge, organised a plebiscite in the Gullane. The result was interesting since of the 705 persons who cast a vote, an overwhelming majority of 663 were in favour of the immediate restoration of the passenger trains. One can only presume that had some of those persons actually travelled on the branch in the first place then the passenger service would never have been withdrawn. On 20th May, 1935 a petition from these same persons calling upon the company to restore the service was received by the LNER and it was said by the Petitioners that 'the bus service is unsuitable for visitors and that consequently hotels are suffering and there is a decrease in the number of summer lettings of houses'. It was suggested that the service could be provided on a summer-only basis by using a light engine and a single carriage, or alternatively a steam railcar, and that a halt could be built at Saltcoats to cater for the developments taking place on that side of Gullane village.

The company costed the proposals. In order to provide a viable service, it was estimated that 12 daily return trips by the Sentinel-Cammell railcar would be required to be made, resulting in the running of an additional 900 route miles per week. The estimated cost of providing a halt at Saltcoats was £245. The station buildings at Gullane had been let for campers' accommodation in the summer months and this brought a useful revenue. The anticipated balance sheet involved in the annual costs of reinstating the service was as follows:

Estimated expenditure:
Engineers Dept	£ 172	
Locomotive Dept	£1,848	
Traffic Dept	£ 469	
		£2,489

Additional receipts:
Passenger bookings	£ 918	
less Revenue from camping accommodation	£ 61	
		£857

The net loss of providing an all-year round service was thus estimated at £1,632 and if this was reduced to a summer only service the loss would still be some £600. It was further said by the company in an internal memorandum that:

> It is doubtful if much long-distance traffic has been lost. Passengers from English stations to Gullane go to Edinburgh, Longniddry or Drem, thence by road making use of the Passengers Luggage in Advance arrangements from Longniddry. A number of Glasgow people who formerly spent their holidays in Gullane now travel to Dunbar, North Berwick and Fife.
>
> In the case of most of the larger houses in the village, private cars are owned. The smaller houses patronise the [Cooperative] Store and do not require to go to Town for their shopping. The journey to Edinburgh is too far for evening entertainment so they go to North Berwick. The inhabitants prefer to travel by bus . . . and there is a half-hourly service. The proposed Saltcoats Halt is badly situated, being a quarter mile down an unlit road. The station at Gullane was placed in that position in the belief that the main development of the village would be to the South and East of the station, but there was no such development.
>
> The withdrawal of the passenger train service on this branch does not appear to be considered a drawback amongst the villagers and in a great measure the only traffic catered for by the railway would be resident summer visitors, holiday trippers and the comparatively few golfers who do not own private cars.

This was a fairly realistic appraisal of the situation, for East Lothian recorded the second highest county increase in Scotland in the number of motor passenger vehicles (i.e. cars and buses) registered there between the years 1929 and 1936. The only concession that the company was prepared to make, however, was to provide an extra train in the morning between Longniddry and Edinburgh and this duty was later allocated to a steam railcar; even this service faded away for lack of support. No further proposals for the resumption of passenger services on the Gullane branch were put forward again and, although a handful of special trains and excursions used the line in post-war years, the rival SMT bus service enjoyed, and continues to enjoy, a complete monopoly of public transport to and from the villages.

The North Berwick line enjoyed a rather better Indian Summer. In 1929 a new Pullman express named the 'Queen of Scots' was inaugurated between Edinburgh (later Glasgow) and King's Cross, and a special connection was provided to and from North Berwick for passengers wishing to join the Pullman at Drem – this service continued until the war, being conditional in June and September and unconditional in July and August. The 'Lothian Coast Express' continued to run (with a Gullane connection up to the end of the 1932 season, Dunbar being served instead by the 'North Briton' express to Leeds) and in October 1926 the *Meccano Magazine* 'Railway Notes' reported that:

> The 'Lothian Coast Express' has been in charge of various engines this year. On the first day it ran, No. 9417 *Cuddle Headrigg* brought it into Edinburgh and 4–4–2 No. 714 (NER class '2') worked it through to Glasgow. Subsequently, however, Director No. 6401 and Pacific No. 2567 have been seen on it, while No. 9360 *Guy Mannering* brings it in from North Berwick to Edinburgh.

In 1929 the LNER restaurant car was replaced by a twelve-wheel Pullman restaurant car – a strange innovation considering the relative unimportance of the train! The Pullman, for travel in which no supplement was payable by passengers taking refreshments and which was staffed and run by the Pullman Car Company's own employees, appeared again in the following seasons and was mentioned in the public timetables. But loadings on the Express were light (mainly due to the fact that its timings were such that only those in 'superior' forms of employment who started work late and ended early could make practical use of the train) and at the end of the 1934 season, it was announced that the Express would not run again the following season; it never ran again.

Notwithstanding the cessation of the Express, passenger receipts on the North Berwick branch held up remarkably well and although the economic doldrums of the thirties affected the hotel trade in the town, day trippers still made it a popular venue. With commendable initiative the LNER began to issue a series of most attractive pictorial posters, in what would now be called the 'Art Deco' style, publicising both the East Coast in general (with slogans such as 'The Drier Side of Britain') and also specific resorts. North Berwick was graced with some particularly fine examples of colourful posters by Andrew Johnson and Frank Newbould -- these showed typical North Berwick scenes with golfers, holidaymakers and inevitably, picnics on the dunes! Further publicity included a highly stylised menu for use in LNER dining cars which depicted the town and the Law.

Throughout the inter-war period the annual average number of passengers using North Berwick Station remained fairly constant at 55,000 or roughly 180 per working day although there were, of course, seasonal fluctuations. Dirleton Station, despite its splendid isolation, at first continued to handle surprisingly large numbers of passengers in spite of the far more convenient and frequent bus service, but by 1932 only some five passengers were still

A selection of LNER posters.

using the station on an average day, and only four trains each way were continuing to call there.

Goods services on both branch lines were now undergoing a fairly spectacular decline in patronage. The tonnage of general goods dealt with at North Berwick had fallen by a half between 1925 and 1932 and in several years no cattle, horses, calves or pigs were handled there although livestock traffic picked up again in the mid-1930s. At Dirleton in the same period, general goods tonnages fell from 3,800 tons to under 1,700 and at Drem the tonnage of general goods was halved. On the Gullane branch, things were a little better and in certain classes of goods there was a slight increase.

The general decline was nevertheless set to continue as more farms acquired their own motor lorries, and local entrepreneurs, including the son of Mr Seth, the Gullane station master, creamed off more and more trade. In 1926 there were 326 motor goods vehicles licensed by the East Lothian authority and nine motor vans or lorries owned by farmers or the proprietors of market gardens. Twelve years later the figures were, respectively, 691 and 64 and in the words of the *Third Statistical Account of Scotland*.

> . . . the use of lorries for transporting farm produce and requirements has transformed both the quiet by-roads and the farm economy. No longer need many hours and days be spent carting grain, potatoes, fertilisers and feeding stuffs or walking sheep and cattle to markets or railway stations.

As the lorries took away the more profitable trade the branches were left to fulfil the railway's statutory obligations as a common carrier and take the goods that no one else wanted to carry and in the same way that the railway had killed off the horse drawn carrier and coastal shipping of a previous generation it was now being replaced by the more effective motor lorry.

One now vanished aspect of railway operations in the 1930s, was the use of mail bag 'line side apparatus' at Drem and Longniddry. At the former location, post and net devices were installed beside both main lines which enabled mail bags to be uplifted in the up direction and thrown out in the down from the East Coast Travelling Post Offices as they sped past. This provided a convenient method by which North Berwick mail for the South could go direct and avoid sorting at Edinburgh or Dunbar. At Longniddry, the apparatus was situated in the down direction only and was used for the Gullane and Haddington mails. After World War II, the up London Mail left Waverley at 8.05 pm and paid a brief call at Drem Station platform to uplift mails; the corresponding down working left King's Cross at 8.20 pm and used the apparatus to deliver mail into the nets at Drem at the unearthly hour of 4.49 am. The line side apparatus was removed in the 1970s and the mail now travels to and from Edinburgh by road.

The North British 'C15' and 'C16' class tanks continued to give sterling service throughout the inter-war period and on 20th October, 1930, 'C16' No. 9449 had a brief moment of glory when 'A1' Pacific No. 2581 failed on the down 'Queen of Scots' express at Drem and the humble North Berwick branch engine had the task of taking the Pullmans single-handed to Edinburgh.

From January 1931 larger locomotives appeared on the North Berwick branch services, supplementing the former North British stud; these were

Nos. 2905 and 2906, two examples of the handsome LNER 'V1' class – large 2–6–2 tank engines designed by Sir Nigel Gresley and used extensively on Edinburgh and Glasgow suburban services. Fitted on the front with North British pattern brackets for destination boards, the 'V1's and their later superheated sisters, the 'V3's were, for many years, a familiar part of the North Berwick branch scene and they worked many of the services, including at times virtually all of the through trains to Waverley. During the 1930s and 1940s, a pair of 'V1's allocated to St Margarets were outstationed at the North Berwick shed and these included Nos. 2907 and 2908, then Nos. 2929 and 2930, and latterly Nos. 2946 and 2967. Both branches were under the LNER Route Availability classification given a '6' rating and in addition classes 'J37' and 'J38' were also permitted although on the Gullane branch 'N1', 'N2', 'O' and 'Q' classes were prohibited. Many ex-NBR locomotives including 4–4–0s of the 'D32', 'D34' and 'D35' classes and 0–6–0s of the 'J34', 'J35' and 'J37' classes were seen on the North Berwick line. In fact a wide variety of the motive power stationed at St Margarets worked the line from time to time but the drivers of most ordinary services were based at North Berwick and few St Margarets men ever had the chance to work regularly on the branch. The passenger rolling stock had shown great improvements and trains were now almost exclusively bogie carriages of LNER build in teak finish or 'cascaded' ex-North British stock until, well into the LNER period, stock from the pre-grouping lines began to stray into each other's territory, and almost anything was liable to turn up on the branch, especially on excursion trains.

In the summer of 1937, the North Berwick line was still busy. The regular service consisted of 17 return trips with another five on Saturdays. The majority of trains ran through to Edinburgh, including the two steam railcar turns and a couple of odd trips to provide connections at Drem with important main line expresses. The goods service consisted of an early morning trip, working from Portobello to North Berwick which did not stop at Dirleton, but the return working dropped off goods wagons for that station having first taken them to North Berwick. On Tuesdays this return trip was for livestock and arrived at Gorgie (for the markets) at 11.42 am; on other days it worked according to the orders of Control once it reached Drem. A further branch goods working left North Berwick at 3.10 pm and called at Aberlady, arriving at Gullane at 7.35, whereupon the engine immediately worked light back to Prestonpans. On Tuesdays however, the engine ran a cattle train to connect up at Londniddry with the similar North Berwick service. A further complete branch goods trip was worked in the early afternoon by the engine and crew of the Haddington branch goods.

The late 1930s still brought holidaymakers by rail to North Berwick, and, although the pier was no longer used by the pleasure steamers (it having become unsafe by 1937), smaller craft and motor launches still provided trips to the Bass Rock and Fidra; the town had other attractions such as a swimming pool, cinema, tennis courts, entertainments and the perennial sand and golf. North Berwick was, in 1938, the scene of an unusual experiment by the LNER into the use of hybrid gas/electric station lamps in an attempt to improve the lighting while at the same time preserving the link

GAS ELECTRIC LAMPS—NORTH BERWICK

During the past decade, lighting of railway stations has attracted the attention of railway officers throughout the L.N.E.R., and steps have been taken in numerous directions to improve as much as possible station lighting with a view to making the passenger station stations more attractive.

In many cases this has been done by the introduction of electricity in place of gas or oil lighting. One of the difficulties, however, which had to be met was brought about by the fact that the gas-producing companies were in many cases traders with the railway company, and therefore it was to the mutual advantage of the railway company and the gas companies to retain gas as a luminant.

As is well known, gas as a luminant requires a great deal of maintenance and has numerous disadvantages, e.g., variations in the strength of illumination could take place due to bad regulation of the air flow and gas flow into the burners, or due to soot or other foreign substances forming in the flow paths. Mantles become defective or broken, particularly on outside burners, where these are exposed to weather when the cases are opened for lighting purposes. In addition, perhaps the greatest weakness of all is that of the ordinary incandescent burner when the maximum amount of air to be consumed to give the most efficient lighting cannot be obtained. The most economical point is arrived at when one volume of gas to 3½ of air are mixed and consumed, and to arrive at this, experimental lamps have been put up by the electrical engineers. In these lamps the air is applied at pressure, the pressure being obtained by means of a small rotary air blower, and the theory of the operation can be clearly seen from the diagram, a description of which is as follows :—

To bring the lamp into operation, the switch controlling the blower unit A is closed and the pressure in the air pipe line B is thereby increased. This increased air pressure is transmitted to the top of the diaphragm C, thus pushing the gas valve D from its seating and allowing gas to pass from the inlet E through the gas valve D, and thence to the fitting, where it mixes with the incoming air at the venturi tube F. This mixture of gas and air is then forced downwards on to the top of the superheater G, where it is heated before passing through holes on the outside rim of the superheater. The mixture then passes through the jet into the mantle H, where it is ignited by the flame from the by-pass tube J. When the switch controlling the blower unit A is opened, the air pressure is released from the diaphragm C, thus allowing the valve D to re-close and cut off the gas supply from the fitting.

This type of lamp can be made up in large sizes for yard lighting, and the lamp of the large type consumes 27 cub. ft. of gas per hour. The small air blower consumes 40 watts, and a lamp of this type will give slightly more illumination than can be obtained from a 500-watt electric lamp, and can be switched on and off with an ordinary tumbler switch in the same way as an electric lamp.

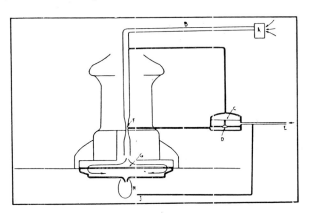

In the case of the experimental units at North Berwick, five lamps have been installed on the platforms. These lamps are single mantle and double mantle, there being two single and three double. The single-mantle lamps consume 5 cub. ft. of gas per hour, and give approximately the same illumination as a 100-watt gas-filled electric lamp. The double-mantle lamps consume 10 cub. ft. of gas per hour, and give a somewhat greater illumination than that which would be obtained by using a 150-watt gas-filled electric lamp. The five experimental lamps installed at North Berwick are fed from one blower, and with this system it is necessary to provide air pipe lines as well as gas pipe lines. These lamps, like the yard lamp, can be switched on and off by means of the ordinary electric light tumbler switches.

Another demonstration of electricity as applied to gas light which has been installed, also at North Berwick in the Scottish Area, is the electric lighting and switching of ordinary incandescent gas lamps.

This scheme is one which might show economies where gases are normally by-passed, as by-passes when operating for 24 hours per day over a considerable number of months in the year, consume a fair quantity of gas. The electric lighting of these lamps also obviates the necessity for opening cases, reduces blackening of mantles and gives better facilities for switching on and off between trains, so far as operations on platforms are concerned, where this could be done without detracting from the general appearance of the station or interfering with the efficient working. J. R. S.

An interesting experiment featured in the *LNER Magazine* in 1938.

LNER railcar No. 36 *Royal Eagle*, on a North Berwick working in the early 1930s, passes beneath the walls of the old Calton Jail near Waverley.　*A.G. Ellis Collection*

between the company and the Gas Works, a valued customer. By 1939 the storm clouds were gathering over Europe, but a correspondent in the *Railway Observer*, in the fateful September of that year, could still comment on the spotless state of the locomotives which he saw at North Berwick.

World War II brought about some important changes to the locality. The airfields at East Fortune, West Fenton and elsewhere brought new traffic, but this was offset by the virtual cessation of the holiday trade and a decline in the number of commuters who were now making other less familiar journeys which, unlike the popular exhortation of that time, could have been said to be really necessary. On the North Berwick branch, the service dwindled to a mere 10 daily passenger trains with only two through services from Edinburgh, although the 8.20 am to Waverley and the 5.12 pm from there, continued to omit the Drem stop and be a substitute for the late lamented express. On Saturdays there were three additional services, all in the early afternoon. Dirleton was now only served by one up and two down trains, but an additional train called there on Wednesdays (presumably for the use of those attending the grain market held in Edinburgh on that day) and on Saturdays. Goods services were virtually unchanged.

Of more general interest, however, was the fact that for security reasons the Royal Train was frequently brought up the branch to Aberlady in the early hours of the morning, in order that the occupants could spend the rest of the night in peaceful surroundings and away from any possible danger. They were taken at a more civilised hour to Princes Street Station in Edinburgh where they would be welcomed by the Lord Provost and then commence their official duties. Aberlady Station was repainted and the surroundings spruced up for this unusual use; when the Royal Train was stationed there the presence of large numbers of Edinburgh CID officers on duty would give local people a good indication of the closely guarded open secret. The late Colonel Barclay of Aberlady, who knew Greece well and was married to a Greek lady, was once asked by the King of Greece where he lived in Scotland, and was delighted to reply that it was close to the railway station where His Majesty, during his wartime exile in Britain, had more than once spent part of the night in the Royal Train. This unorthodox use of Aberlady Station is thought to have continued for a period after the war.

The cessation of hostilities brought back a semblance of normality but passenger services were not augmented, despite the continuing rationing of petrol for private cars. The bus service, which had been reduced in frequency during the war with many buses being converted to running on 'producer gas', was largely restored to pre-war levels and the railway commuters returned. A contemporary writer noted that in connection with this important group of passengers 'one cannot but notice the number of ex-servicemen travelling daily to and from the city and who are clearly not natives of North Berwick'.

The last year of private ownership brought heavy snowstorms, and high winds caused drifting, blocking the North Berwick line on several occasions and disrupting the service; in the following summer, the drought contributed to a spate of lineside fires on the branch. The service continued and, before any developments could take place, the Labour government nationalised the railways. From 1st January, 1948, the North Berwick and Gullane branch lines became part of the Railway Executive of the British Transport Commission or, more popularly, part of the Scottish Region of British Railways.

One of the handsome Gresley 'V1' class 2–6–2Ts, No. 425 (later BR No. 67666) waits to leave North Berwick with an Edinburgh 'residential' on 25th August, 1939.
E.R. Weathersett, RCAHMS Rokeby Collection

Chapter Eight
Owned by the People

THE BRITISH RAILWAYS ERA, 1948–1969

'The railway is a great asset to North Berwick and one which will increase in value as the town grows. The people of North Berwick would be well advised to prepare their defence against Dr Beeching before the axe is lifted instead of waiting until it begins to fall.'

East Lothian Courier, 16th June, 1964

The first outward signs of nationalisation came with the introduction of the new totem symbol and the legend 'BRITISH RAILWAYS' appearing in bold white lettering on the locomotive sides. But little else changed and the two branch lines continued to be operated in much the same way that they had been run by the LNER. What was becoming increasingly apparent, however, was that passenger traffic on the North Berwick line was continuing to decline, especially in the off-peak hours and the reason for this was not difficult to see. As the *Third Statistical Account* for East Lothian, published in 1953, commented:

> Private means of travel are abundant amongst all classes. Most children have a bicycle, many working folk have a car and all farmers have at least one car . . . There has been a big decrease in the size of local trains and the extent to which they are filled.

This latter statement was certainly true and it was not uncommon for mid-morning and afternoon trains between Drem and North Berwick to consist of a tank engine and one composite brake coach, which was more than sufficient for the handful (and even on some occasions the complete absence) of passengers. The decline was most apparent at Dirleton, where the station had always been inconvenient for the village and served little else. The Parish Minister of Dirleton wrote in the *Third Statistical Account* that:

> Only three trains now stop there and they are seldom, if ever, used by the people of the village. Dirleton Station now serves mainly the farms in the southeast of the parish and two close to the village, for the despatch of agricultural produce. The number of people in Dirleton who possess private cars is small, but in Gullane it is large and there is also a good taxi service which can be used by people coming via the main line at Drem, 3½ miles away . . .

The end for Dirleton Station was clearly inevitable and on 22nd January, 1954 BR published the following notice:

CLOSING OF PASSENGER STATION

British Railways (Scottish Region) announce that as from Monday 1st February, 1954 the passenger train service will be withdrawn from Dirleton Station on the North Berwick line. Alternative rail services are available at North Berwick and the area is served by frequent bus services operated from North Berwick and Edinburgh. Traffic (including livestock) in full truck loads will continue to be dealt with at Dirleton but parcels and other passenger train rated traffic and freight train traffic in less than full truck loads will be collected and delivered in the Dirleton area by road motor from North Berwick.

Class 'C16' 4−4−2Ts at North Berwick in the 1950s − (*top*) No. 7494 still in LNER livery but with a BR shed plate (64A St Margarets and sub-sheds including North Berwick); 13th July, 1950 (*middle*) No. 67492 in early British Railways livery on 9th July, 1952 with a fine pictorial poster for Thornton-Cleveleys in the background and (*bottom*) the same locomotive with the North Berwick shed staff after they had cleaned her specially for an RCTS special on 26th August, 1958.

A.G. Ellis (top and middle); W.S. Sellar (bottom)

Accordingly at just after four o'clock in the afternoon of Saturday 30th January, 1954, the last passenger train called at the station and thereafter Dirleton was reduced to the status of an Unstaffed Public Siding for wagonload traffic only and, for the first time in a century, there was no intermediate stop on the branch line.

In the winter of 1954–5 the steam passenger service reached its nadir with a mere eight daily workings (ten on Saturdays); half of the trains ran through to Edinburgh and none to Glasgow. An interesting survivor was the 8.16 am from North Berwick to Edinburgh which called only at Longniddry, Prestonpans and Inveresk – the somewhat less illustrious successor to the 'Lothian Coast Express'. Passenger receipts continued to decline as the cost of running the conventional steam-hauled service on the branch escalated and it had become apparent that unless a fresh approach was taken, the line might be doomed.

The answer was seen to be the diesel multiple unit and a better service. In the summer of 1956, the North Berwick to Edinburgh timetable was completely recast with, for the first time, a service of regular intervals and frequent through trains between North Berwick and Edinburgh, some services being extended for operational reasons westwards to Haymarket and Corstorphine and thereby giving commuters working in the West End of Edinburgh a convenient link. A further innovation was the provision of a summer Sunday service, something that North Berwick had previously enjoyed on a very sporadic basis. The new services were popular but, as yet, were still steam-hauled, with the exception of a few experimental runs made with a Metro-Cammell lightweight twin set multiple unit which appeared for the first time on 23rd July, 1956.

Dieselisation was to follow rapidly. A plan was drawn up in 1957 to convert all local and suburban trains in the Edinburgh area to multiple unit operation in a staged sequence beginning, on Monday 3rd February, 1958, with the North Berwick to Corstorphine service. A local publicity drive was undertaken with illustrated leaflets, extolling the virtues of the new trains, being distributed all along the line and, perhaps with some irony in view of the later conditions of these diesel units, an emphasis was placed on the fact that 'the absence of smoke and steam and the fact that the coaches are of a modern design and construction ensures that they are always bright and clean.'

The new daily service consisted of 17 through trains from Corstorphine to North Berwick and 11 on Sunday. With two additional branch shuttles on a weekday and the combination of the attractive service, the new trains and the good publicity ensured that the new service was an immediate success – so much so that the future of the branch line did not seem to be in any doubt. Fares were revised and a North Berwick to Edinburgh Cheap Day Return fare of 6s. 9d. [34p] first class and 4s. 6d. [22½p] second class was introduced – somewhat remarkably this was not a great increase on the fare a century earlier, despite inflation, and contrasts favourably with the 1991 standard class off-peak return fare of £3.90! Steam was not, however, entirely banished and a couple of passenger trains continued in steam haulage, as did the goods service, but the shed at North Berwick was officially closed as

Two views of a well-groomed 'V1' class locomotive No. 67670 – the famous North
Berwick branch locomotive of the 1950s – as she awaits the departure of the 11.51 am
Drem local service.   *John Edgington*

North Berwick Station from the Ware Road bridge on 17th April, 1955.

C.J.B Sanderson

The same view on 13th April, 1991, shortly before the wires went up.   *Author*

North Berwick in the 1930s showing the famous double scissors curved crossover and the branch passenger set of the time.   *G.E. Langmuir; A.G. Ellis Collection*

The view from the same standpoint in April 1991 with a class '156' 'Super Sprinter' about to depart; the truncated platform, wooden fence and tree are all that has survived.   *Author*

Heaton-based Gresley 'K3' class locomotive No. 61844 leaves North Berwick with an Edinburgh Autumn-Holiday extra on 15th September, 1958 while a Gloucester RCW dmu waits patiently with a Corstorphine-bound local.　　　*W.S. Sellar*

'C16' class No. 67494 waiting at North Berwick on 13th July, 1950 – the goods shed, water crane and tower and the lower-quadrant signals are all in view.　　　*A.G. Ellis*

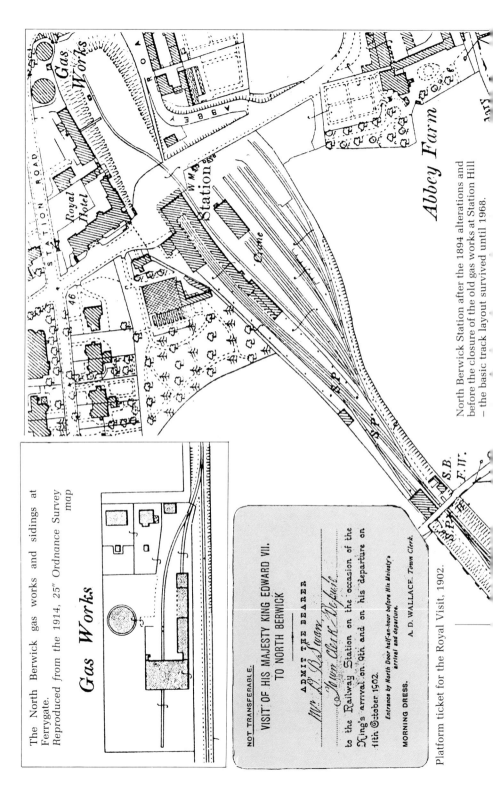

The North Berwick gas works and sidings at Ferrygate.
Reproduced from the 1914, 25" Ordnance Survey map

Gas Works

NOT TRANSFERABLE.

VISIT OF HIS MAJESTY KING EDWARD VII.
TO NORTH BERWICK

ADMIT THE BEARER

Mr. R. Balfour ....

.... Town Clerk's Depute. ....

to the Railway Station on the occasion of the
King's arrival on 9th and on his departure on
11th October 1902.

*Entrance by North Door half-an-hour before His Majesty's
arrival and departure.*

MORNING DRESS.   A. D. WALLACE, Town Clerk.

Platform ticket for the Royal Visit, 1902.

North Berwick Station after the 1894 alterations and
before the closure of the old gas works at Station Hill
– the basic track layout survived until 1968.

from 3rd February, 1958, although it continued in use for several months afterwards.

Local goods services were, however, not flourishing. The start of the decade had been a promising one. The Gullane branch had a daily service, hauled by a veteran North British 'J36' class 0–6–0 from St Margarets; on Saturdays the Prestonpans pilot engine provided the motive power. Additional trips were made as required and these included a regular weekly livestock special for the market at Gorgie. Inward traffic consisted mainly of coal and coke destined for the Aberlady gas works and for Messrs Aikman and Dobson, the two Gullane coal merchants who shared the station goods yard there. Other traffic included fertilisers and agricultural requisites and a small amount of livestock; the principal consignees of this traffic were the farms at Ballencrieff Mains, Craigielaw, Queenstonbank, Fenton, Aberlady Mains and Luffness.

Outward traffic was more varied and included grain (some of which was destined for the whisky distilleries of the north-east), tar from the gas works, and miscellaneous traffic such as the pony belonging to the daughter of the Earl of Wemyss, which made trips by rail to Dunkeld at the beginning of each school term. The traffic in potatoes was in decline and, although the longer-distance haul to Glasgow and the English markets still travelled by rail, the short-haul traffic to Edinburgh had been all but lost to the motor lorry. In contrast, there were two new sources of income – vegetables and sugar beet. After the war a 7.45 pm vegetable special left Drem each weekday night and, calling only at Longniddry and Prestonpans to uplift and Portobello to change crews, arrived at Glasgow High Street at 2.35 am in time for the opening of the early morning vegetable market in that town. Sugar beet was a most valuable traffic and continued to grow in importance throughout the immediate post-war years. The beet was 'graiped' (i.e. loaded by fork) direct from farm trailers into wagons at Aberlady and Gullane and taken from there to the beet factory at Cupar in Fife – a journey which could not readily be undertaken by road in the days before the building of the Forth Road Bridge. There was a return working of beet pulp back to the producers for the purpose of cattle feed and customers of the railway for this traffic included the Wemyss Landed Estates' farm at Craigielaw. The one disadvantage of this traffic was that it was concentrated into the months of October and November and dormant for the remainder of the year; the seasonal nature of this traffic had a parallel in the grain traffic with a harvest and mid-winter peak and a summer slack which became more accentuated with the introduction of the combine harvester to the area in the late 1940s. The North Berwick branch line goods traffic was similar in nature to that on the Gullane branch and was dominated by the inward coal and coke traffic, the gas works again being the biggest single customer.

By the end of the decade, the tide was turning against the railway as a carrier of goods. The traffic had always been varied in nature but enthusiastically sought by the North British and its successors, and yet there was no getting away from the fact that once the motor lorry posed a serious threat to the railway, then the whole operation of goods trains became a highly marginal one. Parcels and sundries traffic destined for a wide area was, by now, being dealt with by BR vans based at North Berwick, which had become the railhead for these goods. Traffic was still holding up well – in contrast, agricultural traffic by rail was dwindling fast and the beet was the last remaining category of profitable activity here. Coal traffic was dealt a severe blow with the closure of the Aberlady gas works in 1958 and subsequently the closure of the North Berwick gas works. This, allied to the continuing decline in the use of coal for domestic purposes, spelt the beginning of the end for local goods services.

In 1958, as part of a BR Freight Traffic Plan review, the Edinburgh district commercial manager commissioned a report on the future of the Gullane branch and although a total of well over 100 tons of goods per week was still being dealt with on the line by a resident staff of two, it was not felt that the line was of sufficient economic attraction to justify its retention. It was thought that additional staff savings could be made by curtailing the activities of the Prestonpans pilot engine and by closing Aberlady Junction signal box; it was felt that 'the two closed stations [i.e. Aberlady and Gullane] might be sold or let as caravan sites which are in keen demand'. The one thing that apparently saved the Gullane branch at this time was, however, the sugar beet traffic, for it was conceded that alternative means of transhipment of the beet would probably result in this traffic being permanently lost to the railways, and so no immediate decision was made to close the line and the 'J36' and its handful of wagons continued to make their dawdling way along the Aberlady and Gullane Railway.

Very occasionally the Gullane branch came alive again. There had been few passenger trains seen on the branch since 1932 other than the wartime Royal trains; the first passenger train seen for many years was a Sunday School special from Edinburgh which visited Gullane in June 1958. This was followed by a Stephenson Locomotive Society enthusiasts' special which visited several local branch lines, including the Gullane line, on 11th June, 1960 which appears to have been the last occasion on which a passenger train traversed that branch. There were, however, other passengers of sorts. Occasionally enthusiasts managed to obtain permits to travel over the line in the brake vans of goods trains and local children were known to have had surreptitious footplate rides from time to time. This activity was, however, insignificant in its economic impact compared to the use made of the station buildings at both Aberlady and Gullane by holidaymakers.

Following the cessation of regular passenger services, the former porters' rooms, ladies and general waiting rooms, and other offices at both stations, were converted into 'Camping Apartments' and were rented out to families on a weekly basis. These proved to be most popular as an inexpensive and interesting means of having a seaside holiday. particularly in an age when the novelty of a holiday at home had not yet worn off. The facilities provided were somewhat rudimentary, although gas was laid on; the cleaning of the apartments between lets was done for a small payment by the wives of the two porters who were still employed at those stations to deal with the goods traffic. In the 1950s, the weekly charges (for up to six persons) were between £5 and £7, according to season. A prerequisite was that campers had to purchase the equivalent of four adult ordinary return tickets from their home station to Longniddry – this, together with the passengers luggage in advance service, brought a not inconsiderable additional revenue to the line. An account of a happy holiday spent at Gullane Station in 1946 appears at the end of this book.

Another innovation was the camping coach which appeared in the siding at Gullane and remained there for many years. This was converted out of an LNER ordinary passenger coach and provided six berths in a somewhat unique environment. The weekly cost in the 1950s was between £7 and £12 10s. per week, according to season, and the same passenger ticket requirements applied. In the summer of 1963, two converted Pullman coaches made a brief appearance on the branch. These were Nos. SC 42 and SC 46 and were painted in a mid-blue livery lined out in gold and bearing the inscription 'PULLMAN CAMPING COACH' – the only occasion when Pullmans were referred to as coaches rather than cars. Rather shabbier than their name might have suggested, they were part of an allocation of vehicles sold by the Pullam Car Company to British Railways in 1962 for £900 each. SC 42 started life as a third class coach 'CAR NO. 44' – (only first class Pullmans and the Pullman Restaurant Cars, used in Scotland on services such as the 'Lothian Coast Express' between the wars, carried names) and was built by the Birmingham Railway Carriage & Wagon Company in 1921. SC 46 was a more distinguished car altogether, being built by Cravens of Sheffield in 1911 for the South Eastern and Chatham Railway's London to Folkestone boat train service and named after their then chairman, *COSMO BONSOR*, before becoming the third vehicle to bear the less impressive name of *RAINBOW* after World War II. They remained at Gullane until the following year, and were reputedly the last vehicles to travel over the branch before being ignominiously dumped in the sidings at North Berwick goods yard prior to scrapping.

Towards the end of the steam era, North Berwick shed still had an allocation of steam locomotives and these, together with engines from the parent shed at St Margarets (64A), were employed on all local trains. The North Berwick engines were usually extremely well turned out, the shed staff having a particularly good reputation for this and undoubtedly their swansong was the 'C16' locomotive, No. 67492, which the staff made immaculate, prior to its use on a Railway Correspondence and Travel Society special in August 1958. The Gresley 'V1' and 'V3' class locomotives shedded at North Berwick were famous for their fine state and the last of these, No. 67670, was, in the 1950s, known to be the last locomotive in the Edinburgh area to have 'that embellishment beloved of North British drivers' a domed brass throttle nut which had been engraved with the initials of a former North Berwick driver'; this was fitted to the handbrake. Even in the latter part of the decade the locomotives seen on the branch were all usually of ex-North British or LNER origin and it was uncommon to see any inter-lopers, although a BR Standard '2MT' 2–6–0, No. 78047 from Hawick shed, was seen in 1957 on one of the Sunday workings from Corstorphine. Other unusual locomotives seen on the Edinburgh Autumn Holiday in September 1958 were a Heaton-based Gresley 'K3' 2–6–0 No. 61844, a 'J37' on a, by

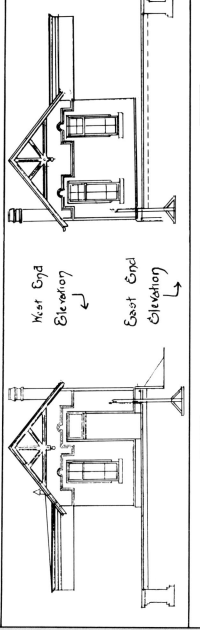
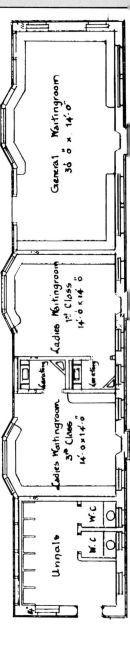

Redrawn by author from original NBR plans.

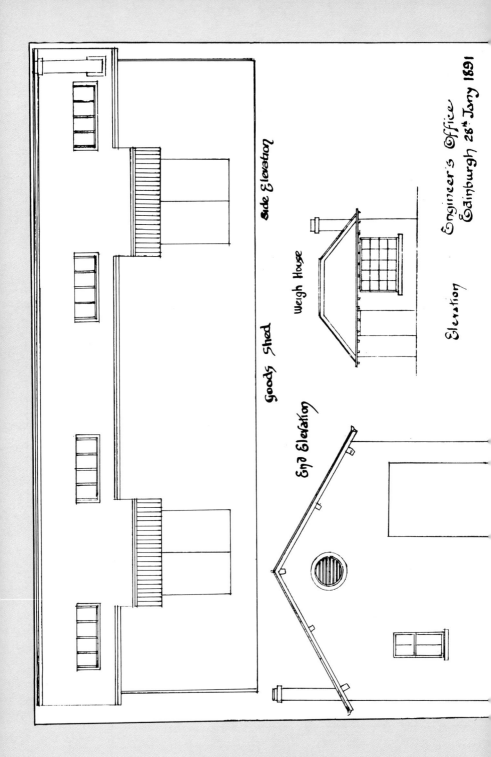

Goods Shed

Side Elevation

End Elevation

Weigh House

Elevation

Engineer's Office
Edinburgh 28ᵗʰ Jany 1891

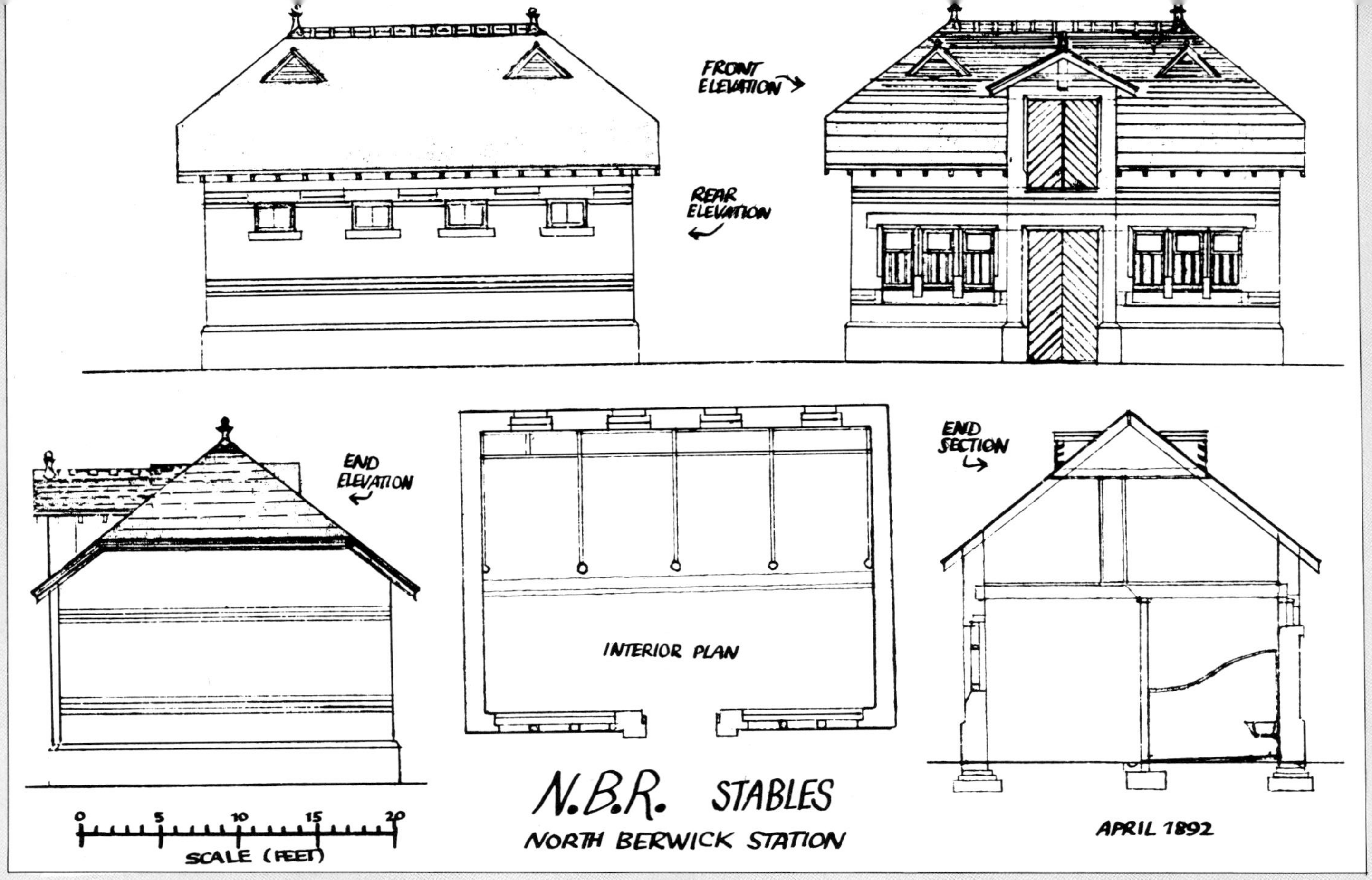

FRONT ELEVATION →

REAR ELEVATION →

END SECTION ↳

END ELEVATION

INTERIOR PLAN

N.B.R. STABLES
NORTH BERWICK STATION

APRIL 1892

SCALE (FEET)

0 5 10 15 20

Redrawn by author from original NBR plans.

The down platform waiting rooms a
North Berwick, January 1967 – th
plans for this building appear on page
130 and 131.   S. Blac

The front entrance to North Berwic
Station, January 1967, with a Triump
convertible, Northern Ireland shippin
timetable and a map of the Londo
Area Network all to be seen.   S. Blac

The buffer-stops at North Berwick i
January 1967 with the modernise
bookstall and waiting room; a pristin
Metro-Cammell dmu in original gree
livery and complete with small firs
class saloon awaits departure. S. Blac

North Berwick engine shed, signal box and the Ware Road bridge in the late 1950s. *Real Photographs*

The station throat, January 1967 — notice how the signalman would have a clear view over the roadbridge. *S. Black*

The view from the Ware Road bridge looking towards Williamston and the holding siding, January 1967. *S. Black*

The goods shed at North Berwick, January 1967 – the plans for this building appear on page 132.   S. Black

The interior of the goods shed, January 1967 showing the ex-NBR hand crane and the variety of general merchandise still typical of the period.   S. Black

Pullman camping coach, No. SC46 showing signs of neglect in 1967 after being dumped at North Berwick – this was once named Cosmo Bonsor and ran in the SECR's Folkestone Boat Trains.
S. Black

nopy details, North Berwick, January
67 – one of the cast-iron supports
w forms the incongruous post for a
tish Rail logo in the car park.
                              S. Black

e goods shed with later additions,
uary 1967.   *S. Black*

trance to the goods yard showing the
yal Hotel, station frontage, weigh-
dge and a car which was, in 1967,
esumably an 'old banger' and would
w be a collector's item!   *S. Black*

Gloucester RCW twin-set posed at Waverley for the front cover of a publicity leaflet issued prior to the introduction of dmus to

Timetable cover for the first summer of diesel services — the slogan is now somewhat quaint!

then, rare passenger working, and the old NBR stalwart *Glen Falloch* ('D34' 4–4–0 No. 62471) in the twilight with the 8.00 pm return special to Waverley. This was literally the twilight for steam, for following the introduction of regular diesel workings on the branch passenger services a few months previously, the shed at North Berwick saw little use and by the end of 1958 it was permanently out of use.

The regular diesel multiple units which served the North Berwick branch were initially from two classes, both based at Haymarket. These two classes were the rather angular Gloucester RCW twin sets of class 100 and the distinctive and ubiquitous Met-Cam two- and three-car sets of class 101. Two classes of accommodation were provided, the first class being in a small saloon situated at the end of one of the motor coaches. The livery adopted for the units was the standard dmu green with the rather quaint 'speed whiskers' on the ends. Later the first class saloons were downgraded to second and the livery altered, first to the plain matt rail blue livery and subsequently to the British Rail blue and grey scheme although only the latter class of unit carried this.

The advent of the diesels did not, however, mean the complete end of North Berwick passenger steam trains and in the 1958 summer season, there were still regular Edinburgh Saturday steam workings and a pair of steam branch shuttles from Drem; the latter survived until 1962 as the 6.55 am from North Berwick and the 8.34 am return working. Goods services remained in the hands of the ex-North British 'D60's and a miscellany of tank locomotives, until late 1964 when Clayton Type 1 diesels made an appearance, as they did on the Haddington line also.

In March 1963 the infamous Beeching Report, *The Reshaping of British Railways* was published and this report condemned not only the Gullane and North Berwick goods services but also the Dunbar local passenger service. By this time, the Cupar sugar beet factory was in the throes of closure; without this traffic the Gullane branch ceased to be economically viable, especially when the other remaining traffic, that of coal, was also tailing off. On both branches part-wagonload traffic was actively discouraged (for economic reasons) and the agricultural traders had deserted *en masse*.

The closure of the Gullane branch to all traffic excited little attention – for all practical purposes the line had long ago ceased to play any real part in local affairs and, with the contemporary closure of so many other branch lines, enthusiasts paid no heed. On 15th June, 1964, a class 'J37' with a handful of wagons, made up the last goods train on the branch and, with its passing, the line was closed to all traffic. The stations at Aberlady and Gullane were retained only for use as camping apartments. All remaining goods traffic was now dealt with by road from Longniddry, Drem and North Berwick, the siding at Ballencrieff having been closed in 1959. Arrangements were now made for the demolition of the Gullane branch and the remaining stock was collected and taken away; the two camping coaches formed the last rail movement on the line. The station platforms and certain overbridges were retained *in situ* but the remaining structures were removed together with all other fittings, fixtures and salvagable materials. The branch was officially taken out of use at Aberlady Junction on 9th November, 1964, and the signal box there was finally abolished some 13 months later after the necessary signalling alterations had been made. A small team of demolition contractors moved in and started cutting up the rails into short lengths for loading onto a lorry and, within a short period of time, the Gullane branch was no more. The two station buildings survived longer but their gradually deteriorating state led to their eventual demolition, that at Gullane lasting until about 1980.

Other local goods facilities were now discontinued as part of the nation-wide retrenchment of BR freight services and this process started with the Dirleton Unstaffed Public sidings which were closed with effect from 1st August, 1964. Some four months later, on 28th December, 1964, the goods yard at Longniddry was closed. Further rationalisation took place and as from 1st January, 1968 all goods facilities were discontinued at North Berwick with Haddington following a couple of months later. This now left Drem as the only handling point for local goods and this yard enjoyed a precarious existence until 6th August, 1979. The wheel had indeed turned a full circle since 1846!

It was now the turn of the North Berwick passenger service to come under scrutiny as one of the many lines earmarked in Scotland for early closure. In June 1964 BR discontinued the special holiday train service between Edinburgh and North Berwick on the grounds that it was uneconomical and that is patronage was too dependent on the weather. This prompted the *East Lothian Courier* to warn the inhabitants of the town that they should

No. 67666 seen again at North Berwick with a mid-day local, 2nd December, 1950 – this engine also appears on page 118.   *J.L. Stevenson*

anticipate any full closure proposals and defend their railway. By September 1964 there were no intermediate stations left open between Prestonpans and Edinburgh – Abbeyhill, Piershill, Portobello, Joppa and Inveresk having all been closed. At the beginning of January 1968, the North Berwick branch itself was 'rationalised' with the removal of all sidings and other equipment, leaving a single line between Drem Junction and the former up platform at the terminus; all signalling, with the exception of the approach to Drem Junction, was scrapped.

The expected announcement now came, and in 1968 the British Railways Board intimated their intention to withdraw all local passenger trains between Edinburgh, North Berwick and Dunbar, and to close to all traffic the stations at Prestonpans, Longniddry, Drem and North Berwick (East Fortune and East Linton having already lost their stations by then). This triggered off the start of a long and orchestrated campaign to save the services and the East Lothian County Council planning authority commissioned a report into the economics of the proposed closure of the North Berwick line. The two academics responsible for the report, Professor White of Newcastle University and Professor Anderson of Strathclyde, were able to demonstrate that the BR assertion that £66,000 per annum would be saved by the closure was not an accurate one. The report concluded that the estimated annual savings, before any account was taken of the costs of delays and traffic congestion, would only be £36,000 calculated as follows:

Track and signalling	£ 5,000
Station costs	£14,000
Train movements	£60,000
	£79,000
less revenue	£43,000
	£36,000

On 17th January, 1969 the County Council sent a copy of the report to the Minister of Transport, Barbara Castle, with the suggestion that the line should receive a subsidy and they supported a suggestion, to the same effect, made by the Transport Users Consultative Committee.

No firm decision had yet been made and, in what the *East Lothian Courier* described as a 'Last bid to save the passenger service', the Town Councils of both North Berwick and Prestonpans touchingly, if rather naively, proposed a twopenny surcharge on their domestic rates in order to provide an annual subsidy for the line of £13,000. These local authorities, the county, the North Berwick Negotiating Committee (an umbrella organisation covering most of the local residents, traders and politicians interests) and the Labour Member of Parliament for East Lothian, John P. Mackintosh, all kept up the pressure on the Minister. Their efforts ultimately paid off when, on 19th September, 1969, it was announced that the Minister had refused BR permission to close the line. The *East Lothian Courier* referred to this as 'a victory for strong local opposition' and the Minister's official statement read as follows:

> After taking into account the availability of existing bus services, the Minister considers that the essential needs of rail users could be met by the provision of a

modified peak-hour rail service, stopping at Prestonpans, Longniddry and Drem, consisting of two morning trains from North Berwick to Edinburgh on Mondays to Saturdays, two evening returns from Edinburgh to North Berwick on Mondays to Saturdays and three afternoon return trains from Edinburgh to North Berwick on Saturdays.

Although the line had been saved, many regarded this as something of a false dawn, for the proposed service had been so drastically reduced as to render it virtually useless to all but daily commuters. One particular concern was the fact that many children attending private schools in Edinburgh were regular travellers on the line and that there was no convenient return service for them to use. John Mackintosh attempted to persuade BR that a 4.30 pm Edinburgh to North Berwick service was needed for these schoolchildren but the official reply was that this service would cost £5,500 annually to provide and that the County Council had been approached for a 50 per cent contribution to this, but had stated that such a contribution 'was out of the question'. The criticisms grew, especially from those who lived in Dunbar and had all but lost their local service. These criticisms culminated in the statement by the Scottish Nationalist Prospective Parliamentary Candidate for East Lothian who denounced the whole affair with the words, 'The reprieve of the North Berwick service looks as though it will last no longer than the next General Election.'

Thus, at the eleventh hour, the North Berwick line had been saved but even now there was no guarantee that this, the last survivor of the seven branches authorised by the 1846 Act, would have anything more than a short term future. Few at that time would have expected the fortunes of the line to be as dramatically reversed as they later came to be.

The bleak 'rationalised' terminus on 5th December, 1970.   *J.L. Stevenson*

Chapter Nine

Railway Renaissance

THE RISE OF THE NORTH BERWICK BRANCH SINCE 1970

'We expect the North Berwick line to be in profit within a few years.'

B.R. Area Operations Manager, March 1984

The reduced passenger service came into operation on the due date, Monday 4th January, 1970, and continued financial support was given to the service by means of a grant from central government made in terms of Section 39(1) of the Transport Act 1968. For 1971 the grant for the Edinburgh to North Berwick and Dunbar service amounted to £70,000. Various suggestions were put forward locally to improve the few services which did remain, including the strengthening of rush-hour services by running two multiple units together in six-coach trains to prevent overcrowding, and the use of North Berwick station as a rail-bus interchange. These suggestions were followed up and six-car trains did appear on occasions, but although BR were in favour of the interchange idea 'provided that they are not asked to keep the station open at times when it is not needed for train passengers', nothing eventually came of it. What was, more surprisingly, rejected was the suggestion that to cut costs and therefore release more money for other services, conductor-guard working could be introduced thus obviating the need for station staff to be in attendance. This idea was rejected by BR on the grounds that they doubted if all the fares could be properly collected on such a short journey and that, in any event, the staff costs referred to were minimal and that in consequence the savings would only be marginal – an odd view given the commercial success of similar conductor-guard 'Pay-trains' in East Anglia.

The service continued on the same minimal basis for several years; it was interesting to note that during a Scottish bus strike in February 1974, when all Eastern Scottish local buses were cancelled and traffic congestion was rife, something of the true potential of the line was shown. All evening trains to North Berwick had to be strengthened to six coaches (and were full!) and the 5.10 pm Edinburgh to Leeds 'North Briton' express had to make additional calls at Prestonpans and Longniddry in order to deal with those wishing to be set down there.

In October 1975 a by no means untypical accident occurred at North Berwick when, yet again, a train ran through the buffer stops. It was a damp and foggy day and a diesel multiple unit made up of two 3-car sets was entering the station down the 1 in 66½ decline when it failed to stop, causing the leading power car to mount the buffer stops and suffer extensive damage. There were no casualties. The investigation into the accident concluded that the driver had failed to make the necessary allowance for the adverse weather conditions when making his final brake application. A similar accident happened in 1986, after the station had been rebuilt, and this time it was three parked cars which sustained the damage when the train hit them. Other similar incidents have occurred, especially in damp or icy conditions, but not, fortunately, with such spectacular results.

The line slumbered on throughout the 1970s and, although there were minimal improvements, a re-awakening was still a long way off. The class '100' and '101' multiple units continued to work the service but the former class, being of a 'non-standard' design, did not survive the decade and suffered an early withdrawal. For a time the '101' 'Met-Cams' enjoyed a monopoly, and refurbished units in the reversed white and blue livery were seen on the branch, together with corporate livery units with inappropriate Greater Glasgow Passenger Transport Executive branding; the same units operated Dunbar locals. At the end of the decade, other types of multiple unit began to make regular appearances and these included classes '104', '105', '107', '108' and '120' – often different types would be combined into curious hybrids both of design and livery. Single unit railcars occasionally made forays onto the branch either on their own or joined to twin sets. More bizarre motive power included at least one HST '125' set on the branch (for reasons which are inexplicable!) and, to the delight of railway enthusiasts, class '55' Deltic locomotives were seen working out their last few months on Dunbar locals. After the closure of the branch to goods traffic, the only locomotives still seen at North Berwick were the BRCW Type 2 (class '26') diesels employed on weedkilling trains and engineer's specials and, latterly, the Hunslet class '20's, again on weedkiller duties, but the lack of runround facilities, holding sidings and the short platform length at North Berwick precluded passenger locomotive hauled trains and excursions*.

A welcome development came in January 1979 when, in an experiment to test the potential for a through service from the West End of Edinburgh, a single weekday morning train from North Berwick was extended from Waverley to Haymarket and a similar return working was also provided. This proved to be a popular move (and of course had the additional benefit of not blocking a through platform at Waverley) and within a few years virtually every train from North Berwick was extended through to Haymarket.

During the early 1980s, there were definite signs that patronage of the branch passenger service was growing, largely due to the external factors of road congestion and parking problems of Edinburgh and, at long last, it became clear that British Rail themselves were now taking a more sympathetic approach to the service.

In March 1984 they, somewhat unexpectedly, announced that the future of the North Berwick to Edinburgh service was secure and that extra trains were to be provided from May. It was said that the line had been chosen as an experiment into local accountability, being run as a separate business responsible for its own losses and profits. According to a report in the *East Lothian Courier*, the BR Area Operations Manager stated that it was expected that the line would be in profit within a few years. The new service included a daily lunchtime train for the first time for many years; to help to publicise this facility, passengers were allowed to travel free in the first week of operation. The fares structure was altered and the self-validating 'Ten Journey' ticket, designed to encourage the less regular passenger to make occasional single journeys, was withdrawn. A letter in the *East*

---

* Multiple units, however, have appeared on 'specials' from time to time and these have included a diesel unit in 1980 and an electric unit in 1992, the latter on an excursion from Glasgow via Ayr and Carstairs!

The old station at North Berwick in its declining days as the 11.05 am to Haymarket waits to depart on 30th January, 1981.   *Brian Morrison*

A class '156' in Strathclyde orange livery on a Sunday service at North Berwick in December 1990 – the extraordinary configuration of the trackwork following the slewing of the lines for the electrification works can be clearly seen in the winter sunlight.   *Author*

Lothian Courier commented that this withdrawal was inevitable due to the abuse of these tickets and that 'a swoop on Prestonpans a few years ago confirmed BR's worse fears and it was interesting that most of the culprits came from North Berwick.'

The condition of the station buildings at North Berwick was now giving serious cause for concern. In February 1984 local councillors had expressed dismay at the deteriorating condition of the station roof, and the fact that large areas of the platform were cordoned off for safety reasons, and they called upon BR to take action. In May 1984 British Rail announced that they were seeking to demolish the station and replace it with a new structure, commenting that this would be an exercise in good housekeeping, since it would cost 'thousands of pounds' to keep the old station in good repair. Its replacement would be much cheaper to maintain and therefore money would be available to put back into the train service itself. With some local dismay, demolition of the station buildings began in January 1985 and the buffer stops on the one remaining line were moved some 50 yards closer to Edinburgh. The existing up platform was retained although by cutting it short, it was now only capable of accommodating a four coach train. Most of the station and goods yard area was now sold off to Walker Homes for housing and a new residential development, known as Station Court, built on the site. A new fibreglass prefabricated structure, containing a small waiting area and a bookstall, was provided (the latter being a popular local facility given the absence of other shops in the vicinity) and a bicycle shelter was also built. A great deal of free car parking space was made available in order to attract what was by now being called 'park-and-ride' passengers. In 1987 the station area was landscaped under a Manpower Services Commission scheme, but the car park remained windswept and unattractive. In retrospect, it is a pity that alternative uses for the original station buildings were not found and that such an unworthy (and already dilapidated) successor was chosen. One can only hope that sooner, rather than later, a more fitting terminus for the branch line will be provided.

Other changes to local station buildings also took place. Longniddry lost its entire buildings, the up side (which had survived longer than the island down platform structure) being demolished and replaced with a glass and steel 'bus-stop' shelter. At Drem, a listed building, the down side waiting rooms, were accidentally partially demolished in 1985 due to a 'misunderstanding' and BR were subsequently obliged to provide a replica on the same site; the up side buildings were boarded up. Staff were withdrawn from North Berwick, Drem (which had already been partially unstaffed for the previous four years), Longniddry and Prestonpans stations on 27th May, 1985 when conductor-guard working was introduced on the Edinburgh to North Berwick service, making it, incidentally Scotland's first 'Pay-Train'.

The service continued to improve and, with an attractive fare structure, more road problems in the capital (leading to serious consideration of introducing a 'road pricing' policy to discourage car commuters) and a number of innovations including the running of year-round Sunday trains, passenger levels continued to increase. Late evening services, first run in connection with the Edinburgh International Festival, later became seasonal and then permanent, and a new station at Musselburgh, opened in 1988 half a mile from the site of the original Inveresk Station, proved within months to be a commercial success.*

By the mid 1980s the diesel multiple units, which were by now nearly 30 years old, were giving cause for concern as increasing mechanical unreliability and a deteriorating passenger environment, coupled with the escalating cost of merely keeping the units running, led to the introduction in 1988 of the class '150' 'Sprinter' units on North Berwick services where they ran selected trains along with the old 'first generation' dmus. As from Monday 15th May, 1989, a new timetable was introduced and virtually every train was now Sprinter worked. The service consisted of a virtually hourly Haymarket to North Berwick shuttle from 7 am until nearly midnight with additional peak hour workings and a two-hourly Sunday service; on weekdays certain trains were extended to destinations such as Bathgate, Cardenden and Stirling for reasons of operational efficacy.

The Sprinters were popular with the travelling public and in the next two years, the '150's in their BR Provincial livery with 'ScotRail' markings became a common sight. Unfortunately, however, the poor interior design of these units did not always endear them to regular travellers and the fact that two-car units replaced the previous three-car dmus, led to severe overcrowding on peak-hour services resulting in irate letters to *The Scotsman* newspaper and, on at least one occasion, a train crew refusing to start a train until an additional unit was provided. Some of the problems were alleviated when the vastly superior class '156' 'Super Sprinters' were used and in peak hours, the 5.10 pm and 5.40 pm departures from Waverley were usually run by Derby class '107' units – these had a monopoly of 'heritage' units after the departure of the faithful 'Met-Cams' in 1990. Liveries were still varied and Strathclyde orange '107' and '156' units made regular appearances.

The age of the North Berwick diesel train was now, however, drawing to a close. On 27th July, 1984, and laying the spectre of the Serpell Report finally to rest, government approval had been given to an ambitious scheme to electrify the whole of the Kings Cross to Edinburgh main line on the 25 kV ac' overhead wire system, and it was envisaged that the final section to Edinburgh would be in operation by May 1991. By the end of the decade, the signs of change were apparent throughout the Scottish sections of the line and, as the wires went up, many older structures, particularly bridges, were removed in order to provide the necessary clearances. Several footbridges disappeared and were not renewed – those at Drem Junction and Aberlady Junction being the most obvious and resulting in the stopping up of local footpaths, while at the station at Drem, the original footbridge was replaced in May 1989 by a metal bridge of novel design manufactured by the Kerse Engineering Company of Grangemouth and the original bridge dismantled, for possible future use at Settle in Yorkshire. The Longniddry Station footbridge was replaced by a more conventional structure; the bridge at Prestonpans was donated to the nearby Prestongrange Mining Museum, having been replaced with a similar bridge to that at Drem. The line between

* The station was originally to have been called Musselburgh West (Inveresk) and a second station, Musselburgh East, was planned to serve the Wallyford area; at the time of writing the Wallyford Station was still under serious consideration.

Regional Express unit No. 158 734 with the 9.24 am to Haymarket on 3rd July, 1991; in the weeks prior to the electric service commencing these units operated almost all services on the branch and until May 1992 continued to operate the 7.07 am to Glasgow, successor to the 'Lothian Coast Express'. *Brian Morrison*

Signs of the times at North Berwick, July 1991. *Author*

The first electric train to North Berwick – unit 305 501 waits at the terminus on Monday 8th July, 1991. *Author*

Millerhill, near Edinburgh, and Belford in Northumberland was energised in October 1990 and a sign was erected at Drem Junction prohibiting entry to the branch for electric trains – as events transpired, this sign was to have a short period of use!

The 'Lanark card' was now played. In the 1970s, it had been decided that there was little sense in working by diesel power the short Lanark branch off the electrified West Coast main line, especially when the branch dmus would be required to run in the path of electric trains on the main line. It was now recognised that, notwithstanding the success of Sprinter working, similar considerations would apply to the North Berwick branch, especially when the limited paths available between Drem and Edinburgh were taken into account. The decision to electrify the North Berwick line therefore came quickly and surprised few, notwithstanding the problems of finance and the fact that no local Scottish train service outside Strathclyde Region had ever been run with electric traction. In May 1990 the press carried reports that British Rail were giving serious consideration to the electrification of both the Edinburgh to North Berwick and the Edinburgh to West Calder services, with the possibility of running them as a joint through service. Negotiations then followed with the Lothian Regional Council, the authority having a local transport function. Fortunately Lothian were, at that time, rail-minded and had been responsible for funding other railway projects, such as the opening of several new stations within the region and the high profile reopening of the Edinburgh to Bathgate line. In September 1990 it was announced that a provisional agreement had been reached whereby British Rail and Lothian Region would each meet one-half of the estimated £1,300,000 capital cost of electrification between Drem and North Berwick, and the final go-ahead for the scheme was given on the 27th of that month.

Given that the main line electrification gangs were still present in the area, it was possible to make an early start on the works, with the aim of having the branch electric service commencing on the same day as the projected start of the main line service between London and Edinburgh, and various civil engineering works were undertaken almost at once. At the end of November 1990, the branch was closed for a whole week, a replacement bus being used to take passengers between North Berwick and Drem where a modified local service then took them to Edinburgh; during this week essential preparatory works, including drainage, the cutback of vegetation and the general upgrading of the trackbed, were undertaken by the main contractors, Pirelli Construction. On the main line, it had been necessary to rebuild overbridges in order to provide the necessary overhead clearances for the catenary wires but, when it came to the North Berwick branch, it found that no rebuilding was required for, by slewing the running line to run beneath the centre of each bridge arch, the required clearances could be obtained. At long last the initial decision of the North British to build the line to double-line standards was vindicated, and the workmanship of James Gowans' bridges was such that the only modification they required was to raise the parapets so that the wires could not be touched from above, but on the debit side the previously straight configuration of the line was sacrificed! The only bridge not to be rebuilt was that at Williamston which carried a farm road over the line close to the site of the original temporary terminus; despite strong local opposition (and correspondence in the *East Lothian Courier!*), the road was closed and the bridge entirely demolished, leaving no public crossing over the line between the Dirleton Station bridge and North Berwick.

Further weekend closures took place over the winter months and, by Easter, the first of the overhead line support masts had been erected near Drem Junction. Work then progressed at a fast pace and within weeks all the masts were in place and the wires were up and at one minute past midnight on the morning of Sunday 18th May, 1991, the electric current was switched on.

Unfortunately financial constraints ruled out the possibility of new stock being built for the Edinburgh to North Berwick service, at least for the first few years and in consequence BR began to consider the possibilities of various redundant ac suburban electric multiple unit stock which was surplus to their requirements. Initially redundant electric units of classes '303' and '311' from Strathclyde (the original Glasgow 'Blue Trains') were examined but rejected on a number of grounds; the net was cast wider and it was decided to use class '307' units which had formerly worked services on the Great Eastern line out of London's Liverpool Street and which were now lying in store at Carlisle. For several weeks unit No. 307 117, in the full Network South East livery of red, white, and blue and bearing the inappropriate destination of 'Clacton', was seen at Waverley. Further examination of these redundant units, and the basic unreliability of similar refurbished units in use on local services in West Yorkshire, led to their eventual rejection for the North Berwick service and once again, the net was cast. Class '310' units were next considered and rejected before an eventual decision was taken to use five refurbished sets of class '305/2' units which had been built at Doncaster works in 1960 and which had spent their entire working lives up to then on the London, Tilbury and Southend and Great Eastern suburban lines out of London. Units Nos. 501, 502, 508, 517 and 519 were chosen for the new service and they were rebuilt with internal gangways (a necessary prerequisite for conductor-guard operation) and provided with new seating and a revised internal layout. The four-coach units were sent to BRML Wolverton for this work to be done and each emerged resplendent in the new Regional Railways two-tone blue and grey livery; once in service ScotRail markings were added. Unfortunately, an earlier suggestion that the units, which formed a separate sub-class used only on the North Berwick service, should bear a madder and white livery similar to Lothian's buses, or at the least a madder band, were not followed through but the line's '305's were at least unique and in their first few months of service proved to be a popular subject for railway photographers.

Driver training was undertaken with surplus Strathclyde units and on several occasions the celebrity unit '303 048', restored to its original Glasgow Blue Train 'Caledonian' livery, made trial trips along the branch. A break with tradition now followed – due to the fact that there were no other electric multiple units to be stabled in Edinburgh it was decided that the North Berwick '305's were to be shedded at Glasgow's Shields depot, reached via the newly-electrified Carstairs link and Haymarket depot was to remain solely for use by Sprinters. Doubts began to be expressed as to the likelihood of the electric service beginning on time, especially after a fire at Shields and the apparent delay in the new units being sent up from the South but the full electric service was advertised to commence concurrent with the inauguration of the full Kings Cross to Edinburgh electric service.

In May 1991 an interim timetable for the last two months of diesel working was brought into use and an interesting new working appeared. This was the 7.07 am, the first down working from North Berwick, which was extended through Edinburgh to Glasgow Queen Street where it arrived at 8.48 am having stopped at all twelve intermediate stations. This service, which ran as empty coaching stock from Haymarket to North Berwick, was operated by class '158' 'Express' units and carried both first-class accommodation and a refreshment trolley thereby providing a curious evocation of the long-vanished 'Lothian Coast Express' and even the timings, despite the frequent stops, compared credibly. The service continued into the electric era, and became the only scheduled diesel departure from North Berwick; there was, however, no return working in the evening.*

On Monday 8th July, 1991 the full electric service commenced with unit 305 501 leaving North Berwick on time (but in torrential rain) with the 7.38 am to Haymarket. Perhaps fortunately there was no opening ceremony that day for the timetable soon degenerated into farce – the first up working from Edinburgh was cancelled without notice (thereby disappointing several intrepid 'first day' travellers who had hoped to arrive at North Berwick on the first scheduled service) and thereafter bus substitutions and a disrupted train service ran. Later in the day advertised services were operated and on the following day Councillor Ron Muir, the Chair of the Lothian Regional Council Transportation Committee, unveiled a commemorative plaque at North Berwick station. Within days there were public protests that the service had deteriorated dramatically since electrification and cancellations, late-running and diesel substitutions were all too common. The reasons for this inauspicious start were not difficult to find and these included a shortage of drivers trained to drive emus and a lack of units. In an echo of earlier times a petition was drawn up and protests made to BR about the poor timekeeping and cancellations and this brought the frank admission from the Director of ScotRail in October of that year that the service since electrification had frequently been 'dismal' and a promise of improvement was made; in early November 1991 the fifth and final unit, 305 519, was delivered from Wolverton and it was claimed that the availability of units for the service was now 100 per cent. Another problem, that of delays and cancellations caused by pathing difficulties through Waverley station, was finally solved in February 1992 when, for the first time. North Berwick services were diverted from the main station to the 'suburban' platforms 20 and 21.

Despite these difficulties, however, the new electric units proved popular with the travelling public and their somewhat antiquated features such as slam-doors and a lack of air conditioning were overlooked in favour of such old-fashioned virtues as comfortable seats, opening windows and space for

* The service was discontinued as from 11th May, 1992.

bicycles – a very positive advance over the class '150' Sprinters! Perhaps their greatest virtue was the high capacity of each four-coach set, something which helped to eradicate the previously endemic rush-hour overcrowding.

With the advent of the electrics we come, for the time being, to the end of the North Berwick branch line story in an age when the line is being worked by its fourth form of motive power and hopes are again high for the future of the service. Whether or not it will survive another century and a half depends on how adequately it continues to fulfil its original function of carrying both commuters and 'excursionists' between the East Lothian towns and villages and the capital and although it undoubtedly has the potential for this, local railway management must ensure that the trains continue to run on time and at all, for even the most pro-rail local passenger can become easily alienated by often justified and long-running complaints. In the meantime, however, as the daily travellers watch the familiar countryside slipping past in the early morning mist and haar* and look out on their return for the welcoming sentinel of the Law bathed in the evening sunlight, perhaps a few reflect on how Scotland and indeed the whole world has changed dramatically since those few intrepid passengers sat huddled beneath the single flickering oil-lamp in the Dandy Car as the weary horse trudged its way home along the very same line of railway in the darkness of the bleak mid-winter long, long ago.

* cold sea-fog on east coast of Scotland.

Electric train on a North Berwick–Haymarket evening working at Longniddry Station, August 1991.   *Author*

Chapter Ten

A Journey to the Sea

THE NORTH BERWICK AND GULLANE LINES DESCRIBED

'Faster and faster the train went, farther and farther away from home, till at last Nelly, who was watching eagerly at the window cried "I can see the sea, Jim, I can see the sea!"'

Mary Heugh Aitken, 'Adventures at North Berwick', 1880

A typical Saturday afternoon journey to at the end of the diesel era, begins as the vintage Met-Cam multiple unit departs in a cloud of smoke from Platform 1 at Waverley. The three coach train, with its mixed load of tired shoppers returning home, a handful of cyclists and walkers out for a day in the country, and several beleaguered parents with their children already excited by the prospect of a trip to the seaside, plunges into the gloom of the Calton North tunnel, before emerging again into daylight, passing the backs of tenements on one side and the vista of the Queen's Park and Holyrood Palace on the other. Soon the abandoned Abbeyhill loop diverges to the left, and Meadowbank Stadium and House are passed, with few reminders now of the once great steam shed at St Margarets, which has long gone. The goods line from Leith, and the sidings at Craigentinny and Portobello, now pass by and in the distance the sea beckons invitingly. 'Each a glimpse and gone for ever' as the abandoned Joppa Station and the lines to Millerhill and Bilston Glen pass by. Before long, the train is slowing down for its first stop, the new station at Musselburgh, close to where the course of the original branch line to the 'honest toun' can still be seen.

At Musselburgh, as usual, a fair number of passengers alight and soon the train is on the move again, passing Monktonhall, crossing the River Esk and hurrying past the site of the battle of Pinkie where, in 1547, the English routed the Scots with great slaughter. The village of Prestonpans now comes into view and soon the train comes to a halt here beside the original (but boarded up) station buildings. Once more the train is under way, and to the right can be seen the ruins of Bankton House, the headquarters of Colonel James Gardiner, who died in 1745 in the great battle of Prestonpans which marked the high point in the last campaign of Prince Charles Edward Stuart. More prosaic is the sight of the Meadowmill Sports Complex and, in the last small pocket of industrialisation left in East Lothian, a line diverges on the left to the clearly visible Cockenzie Power Station, and to the right to the Coal Board sidings at Blindwells; it is strange to think that one of Scotland's earliest railways, the 18th-century Cockenzie and Tranent wagonway, crossed the main line at this point.

A long and fast run now follows and soon the train is racing the cars along the short dual carriageway section of the A198 main road. At St Germains crossing the barriers rise with its passing and soon the village of Longniddry, which has expanded considerably in recent years and is now a favoured residence for Edinburgh commuters (particularly those who like golf!), comes into view. *Sic transit gloria* – Longniddry Station is now a spartan affair, with bare platforms and small bus-stop shelters, sadly depleted since the days when passengers were exhorted to change for the Gullane and Haddington branches by the cries of the porter. The elderly diesel now splutters into life again and to the right can be seen the grassy embankment of the former Haddington branch, curving away sharply towards the county town, while to the left lies farmland and, on the horizon, the shimmering sea backed by the distant coast of Fife. The impressive ruins of the Redhouse Castle pass by and, at Spittal, the train passes the site of Aberlady Junction and the overgrown embankment of the Gullane branch falls away to the left before swinging towards the coast where both Aberlady and Gullane can be seen quite clearly. On the landward side, the Garleton Hills rise up abruptly, and a gate and an overgrown strip mark the sole remains of the Ballencrieff siding.

Within a couple of minutes, the train wheezes to a halt at Drem where, according to the late architectural historian, Colin McWilliam, the station still 'dominates the village in a friendly way' – and what a station and what a village! The 1846 buildings all survive in recognisable form and the presence of a siding, complete with tracklaying machines, a proper waiting room on the down platform, the goods shed and a newly painted picket fence, all contribute to a feeling that this traditional country station has been caught in a timewarp, notwithstanding the new footbridge, the electric wires, the continual procession of passenger trains thundering through and the slow rumbling of the occasional class '37'-hauled freight. Outside the village is a charmingly grouped collection of typical stone and pantile East Lothian cottages, complete with country gardens, and a traditional village post office – the only incongruous note being the BR posterboard labelled 'Bishopbriggs' in recognition of its presumably previous incarnation.

The train starts up again and lurches over the points onto the up loop in order to gain the branch line. A wide vista of farm, field and ocean now opens up and to the left Dirleton and its castle can be seen with the 'model holding' at Fenton Barns, in the foreground. The Peffer Burn is crossed; the single track and the frequent wheel beats on the short rails add to the branch line atmosphere. Soon the diesel's exhaust reverberates through the deep cutting at Kingston – 'the gradient's against her, but she's on time!' Under another of James Gowans' bridges and the site of Dirleton Station is passed; the tall chimneys of the station master's house, together with the edges of the loading bank, are both clearly seen, while a donkey grazes where once the local farmers loaded the railway wagons. To the right the bulk of the Law looms up unmistakably and the whalebone at its summit can be discerned, while to the left the island of Fidra, with its white painted lighthouse, comes into view. The remains of the 'new' gas works at Ferrygate are now passed and, at Williamston, the train again enters a cutting. The brakes are applied and the elderly dmu slows to walking pace as it enters the much reduced terminus at North Berwick, where the short single platform and wooden fence are the only reminders of the previous station, apart from a solitary cast iron column which formerly supported part of the canopy and now supports a British Rail logo. The never completed harbour extension embankment and the Royal Hotel are passed by the passengers as they hurry towards the town and beach and, as the sun shines benignly on the burgh, the gleaming blue Firth, the white ramparts of the mighty Bass Rock and the seagulls wheeling overhead, all combine to lend an air of excitement and expectation in much the same way as they have done for train travellers arriving at North Berwick over almost a century and a half.

The Gullane branch has, in contrast, largely reverted to nature and although it has no right of way along its length (unlike the neighbouring Haddington branch which is now a public footpath named 'The Railway Walk'), it is still possible to walk on isolated sections of the trackbed. At Gullane the station site is a sorry spectacle – a few sections of platform edge and other rubbish strewn debris mark out the remains of what was once a beautifully kept station, where John Seth regularly won prizes for his efforts and the flower displays cheered the traveller. Leaving this area, which may well disappear beneath new housing in the near future, the trackbed continues under a footbridge, which still carries a path across the line, before leaving the outskirts of the village. Passing Saltcoats Farm and Castle, the route then runs through prime golfing country, past the Luffness Links where the site of the platform is now only marked by a single upright of bullhead rail which once carried a warning notice. The line now skirts Peffer Bank Wood and crosses the burn on the still extant Bridge No. 6 before becoming somewhat overgrown – this section is popular with dogwalkers and ramblers and the presence of spent shotgun cartridges speaks of other pursuits too. At Bridge No. 5, carrying the Luffness to West Fenton road over the line, the trackbed peters out and from here on, the route is difficult to follow, ploughing having all but obliterated it. Bridge No. 4, close to the Myreton Motor Museum, still stands and some remains are visible thereafter in the curiously named Maggies Waa's Wood before the site of Aberlady Station, next to the A6137 Aberlady to Haddington road, is reached. Here the station platform, station master's house and goods bank all stand, although a new bungalow has been built where the station buildings once were and the goods yard site is used as a yard for lorries. From Aberlady Station the route skirts the Gosford Estate and, close to the farm at Ballencrieff Mains, part of the trackbed is now in use as a farm road. The overgrown embankment now rises to join the main line and merges imperceptibly with it, close to the vanished Aberlady Junction and the new bridge at Spittal.

The spirit of the Gullane branch can, perhaps, best be savoured from the overbridge at Aberlady Station and, with a little imagination, the sights and sounds of the past can be conjured up – the small station bustling with summer visitors, the goods engine leisurely shunting its few wagons and the impressive Royal Train carriages awaiting patiently with their important passengers on a misty wartime morning. Here on this bridge, where the waving and cheering children greeted the first train over 90 years ago, one can reflect on the all too brief life and the long demise of this little line and remember the words of that most eminent of railway historians, Hamilton Ellis, who said 'Alas for the days when Gullane had not only a train service, but even a named express!' And yet all is not lost for in the distance, a London-bound '125' streaks across the horizon, and one is reminded that, whatever other changes have taken place, at least somewhere in the tranquil Vale of Peffer the railway is still alive.

North Berwick on 17th June, 1976 as a Metro-Cammell dmu prepares to brave the
elements on the 10.55 am to Waverley. *Tom Heavyside*

The basic railway – the 6.18 pm Sprinter from Waverley arrives at North Berwick on
2nd July, 1991 in the last week of diesel working. *Brian Morrison*

Chapter Eleven

'Line Clear'

SOME NOTES ON THE BRANCH SIGNALS AND SIGNAL BOXES

'Hand signals – Any signal or the arm, or anything in the hand, waved violently denotes Danger and the necessity of stopping immediately.'

NBR Rule 48

When the North Berwick line was opened, railway signalling was still in its infancy and the basis of local train movement control was the telegraphed message. From about 1860 the staff and ticket system was introduced in order to work the single line in a more structured manner, and the 1863 Working Timetable states that for use on the branch was a 'Green train staff and train ticket – No. of staff 5'. The engine driver was required to carry the train staff (or, in the case of a train being followed by another in the same direction, a train ticket), which showed that he had the necessary authorisation to travel the North Berwick to Drem Junction section. The staff was fixed to a socket on the engine, the ticket being placed in a spring clip. When staff and tickets were not in use, they were kept in the booking offices of the stations at each end of the section and they were to be issued only under the supervision of the respective station agents.

On entering the branch, it was the duty of the Drem station master 'to have the Train Staff or Ticket ready beforehand, and to exhibit it to the Driver who must not, under any circumstances, proceed until the Guard shows him the "All Right" signal.' Later on, the branch was operated with standard three-indicator needle block telegraph instruments and, following the implementation of the Regulation of Railways Act 1889 and the reconstruction of the terminus, the tablet system was adopted and Tyer's No. 1 instruments (referred to by the North British as 'old pattern') were provided. These were replaced in about 1901 by a modernised version of the same (the NBR 'converted tablet') and, in turn, by Tyer's No. 6 after World War I. The signals themselves were standard Stevens-pattern NBR lower quadrants; some of these were replaced by upper quadrants, on the same posts, in the 1950s.

Drem Junction signal box was situated at the eastern end of the down platform opposite the entrance to the goods yard. The original Stevens frame of about 1890 was replaced as part of a resignalling scheme by a new-pattern 45-lever 4¼ in. frame in November 1918. Small wooden tablet stages were provided at the east end of each platform, and the 'residentials' and other trains which omitted the Drem Station stop were required to reduce their speed to 3 mph while passing the stages, to enable the driver to receive or hand back the tablets. The box was open continuously on weekdays but was closed 'from the passing of the 6.09 am ex-Berwick until 5 am on Mondays'. In earlier days a pointsman had been in charge of operations at the junction and would have had to observe the old Rule 69. This stated that 'In the case of Engines or Trains approaching a junction or the Main and Branch Line at the same time, preference must be given to the train which first came in sight.' A complicated code of whistles was to be observed by steam engines on the approach to the junction so that all concerned would be aware of their identity and at Drem this code required that the following number of whistles be made:

1 = Main line
2 = North Berwick branch
3 = Up to Down crossover or vice versa
4 = Up line shunting siding
5 = Goods siding
6 = Down-line shunting siding
7 = Down-line carriage siding

A speed limit of 15 mph was in force over the up and down line crossovers and over the junction with the branch line.

At Dirleton the sidings were worked by ground frame controlled by a tablet lock, and similar arrangements applied to the gas works sidings. North Berwick signal box was a tall structure situated next to Ware Road bridge and opposite the engine shed. Commanding a good view over the station approaches and yard, and fitted with a 25-lever frame, the box was open in the 1930s between 6.15 am and 4.55 pm and again from 5.35 pm to 11.35 pm on weekdays and 6 pm to 12.15 am on Saturdays but was normally closed on Sundays. After the war the operating hours were simplified to 6.10 am to 11.50 pm on Mondays to Saturdays. An advanced starting signal controlled the exit from the station and this marked the outer limit beyond which engines assisting down passenger trains were not allowed to pass.

With the rationalisation of trackwork at North Berwick in January 1968, the box there was closed as from the 7th of that month and subsequently demolished; the branch was then worked on the 'one engine in steam' principle. Drem Junction box remained in use until 21st November, 1977, when 4-aspect colour light signalling, controlled from the signalling centre at Waverley, came into operation. The only remaining signal on the branch controls the entry to the junction at Drem.

The Gullane branch was from the outset operated by Tyer's No. 6 instruments and the 'Aberlady & Gullane No. 0' staff. Aberlady Junction box was a brick structure on the down side of the main line close to Spittal overbridge and opened on 23rd September, 1897. It was oil-lit and fitted with a Stevens old-pattern 5¼ in. frame and the signalman here was rather quaintly described as being 'the train staff custodian'. In December 1911 the frame was extended and relocked, 25 levers now being provided, and outer homes were placed on both the branch and main lines, together with a trailing crossover provided at the suggestion of Major Pringle, the Board of Trade Inspector.

After cessation of the branch passenger service, the box was switched in on weekdays only between 7 and 11.25 am and 12.25 to 4 pm (i.e. a single 8-hour shift). In November 1943 the signalling at the junction was simplified and the opening hours were extended, from 7 am to 6.05 pm, on weekdays only. The box was finally abolished on 12th December, 1965, some 13 months after the branch itself had been taken out of use.

Aberlady Station signal box was situated on the platform and had a 17-lever frame (of which 14 were actually in use and 3 were spare). The original purpose of the box was to act as an 'outer home' for the junction, allowing trains to approach the junction when the main line was still blocked – this still being an age when actual outer home signals were regarded with suspicion. Following the 1911 alterations at the junction, the main *raison d'etre* of the box disappeared and it was replaced, on 3rd October, 1921, by ground frames controlled by Annett Key; these worked the station sidings and loops at their east and west ends. An odd survival, however, was the fact that, as late as 1959, the main line signal lamps at Aberlady Junction were still being serviced by the sole member of staff at Aberlady Station until this duty was taken over by the Longniddry Station staff.

Gullane signal box was a brick and wooden structure situated at the west end of the passenger platform and it had a relatively brief life, being closed on 7th May, 1929. The loop and sidings were then worked by a ground frame controlled by Annett Key; from that date until closure, the whole branch was operated on the 'one engine in steam' principle. At Longniddry Station, the signal box, known as Longniddry Junction, was opened in 1881 and extended and raised in 1922. This box was, like Drem, open continuously until being finally closed on 8th September, 1968, six months after the Haddington line was taken out of use.

North Berwick signal box, January 1967.   *S. Black*

North Berwick Law and a charabanc from a commercial postcard of about 1926.

Marine Parade, North Berwick at the turn of the century – then, as now, many of the inhabitants of these villas would have been regular commuters on the train.

Quality Street in the early 1950s – the bus is a 1948 AEC on Stark's Haddington service but painted in full SMT livery – compare with the similar view which appears on page 38.

Endpiece

The following account of a happy family holiday spent in the Gullane Station 'camping apartments' in the summer of 1946 was written by the late Mrs Margery Rorke of Dollar and appears here with the kind permission of her daughter, Mrs J. Carolan, who was one of the children mentioned.

Station Holiday

One summer we rented the railway station of a small seaside village for a fortnight for our family holiday. There were six of us to start with, but after the first week we were joined by some friends who brought our numbers up to 12; four adults, six children under eight years of age, and two dogs of uncertain parentage but great character.

We were given four rooms, all opening onto the platform. There was a large waiting room, which we used as a living room and in which we had three camp beds. Off this was a small room containing a penny-in-the-slot gas cooker and an enamel basin in which we washed ourselves, the dishes and the clothes. The two other rooms were dormitories, and some of the smaller children shared beds, sleeping feet to feet with a pillow in the middle to stop them kicking each other.

Washing six children one after another in the evening was reduced to a fine art, and it was a strange sight to see them dancing along the platform in their nighties and pyjamas on the way to bed. Housework was easy – we just swept the dust from the rooms on to the platform and from there on to the line.

The railway company looked after us well, providing us with plenty of clean linen, coal, necessary china, cutlery and cooking utensils. The station master, porter and clerk were most helpful and friendly, and were not at all disturbed by the children's visits to their office, their questions and pranks.

Ours was the last station on the line and the passenger service had been suspended owing to the popularity of the buses, but we had one goods train a day, and its arrival was the big moment for the young fry. They used to rush down the platform to meet it, having pestered the station master to let them know when it was due. They then would climb into the engine and spend a blissful and exceedingly dirty half hour or so shunting and taking in water from the big tank at the end of our platform.

We were about a mile from the sea and we usually took a picnic to the beach and spent a large part of the day paddling and bathing, climbing on the rocks or playing hide-and-seek on the sand-dunes. Other days we were content to sit in deck chairs on the platform and watch the children playing 'trains'.

There was never a dull moment. In fact our adventures started a few minutes after we arrived. We had sent the bigger boys' bicycles in advance, and while I was unpacking they started riding up and down the platform. Suddenly there was a crash and a yell. I rushed out to find my son and heir lying on the line with a somewhat battered bicycle on top of him. He was badly winded and bruised but otherwise undamaged, and cycling on the platform was put onto the 'don't' list.

Though it was hardly a rest-cure for the adults, we all decided it was one of the most amusing, inexpensive, free-and-easy and out-of-the-ordinary holidays we had ever spent, and even the youngest child still remembers the rides on the engine.

Two views of the Aberlady Station buildings when in use as camping apartments in the 1950s.   *RCAHMS, Rokeby Collection*

Appendix One

The West Fenton Narrow Gauge Line

One of the lesser-known railway byways of East Lothian was the 2 ft gauge West Fenton line which remains almost completely undocumented and, had it not been for the fact that two local children had taken a keen interest in it during its short existence nearly three-quarters of a century ago and were able to give the author much useful information during the writing of this book, it is possible that the details of this line would have disappeared into permanent obscurity.

In 1915 the War Department decided to build an airfield at West Fenton, about 1½ miles south of Gullane, apparently for the purpose of training pilots in connection with the nearby East Fortune aerodrome. In the following year this installation was officially designated a 'Home Defence Landing Ground'. In order to convey the construction materials to the site, the North British agreed to make deliveries to Gullane station, where the loading bank to the south of the passenger platform was specially extended in May 1915 at a cost of £245. A 2 ft gauge tramway or light railway was then laid from here to the airfield and this ran virtually on top of the ground with minimal earthworks. The course of the line, which is barely discernible today, largely followed the contours of the land; starting at the station the rails ran eastwards for 200 yards or so before reaching the Fenton road close to Muirfield Farm Cottages. The line then swung to the south and ran parallel to the road on its western side for ¾ mile until it crossed the road on the level and travelled a short distance along the north bank of the Peffer or Mill Burn. The line then turned south, crossing the Burn on a wooden trestle bridge (which provided the only substantial engineering feature on the whole route) and continued south across the public road close to Craighead Cottage, before entering the airfield site. Both level crossings were ungated and apparently unprotected.

The contractors responsible for building and operating the line and constructing the airfield, were the then well-known Glasgow firm of F.D. Cowieson and Company, who were also responsible for several other works in the Gullane area. Initially the line was run by a combination of horse power and gravity, and a typical operation consisted of several wagons laden with timber, cement and bags of lime which were taken by the horse to the Fenton road. Here the horse was unhitched and the wagons were allowed to run free down the gradient. Halfway down this section, the road and railway took a slight kink and here, to the delight of local children, the wagons would occasionally derail and scatter their contents far and wide. For some reason bricks were not taken by the railway but, after being unloaded by hand at Gullane Station, they were loaded onto road trailers which were then hauled along the road by a commandeered showman's engine. Later a small 0–4–0 saddle tank engine, William Bagnall No. 2046 of 1918, and of a similar pattern to those used elsewhere in army installations and at the fronts, replaced the horse and this was immediately given the name of 'the pug' by villagers. The reign of the pug was, however, only a short one for, by 1920, the line was apparently out of use and the small locomotive was sent south to end its days at a works in Staffordshire. The rails were then lifted and few traces now remain of the line. In World War II West Fenton Airfield became RAF Drem (also known as RAF Gullane) and another short tramway was built, although this was solely for the purpose of transporting ammunition within the compound.

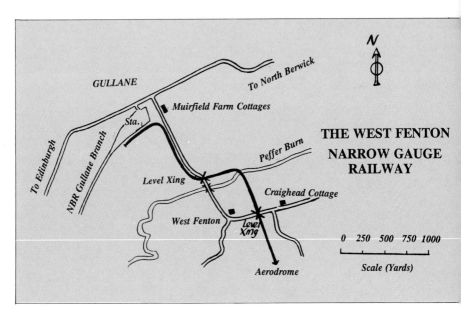

Bagnall narrow gauge 0−4−0ST No. E25058/17 supplied to the War Department for use at Corbridge timber depot and similar to the West Fenton 'pug'.
J.L. Stevenson Collection

Appendix Two

The Fidra Island Tramway

Even more obscure than the West Fenton line, but enjoying a much longer, if less busy, life, was the tramway which existed and exists on the Island of Fidra. The *Ordnance Gazeteer of Scotland* of 1895 contains the following entry:

> Fidra or Fetheray, a rocky basaltic islet of Dirleton parish, Haddingtonshire, 3 furlongs from the coast, and 2¾ miles WNW of North Berwick. It has ruins of a small old chapel; and there is a lighthouse, with group flashing light, showing two flashes in quick succession, with intervals of about 15 seconds between the groups, visible for 17 nautical miles.

The lighthouse was, and is, operated by the Northern Lighthouse Board and to connect this building with the landing place, a paved tramway track some 750 ft in length was constructed up a fairly steep incline. Supplies were then loaded upon a bogie which was connected to a haulage rope and drawn up by an Ace winch, powered by a Lister 10 hp twin-cylinder diesel engine. Of a similar pattern to other installations owned by the Board, the Fidra tramway had a rudimentary signalling system – inside the hollow tube handrail which paralleled the track was a bell wire, which ran right up to the terminus adjacent to the lighthouse. The tramway still exists although it has been out of use for several years and the bogie has been disposed of.

The Island of Fidra showing the lighthouse and tramway.

John Wilkie

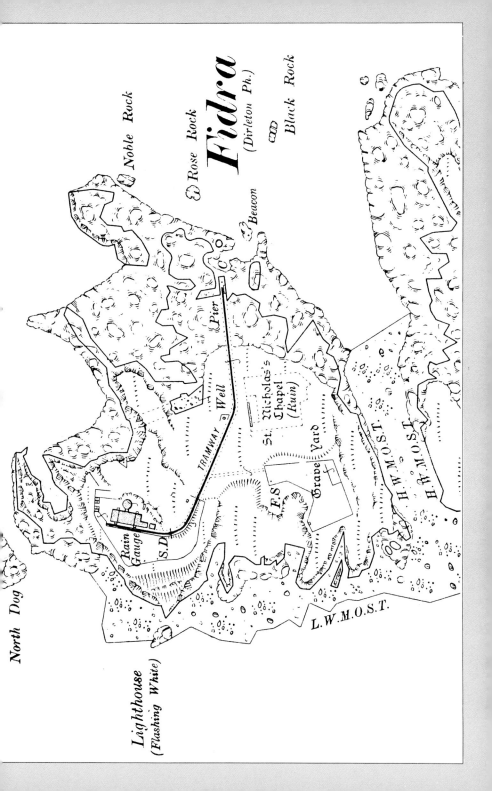

Appendix Three
Chronology of Important Dates

16th June, 1846	Act authorising North Berwick branch passed.
22nd June, 1846	Longniddry, Drem and Ballencrieff stations opened to passengers and goods.
20th January, 1847	James Gowans' tenders for construction of North Berwick branch accepted.
1st November, 1847	Ballencrieff Station closed.
13th August, 1849	Line opened Drem Junction to Williamston.
17th June, 1850	Line opened from Williamston to North Berwick; Dirleton and North Berwick stations opened to all traffic and Williamston (temporary terminus) closed.
1st November, 1856	Horse drawn Dandy Car commences operations between Drem and North Berwick.
1st May, 1857	Dandy Car withdrawn.
9th August, 1884	First accident at North Berwick Station.
7th June, 1893	Aberlady, Gullane and North Berwick Railway Company founded.
March 1894	New buildings at North Berwick Station completed.
24th August, 1894	Gullane branch authorised by Parliament.
18th November, 1896	Draft contract for construction of Gullane branch by John Howard approved.
23rd September, 1897	Aberlady Junction signal box opened.
1st April, 1898	Line between Aberlady Junction and Gullane including Aberlady and Gullane stations opened to all traffic.
1st August, 1900	Aberlady, Gullane and North Berwick Railway Company absorbed by North British Railway.
1st September, 1903	Luffness Platform opened.
May 1904	New North Berwick Gas Works siding opened and old siding closed.
20th August, 1904	Accident at North Berwick Station.
14th June, 1905	NBR Aberlady to North Berwick motor bus service commenced.
30th September, 1910	NBR bus service finally withdrawn.
3rd June, 1912	'Lothian Coast Express' inaugurated.
1st July, 1913	Through North Berwick to Kings Cross carriages first run.
21st September, 1921	Accident between Drem and Dirleton.
3rd October, 1921	Aberlady Station signal box closed.
1st January, 1923	North British Railway absorbed by LNER.
June 1928	Steam railcars commence trials on North Berwick branch.
7th May, 1929	Gullane signal box closed and branch operated on 'one engine in steam' basis.
November 1930	Regular steam railcar service on North Berwick branch inaugurated.
1st June, 1931	Luffness Platform closed.
12th September, 1932	Gullane branch and Aberlady and Gullane stations closed to passenger traffic.
30th September, 1934	'Lothian Coast Express' withdrawn.
10th September, 1939	North Berwick sleeping car service withdrawn.
1st January, 1948	LNER nationalised; became British Railways.
1st February, 1952	Dirleton Station closed to passengers; goods yard reduced to Unstaffed Public Sidings for wagonload traffic only.
3rd February, 1958	Hourly diesel service from North Berwick to Corstorphine inaugurated; North Berwick engine shed closed.

Class 'C15' 4−4−2T No. 9053 brings an era to an end as she heads the 6.35 pm Gullane to Longniddry on Saturday 10th September, 1932; this view of the last passenger train on the branch was taken by the fireman.   *J. Fleming*

1st June, 1959	Ballencrieff Siding closed.
15th June, 1964	Gullane branch and Aberlady and Gullane stations closed to all traffic.
1st August, 1964	Dirleton Sidings closed.
9th November, 1964	Gullane branch officially 'out of use'.
28th December, 1964	Longniddry closed to goods.
12th December, 1965	Aberlady Junction signal box abolished.
1st January, 1968	North Berwick goods yard closed.
8th January, 1968	North Berwick signal box closed; line rationalised and worked by 'one engine in steam'.
8th September, 1968	Longniddry signal box closed.
19th September, 1969	North Berwick passenger service reprieved by Minister of Transport.
4th January, 1970	Reduced Edinburgh to North Berwick passenger service comes into effect.
21st November, 1977	Drem signal box closed.
6th August, 1979	Drem goods yard closed.
5th February, 1985	Demolition of North Berwick Station buildings commenced.
27th May, 1985	Paytrain service with conductor-guard operation comes into use between Edinburgh and North Berwick; stations at Prestonpans, Longniddry, Drem and North Berwick all become unstaffed.
15th May, 1989	'Sprinters' commence regular operations on North Berwick line.
27th September, 1990	Agreement reached to fund electrification of North Berwick to Drem Junction section.
18th May, 1991	Line between North Berwick and Drem 'energised'.
8th July, 1991	Regular service of electric trains between Haymarket and North Berwick commences.

Appendix Four

Mileages

North Berwick Branch

	Miles	Chains	Miles
DREM Station	0	00	0.0
Drem Junction	0	27	0.3
DIRLETON Station	2	40	2.5
Gas Works Siding	3	54	3.7
Williamston	4	20	4.2
NORTH BERWICK Station	4	60	4.7
* NORTH BERWICK Harbour	5	07	5.1

* Section between North Berwick Station and Harbour never constructed.

Aberlady, Gullane and North Berwick Railway

	Miles	Chains	Miles
LONGNIDDRY Station	0	00	0.0
Aberlady Junction	1	40	1.5
ABERLADY Station	3	07	3.1
LUFFNESS Platform	4	53	4.7
GULLANE Station	6	25	6.3
* NORTH BERWICK Station	9	24	9.3

* Section between Gullane Station and North Berwick Station never constructed.

Appendix Five

Facilities at Local Stations

The following are the entries which appear in the 1904 Railway Clearing House Handbook.

Station						Crane cap.	Notes
ABERLADY	G	P	F	L	H	C 2t. 10cwt.	
Aberlady Junction							
Ballencrieff Siding	G						
DIRLETON	G	P		L	H	2t.	
DREM	G	P	F	L	H	C 1t. 15cwt.	
GULLANE	G	P	F	L	H	C 2t. 10cwt.	
LONGNIDDRY	G	P		L	H	C No crane	[a]
– Harelaw Lime Siding							
– Longniddry West Siding							
– Longniddry Junction							
NORTH BERWICK	G	P	F	L	H	C 3t.	
– Gas Sidings							

Key:

G – Goods; P – Passengers and Parcels; F – Furniture vans, carriages, portable engines and machines on wheels; L – Live stock; H – Horse boxes, prize cattle vans; C – Carriages by passenger trains. [a] – only trucks not exceeding 12 ft wheelbase.

Timetables

WEEK-DAYS.

Stations and Sidings.	Distance from Drem.	South Leith and North Berwick. Min.	1 Pass. a.m.	2 Pass.	3 Pass.	4 Pass.	5 Pass. Mixed	6 Pass. Sat. only. p.m.	7 Goods p.m.	8 Exp. Pass. Sat. only.	9 Pass. p.m.	10 Fast Pass. p.m.	11 Pass. p.m.	12 Fast Pass. p.m.	13 Pass. p.m.	14 Goods	15 Pass. p.m.	16 Exp. Pass. Sat. only.
Edinburgh ... dep.			...	6 55	9 20	10 33	...	12 30	...	1 40	1 45	4 35	5 5	4 5	6 30	...	8 15	10 25
Berwick ... ,,			...	5 45	7 40	...	...	...	...	...	12 30	...	...	...	5 35	...	...	...
—Drem Junction dep.			7 28	7 50	10 7	11 15	11 35	1 4	1 10	2 12	2 30	5 13	6 0	6 19	7 17	8 25	8 57	11 0
Dirleton ... ,,	2 40		7 38	7 56	10 13	11 21	11 41	1 10	1 20	2 18	2 36	5 19	...	7 23	8 37	9 3	...
—North Berwick arr.	4 50		7 48	8 3	10 20	11 28	11 48	1 17	1 30	2 25	2 43	5 26	6 9	6 28	7 30	8 50	9 10	11 7

No. 1.—Shunts Station Sidings at North Berwick.
No. 4.—On Saturdays the Engine with empty vehicles returns from North Berwick to Edinburgh to work 1-40 p.m. Saturday Train from Edinburgh to North Berwick. † No. 7.—*On Saturdays follows No. 6.*
Nos. 4, 6, 8, 10, 12, 15, and 16.—Through Trains from Edinburgh to North Berwick.
Through Carriages are run from Edinburgh to North Berwick by Nos 3 and 9.

Down Trains.

WEEK-DAYS.

Stations and Sidings.	Distance from North Berwick.	1 Pass. (Mixed) a.m.	2 Exp. Pass. a.m.	3 Exp. Pass. a.m.	4 South Leith and North Berwick. Min. a.m.	5 Pass. a.m.	6 Pass. a.m.	7 Goods p.m.	8 Pass. p.m.	9 Pass. p.m.	10 Pass. p.m.	11 Pass. Mixed p.m.	12 Pass. Sat. only. p.m.	13 Pass. ex. Sat. p.m.	14 Goods p.m.	15 Pass. Sat. only. p.m.
—North Berwick dep.		7 10	8 5	8 45	9 7	9 40	11 0	12 35	1 45	3 20	4 15	5 35	6 45	6 45	7 50	9 15
Dirleton .. ,,	2 20	7 19	8 +9	8 49	9 20	9 46	11 6	12 45	1 51	...	4 21	5 44	6 51	6 51	8 2	9 21
—Drem Junction arr.	4 60	7 28	8 13	8 53	9 30	9 52	11 12	12 55	1 57	3 30	4 27	5 53	6 57	6 57	8 15	9 27
Berwick ... arr.		9 20	...	...	...	11 48	...	...	4 11	...	6 43	7 52	8 50	8 50	...	...
Edinburgh ,,		8 24	8 44	9 23	...	...	12 18	...	2 54	4 15	5 19	...	7 43	7 55	...	10 9

† Nos. 2 and 3.—Call at Dirleton when required to pick up but not to set down Passengers.
Nos. 2, 3, 10, 12, and 15.—Through Trains from North Berwick to Edinburgh.
No. 6.—North Berwick will wire Dunbar the number and description of all extra Vehicles on this Train going in the direction of Edinburgh.
No. 13.—On Saturdays the Engine with empty vehicles of this Train will run *light* to Drem to work the 7-17 p.m. Passenger Train, Drem to North Berwick.
Through Carriages are run from North Berwick to Edinburgh by Nos. 6 and 13.

ABERLADY AND GULLANE RAILWAY.

Up Trains.

WEEK-DAYS.

Stations and Sidings.	Distance from Longniddry. Ms. Chs.	1 Cattle Tues. only. a.m.	2 Pass. a.m.	3 Pass. a.m.	4 Exp. Pass. Sat. only. a.m.	5 Pass. a.m.	6 Pass. a.m.	7 Pass. a.m.	8 Pass. Sat. only. p.m.	9 Pass. p.m.	10 Pass. Sat. only. p.m.	11 Pass. ex. Sat. p.m.	12 Pass. p.m.	13 Pass. p.m.	14 Pass. Sat. only. p.m.
Edinburgh (Wav.) dep.		...	6 55	...	9 5	9 20	10 20	10 33	12 30	1 45	4 0	4 35	5 15	6 30	...
Berwick ... ,,		...	...	5 45	...	7 40	...	...	12 30	...	2 10	2 10	...	...	...
Longniddry ... dep.	40	7 25	7 50	8 30	9 45	9 58	10 45	11 45	1 0	2 25	4 50	5 7	5 55	7 10	9 40
Aberlady Junction ... ,,	1 40	7 30	7 53	8 33	9 48	10 1	10 48	11 48	...	2 28	4 53	5 10	5 58	7 13	9 43
Aberlady ... ,,	3 7	7 35	7 58	8 37	9 32	10 5	10 52	11 52	1 7	2 32	4 57	5 14	6 2	7 17	9 47
Gullane ... arr.	6 18	7 45	8 4	8 44	9 39	10 12	10 59	11 59	1 14	2 39	5 4	5 21	6 9	7 24	9 54

No. 4.—After arrival at Gullane the Engine of this Train must make a Special Goods Trip from Gullane to Longniddry and back as required.
No. 7.—After arrival at Gullane the Branch Engine and Guard must make a Special Goods Trip daily except Saturdays from Gullane to Longniddry and back.

Down Trains.

WEEK-DAYS.

Stations and Sidings.	Distance from Gullane. Ms. Chs.	1 Pass. a.m.	2 Pass. a.m.	3 Pass. a.m.	4 Cattle Tues. only. a.m.	5 Pass. a.m.	6 Pass. a.m.	7 Pass. Sat. only. a.m.	8 Pass. p.m.	9 Pass. p.m.	10 Exp. Pass. Sat. only. p.m.	11 Pass. p.m.	12 Pass. p.m.	13 Pass. Sat. only. p.m.
Gullane ... dep.		7 10	8 10	8 50	9 10	10 16	11 18	12 35	1 50	4 15	5 10	5 28	6 40	9 15
Aberlady ... ,,	3 11	7 17	8 17	8 57	9 30	10 23	11 25	12 42	1 57	4 22	5 17	5 35	6 47	9 22
Aberlady Junction ... ,,	4 58	7 21	8 21	9 1	9 39	10 27	11 39	12 46	2 1	4 26	5 21	5 39	6 51	9 26
Longniddry ... arr.	6 18	7 24	8 24	9 4	9 45	10 30	11 32	12 49	2 4	4 29	5 24	5 42	6 54	9 29
Berwick ... arr.		9 20	...	11 48	...	11 48	...	...	4 11	6 43	...	7 52	8 50	...
Edinburgh (Wav.) ,,		8 24	8 58	9 49	...	12 18	...	2 54	5 19	5 49	...	7 55	10 9	...

No. 4.—Takes forward Traffic for Haymarket to go on from Longniddry by Berwick and Haymarket Train.
† No. 12.—Arrives Edinburgh 7-43 p.m. on Saturdays.

From the June 1899 NBR Working Timetable.

ABERLADY AND GULLANE RAILWAY

† After 31st August leaves at 11 0 a.m.

§ On Sats. Passengers for Aberlady and Gullane leave Edinburgh (Waverley) at 9-5 a.m.

‡ Five minutes later on Saturdays.

WEEK-DAYS.

Miles from Longniddry				Sat.		Sat.		Sat. only.		Sat. only.					
			a.m.	a.m.	a.m.	a.m.	a.m.	a.m.	a.m.	p.m.	p.m.	p.m.	p.m.	p.m.	p.m.
38	..	Glasgow (Queen Street) leave	......	......	6a20	7 45	8 45	11 a 0	11+38	12p27	2 15	4 0	5 0	6 0	6 0
12	...	Edinburgh (Waverley) ,,	6 55	.....	9 6	9 17	11 0	12p40	1p30	2 6	4 45	5 15	6 30	8 10
14	...	Berwick ,,	......	......	7 32	...	...	12 30	...	2 8	5 25	...	
...	...	LONGNIDDRY .... leave	7 38	8 25	...	9 58	11 35	...	2 10	2 50	3 11	5 47	7 20	8 50
3	...	ABERLADY ,,	7 45	8 32	9 39	10 5	11 42	1 10	2 17	2 57	5 18	5 54	7 27	8 57
6	...	GULLANE .... arrive	7 52	8 39	9 46	10 12	11 49	1 17	2 24	3 4	5 25	6 1	7 34	9 4

NORTH BERWICK BRANCH.

WEEK-DAYS.

Miles from Drem.			1	2	3	4	5	6 Sat. only.	7	8		9	10	11	12	13	14	15 Sat. only
			a.m.	a.m.	a.m.		a.m.	a.m.	a.m.	a.m.	After 31st August leaves at 11.0 a.m.	p.m.	p.m.	p.m.	p.m.	p.m.	p.m.	p.m.
38		Glasgow (Queen St.) ... leave			7 45	...	8 45	11 0	11+38	12p27		2 15	4 0	5 0		6 0	6 0	8 20
12		Edinburgh (Wav.) .... ,,	6 55		9 17		11 0	12p30	1 30	2	Saturdays only	4 35	5 15	6 30		8 10	10 22
14		Berwick .... ,,			7 32			12 30				2 8		5 25	6 39	
...		DREM .... leave	7 45	8 55	10 7	11 20	11 42	1 9	2 7	2 50		3 7	5 54	7 17	7 50	8 52
2½		Dirleton .... ,,	7 51	9 1	10 13	11 26	11 48	1 15	2 13	2 56		5 13		7 23	7 56	8 58
4½		NORTH BERWICK ...arrive	7 58	9 8	10 20	11 33	11 55	1 22	2 20	3 3		5 20	6 3	7 30	8 3	9 5	11 7

MOTOR CAR SERVICE between NORTH BERWICK,

	1	2	3	4	5	6	7	8	9	10	11	12	13	14	15
	a.m.	a.m.	a.m.		a.m.	p.m.	p.m.		p.m.	p.m.	p.m.		p.m.	p.m.	p.m.
NORTH BERWICK STATION ...... leave	7 20	9 20	10 20	...	11 20	12 20	1 20	...	2 20	3 20	4 20	...	5 20	6 20	8 20
Dirleton	7 32	9 32	10 32	...	11 32	12 32	1 32	...	2 32	3 32	4 32	...	5 32	6 32	8 32
Gullane	7 45	9 45	10 45	...	11 45	12 45	1 45	...	2 45	3 45	4 45	...	5 45	6 45	8 45
ABERLADY .... arrive	8 0	10 0	11 0	...	12 0	1 0	2 0	...	3 0	4 0	5 0	...	6 0	7 0	9 0

FARES—
Between North Berwick and Dirleton, 4d. North Berwick and Gullane, 8d. North Berwick and Aberlady, 1s.

From the NBR public timetable for Summer 1905 – the only year in which the 'Motor Car Service' operated by the pioneer NBR buses features.

ABERLADY AND GULLANE RAILWAY.

§ On Saturdays arrives 2-22 p.m.

WEEK-DAYS.

		1	2	3	Sat. only.	Ex. Sat.	6	7	8	Ex. Sat.	Sat. only.	11	Sat. only.
		a.m.	a.m.	a.m.	a.m.	a.m.	p.m.	p.m.	p.m.	p.m.	p.m.	p.m.	p.m.
GULLANE .... leave		7 10	8 6	8 55	11 a 0	11 a 0	1 43	...	4 15	6p40	6p42	8 5	9p55
ABERLADY .... ,,		7 17	8 12	9 2	11 7	11 7	1 50	...	4 22	6 47	6 49	8 12	9 47
LONGNIDDRY .... arrive		7 24	8 19	8 9	11 14	11 14	1 57	...	4 29	6 54	6 56	8 19	9 49
Berwick .... arrive		9 6	...	11 52	...	...	4 21	...	6 43	8 50	8 50	...	...
Edinburgh (Waverley) ,,		8 24	8 46	9 52	11 44	1 2	2p33	...	5 5	7 53	7 40	9 4	10 28
Glasgow (Queen Street) ,,		...	10 10	11 15	2 10	2 10	5 15	...	7 35	9 32	9 32	10 25

NORTH BERWICK BRANCH.

WEEK-DAYS.

		1	3	4	5	6	7	8	9	10 Ex. Sat.	11 Sat. only.	12	13 Sat. only.		NOTE
		a.m.	a.m.	a.m.	a.m.	a.m.		p.m.	p.m.	p.m.	p.m.	p.m.	p.m.		
NORTH BERWICK ...leave		7 10	8 3	8 45	9 35	10 50	12 35	...	1 40	4 45	6 40	6 46	8 10	9 15	† Call at Dirleton to pick up, but not to set down Passengers.
Dirleton .... ,,		7 15	8 +7	8†49	9 40	10 56	...	...	1 46	4 51	6 46	6 52	8 16	9 21	
DREM .... arrive		7 23	8 12	...	9 47	11 2	1† 44	...	1 52	4 57	6 52	6 57	...	9 27	
Berwick .... arrive		9 6	...	11 52		p.m.	1 49	...	4 21	8 43	8 50	8 50	...	...	
Edinburgh (Wav.) .... ,,		8 24	8 58	9 23	...	12 1	...	...	2 33	5 48	7 53	7 37	9 4	10 8	
Glasgow (Queen Street) ,,		10 10	10 10	11 15	...	2 10	...	...	5 15	7 35	9 32	9 32	10 25		

DIRLETON, GULLANE, and ABERLADY.

		1	2	3	4	5	6	7	8	9	10	11	12	13	14	15
		a.m.	a.m.	a.m.		a.m.	p.m.	p.m.	p.m.	p.m.	p.m.	p.m.	p.m.	p.m.	p.m.	p.m.
ABERLADY .... leave		8 5	10 5	11 5	...	12 5	1 5	2 5	...	3 5	4 5	5 5	...	6 5	7 5	9 5
Gullane		8 20	10 20	11 20	...	12 20	1 20	2 20	...	3 20	4 20	5 20	...	6 20	7 20	9 20
Dirleton		8 33	10 33	11 33	...	12 33	1 33	2 33	...	3 33	4 33	5 33	...	6 33	7 33	9 33
NORTH BERWICK .... arrive		8 45	10 45	11 45	...	12 45	1 45	2 45	...	3 45	4 45	5 45	...	6 45	7 45	9 45

FARES—
Between Dirleton and Gullane, 4d. Dirleton and Aberlady, 8d. Gullane and Aberlady, 4d

NORTH BERWICK BRANCH.

July 1914

UP TRAINS. — WEEK-DAYS

Stations.	Distance from Drem Chs.	Distance from Drem Mls.	1 Min.	2 Pass.	+3 EXP. PASS.	4 EXP. PASS.	5 Pass.	6 Pass.	7 Goods	8 Pass.	9 Pass.	+10 EXP. PASS.	+11 EXP. PASS.	12 Pass.	13 EXP. PASS.	14	15	16	+17 EXP. PASS.	18 Pass.	+19 Pass.	+20 Pass.	21 Pass.	22 Pass.	23	24 EXP. PASS.	25 EXP. PASS.	26
Departs from...			*Portobello* a.m. 4 55		*Glasgow* a.m. 7 54	*Edinburgh* a.m. 9 7		*Edinburgh* a.m. 11 5		*Edinburgh* p.m. 12 35	*Edinburgh* p.m. 1 34	*Glasgow* p.m. 12 37	*Edinburgh* p.m. 1 50		*Edinburgh* p.m. 4 30				*Glasgow* p.m. 3 53			*Edinburgh* p.m. 6 50		*Edinburgh* p.m. 8 10		*Edinburgh* p.m. 10 20	*Edinburgh* p.m. 11 0	
Drem Jun. dep.	—	—	a.m. 6 30	a.m. 7 38	a.m. 8 52	a.m. 9 44	a.m. 10 51	a.m. 11 46	p.m. 1 10	p.m. 1 16	p.m. 2 14	p.m. 2 16	p.m. 2 22	p.m. 2 48	p.m. 5 0				p.m. 5 29	p.m. 6 0	p.m. 7 19	p.m. 7 22	p.m. 7 45	p.m. 8 52		11 2	11 38	
Dirleton	40	2	6 50	7 43			10 11	11 52	1 20		2 20		2 28	2 49	5 6						7 25	7 28		8 58					
No.Berwick arr.	60	4	7 0	7 49	8 9	9 53	10 18	11 59	1 35	1 24	2 27	2 28	2 30	2 56	5 13				5 37	6 9	7 32	7 35	7 54	9 5		11 2	11 38	

No 1.—Performs necessary shunting at Dirleton, and shunts Station Sidings at North Berwick.

No. 7.—If time permit works North Berwick Gas Works Siding, leaving three at 1-30 p.m. If there is not time to work this Siding it must proceed direct from Dirleton to North Berwick in order to admit of the 1-41 p.m. Passenger train from North Berwick starting punctually, arrangements being made for the Gas Works Siding being worked at a later hour.

+ No. 10.—Ceases after 12th September.

No. 11.—Runs on 19th and 26th September only.
No. 17.—Ceases after 1st Sept.
No. 20.—Ceases after 29th August.
No. 21.—Calls at Dirleton only when required to set down Through Passengers. When the stop is made the train will arrive at North Berwick 2 minutes later.
No. 22.—Engine and Guard of this train will make Goods trip from North Berwick to Drem and back for Live Stock when required.

‡ No. 24.—No. 19.—Runs daily commencing 1st Sept.

DOWN TRAINS. — WEEK-DAYS

Stations.	Distance from N. Berwick Chs.	Distance from N. Berwick Mls.	1 Pass.	+2 EXP. PASS.	+3 EXP. PASS.	4 Min.	5 Min.	6 EXP. PASS.	7	8 Pass.	9	10 EXP. PASS.	11 Pass.	12 Pass.	13	14 Goods	15	16 Pass.	17 Pass.	18	+19 Pass.	20 Pass.	21 EXP. PASS.	22	23	+24 Pass.	25
North Berwick dep.	—	—	a.m. 7 7	a.m. 7 54	a.m. 8 0	T O a.m. 8 15	T a.m. 8 20	a.m. 8 40		a.m. 9 23		a.m. 10 50	a.m. 12 30	p.m. 1 41		p.m. 3 0		p.m. 4 15	p.m. 4 28		p.m. 8 22	S O p.m. 9 15	TH O p.m. 9 47			p.m. 10 46	
Dirleton	20	2	7 11	8 3	8 9	*Portobello* 8 37	*Portobello* 8 35	8 46		9 29		10 56	12 39	1 47		3 12		4 21	6 34		8 32	9 21	9 17			10 54	
Drem Junction arr.	60	4	7 17	8 9		*Portobello* 1 43		*Edinburgh* 9 24		9 35		*Edinburgh* 11 38	*Edinburgh* 2 88	1 53		3 25		4 27	6 40		*Edinburgh* 9 16	*Edinburgh* 10 11	*Edinburgh* 10 26				

No. 2.—Commences 2nd September.
No. 8.—Daily till 1st September inclusive, thereafter on 7th and 14th September only. Does not convey Passengers to Drem during July and August. On 1st, 7th, and 14th September it will leave at 7·54 and arrive Drem 8·3 a.m., and convey Passengers to Drem.
‡ No. 4.—Calls at Dirleton when required to lift Live Stock.

+ No. 19.—Daily during July and August. S during September.
No. 24.—Commences 13th July. Will not run unless there are Passengers for Newcastle or South thereof. Station Master, North Berwick, will nightly advise the Signalman at Drem, the Locomotive Department, and all concerned, whether the train is to run or not. On Saturdays, when run, it will leave at 10·42 and arrive Drem 10·51 p.m.

ABERLADY AND GULLANE RAILWAY. July 1914

WEEK-DAYS. UP TRAINS.

No.	Type	Origin	Longniddry dep	Aberlady Junction arr	Aberlady arr / dep	Gullane arr
1	Cattle	Portobello a.m. 6 15	…	…	7 15	7 25
2	Goods / Pass.	T O M T	a.m. 7 0	7 6	7 15	7 25
3	Pass.		a.m. 7 25	7 30	7 32	7 38
8	Pass.	Edinburgh a.m. 9 7	9 39	9 44	9 46	9 54
9	Pass.	a.m.	11 40	11 45	11 47	11 55
11	Pass.	Edinburgh p.m. 12 35	S O 1 5	1 10	1 12	1 20
12	Pass.	Edinburgh p.m. 1 27	S O 1 56	2 1	2 8	2 11
13	Pass.	S	2 8	2 13	2 15	2 23
15	Pass.	S O	p.m. 2 40	2 45	2 47	2 53
16	Pass.	Edinburgh p.m. 3 5 S O	3 33	3 38	3 40	3 46
17	Pass.		p.m. 4 55	5 0	5 2	5 8
21 ‡	Pass.	Glasgow p.m. 8 58	S 5 20	5 25	5 26	5 32
22	Pass.	S p.m. 5 58	6 1	6 5	6 8	6 11
24 ‡	Pass.	S O	p.m. 7 17	7 22	7 24	7 30
25 ‡	Pass.		8 56	8 58	9 0	9 6

Distance from Longniddry (Mls. Chs.): Aberlady Junction 1 40; Aberlady 3 7; Gullane 6 25.

No. 1.—Works Road Van Goods from Longniddry to Gullane.

No. 2.—Engine with Guard and Van to work this train leaves Gullane at 6.30 a.m.

Nos. 8, 9, 11, 12, and 13.—Call at Private Golf Club Platform (which is situate between Aberlady and Gullane) only for the accommodation of Members of Luffness New Golf Club.

No. 9.—After arrival at Gullane the Branch Engine and Guard will make a Goods trip from Gullane to Longniddry and back except Saturdays. On Saturdays No. 15 will do so.

‡ No. 21.—Ceases after 1st September.

‡ No. 25.—Daily during July and August. S O during September.

WEEK-DAYS. DOWN TRAINS.

No.	Type	Gullane dep	Aberlady arr	Aberlady Junction arr	Longniddry arr	Arrives at destination
3 ‡	Pass.	a.m. 8 0	8 6	8 9	8 12	Glasgow 9 48 / Edinburgh 8 48
4 ‡	Pass.	a.m. 8 10	8 16	8 19	8 22	
6	Pass.	a.m. 9 37	9 43	9 46	9 49	
10	Cattle	T O 9 5	9 20		9 35	
11	Pass.	a.m. 10 45	10 51		10 57	
15	Pass.	p.m. 1 37	1 43	1 46	1 49	
19	Pass.	p.m. 4 14	4 22	4 25	4 28	Edinburgh p.m. 5 1 / 7 5
20	Pass.	S O p.m. 6 22	6 30		6 36	Edinburgh
22	Pass.	S p.m. 6 24	6 32	6 35	6 38	
23 †	Pass.	p.m. 8 20	8 27	8 33	8 42	
24 ‡	Pass.	S O p.m. 8 30	8 36		8 42	

Distance from Gullane (Mls. Chs.): Aberlady 3 18; Aberlady Junction 4 65; Longniddry 6 25.

‡ No. 3.—Daily till 1st September inclusive, thereafter on 7th and 14th September. The Engine working this train to Longniddry, after placing the Vehicles on the Down Lothian Express, must immediately return to Gullane to work out No. 6, and must on no account be delayed in order to ensure a punctual start to No. 6.

‡ No. 4.—Commences 2nd September, but will not run on 7th and 14th September.

No. 10.—Takes forward Traffic for Gorgie to go on from Longniddry by Berwick and Gorgie Train.

Nos. 19 and 20.—Call at Private Golf Club Platform (which is situate between Gullane and Aberlady) only for the accommodation of Members of Luffness New Golf Club, and No. 22 will call during July only. When required No. 24 will also call.

No. 24.—Commences 5th September.

‡ No. 23.—Ceases after 31st August.

From the July 1914 NBR Working Timetable (cont.).

NORTH BERWICK BRANCH—UP.

WEEK-DAYS.

UP TRAINS.			Distance from Drem.	1	2	4	7	8 O.P. Steam Coach	11	13‡	14	15	16	17	18
				Goods	O.P.	O.P.	O.P.		E.P.	O.P.	O.P.	E.P.	O.P.	O.P.	E.P.
CLASS				C	...	...	...	...	...	...		...	...	...	...
Departs from				Porto-bello a.m. 4 23	Commences July 5.	...	...	Edin-burgh a.m. 8 52	Edin-burgh a.m. 9 35	...	Commences July 5.	Edin-burgh p.m. 12 20	Edin-burgh p.m. 12 21	...	Edin-burgh p.m. 1 14
			M. C.	a.m.	a.m.	a.m.	a.m.	a.m.	a.m.	a m	a.m.	a.m.	S X p.m.	S O p.m.	S X p.m.	S O p.m.
—Drem Junction	...dep.			6 15	7 12	7 28	8 8	9 29	10 5	11 6	11 46	12 45	12 55	1 36	1 40
Dirleton		,	2 40							11 11			1 41		
Gas Works Siding		,,	3 54								11 54				
—North Berwick	...arr.		4 60	6 30	7 20	7 36	8 16	9 39	10 11	11 16	11 54	12 53	1 3	1 46	1 48

WEEK-DAYS.

UP TRAINS.				19	20	21	24	26	28	29	30	31	33 O.P. Steam Coach	34	37	38	39
				E.P.	E.P.	O.P.	O.P.	O.P.	O.P.	E.P.	O.P.	O.P.		O.P.	O.P.	E.P.	O.P.
CLASS				...	...	•	...	...	...	...	...	...	•	...	...	...	...
Departs from				Glasgow p.m. 12 24	Edin-burgh p.m. 2 10			Edin-burgh p.m. 5 3		Edin-burgh p.m. 5 48		Edin-burgh p.m. 7 28	Edin-burgh p.m. 7 28	Edin-burgh p.m. 8 35	Edin p.m. 9 45	Edin-burgh p.m. 11 21	Edin-burgh p.m. 11 21
				S O p.m.	p.m.	p.m.	p.m.	S X p.m.	S O p.m.	S X p.m.	p.m.	S O p.m.	S X p.m.	p.m.	p.m.	Th O p.m.	S O p.m.
—Drem Junction	...dep.			2 8	2 36	2 56	4 32	5 29	6 9	6 14	7 2	7 58	8 0	9 8	10 16	11 48	11 52
Dirleton		,,				3 1	4w037		6 14								
Gas Works Siding		,,															
—North Berwick	...arr.			2 16	2 44	3 6	4 40	5 37	6 19	6 22	7 10	8 6	8 10	9 16	10 24	11 56	12 0

Gas Works Siding.—Except on Saturdays this Siding will be worked, when required, by one of the North Berwick Engines and Guards at the most suitable time.

No. 1.—Dirleton wagons to be taken to North Berwick and left off on return trip. After arrival at Drem, works to orders of Control and finishes at 11.5 a.m. M O (11.35 a.m. M X).

No. 13.—‡ On Saturdays commencing July 10 runs nine minutes later.

No. 24.—‡ Arrives North Berwick 4.42 p.m. on Wednesdays.

GULLANE BRANCH—UP.

WEEK-DAYS.

UP TRAINS.			Distance from Long-niddry.	1	3	4	5	6	7	8	9	10	10a	11	12
				Goods		Goods		Goods							
CLASS				D	...	D	...	D	...	...	...	...	...	...	...
			M. C.	a.m.		S O p.m.		S X p.m.							
—Longniddry	...dep.		... ...	7 0	...	1 22	...	1 40	...	...	...	...	—	...
—Aberlady Junction	... ,,		1 40	7 5	......	1 27	......	1 44	......	......	......	......	—	......
Aberlady	{ arr. dep.		3 7	7 25	...	1 45	...	2 10	...	...	...	...	...	...
Gullane	...arr.		6 25	7 35	...	1 55	...	2 20	...	...	...	...	...	...

No. 1.—Worked by Prestonpans Pilot and Guard and starts from Prestonpans at 6.25 a.m. Light Engine and Guard return immediately from Gullane to Prestonpans except on Tuesdays. On Tuesdays works Live Stock from Gullane and Aberlady to Longniddry to connect with 8.51 a.m. T O, North Berwick and Gorgie Cattle Train.

No. 4.—Worked by Engine and Trainmen of 11.55 a.m. S O Goods, Portobello to Haddington.

No. 6.—Worked by Engine and Trainmen of 12.30 p.m. S X Goods, Portobello to Haddington.

LNER Working Timetable, 3rd May, 1937 until further notice.

NORTH BERWICK BRANCH—DOWN.

DOWN TRAINS.	1 §	2 O.P.	3 O.P.	6 O.P.	8 E.P.	9 O.P.	10 Live Stock	11 Goods	12 E.P.	14 O.P. Steam Coach	15 E.P.	16 E.P.	17 E.C.S.	19‡ O.P.	20 O.P.	21 O.P.
WEEK-DAYS.																
CLASS	...	...	...	...	...	...	A	D	...	...	...	...	...	...	...	...
							TO	TX			SX	SO				
	a.m.	a.m.	a.m.	a.m.	a.m.	a.m.	a.m.	a.m.	a.m.	a.m.	a.m.	a.m.	a.m.	a.m.	a.m.	p.m.
—No. B'wick dp	6 42	7 2	7 12	7 51	8 25	8 41	8 51	8 51	9 15	9 50	10 20	10 20	10 42	11A25	11 58	1 13
Dirleton ,,	......	......	......	7 56	......	8 46	9 6	9 6	......	9 55	......	......	......	......	......	......
—Drem Jct. arr.	6 52	7 10	7 20	8 1	8 33	8 51	9 13	9 13	9 23	10 0	10 28	10 28	10 52	11A33	12p 6	1 21
Arrives at ...	Commences July 5.	Commences July 5.	Crosses after July 3.	Edinburgh 8 58	Edinburgh 9 21	Gorgie 11 42	To Central orders.		Edinburgh 9 46	Edinburgh 10 38	Edinburgh 10 53	Edinburgh 10 56	Works No. 13 up.	...	...	Edinburgh 1 50

DOWN TRAINS.	23 O.P.	24 Goods	25 O.P.	27 O.P.	28 O.P.	29‖ E.P.	30‖ E.P.	32‖ O.P.	33‖ O.P.	34 O.P. Steam Coach	35 O.P.	36 O.P.	37 E.P.	38 O.P.	39 O.P.	40‡ O.P.
WEEK-DAYS.																
CLASS	...	D	...	...	...	...	...	...	...	...	...	...	...	...	...	...
			SO	SX	SO		SO	SO		SX	SO	SO	ThO	SO	MO	MO
	p.m.	p.m.	p.m.	p.m.	p.m.	p.m.	p.m.	p.m.	p.m.	p.m.	p.m.	p.m.	p.m.	p.m.	p.m.	p.m.
—No. B'wick dp	2 23	3 10	3 54	4 10	5 0	6 27	6 40	7 29	7 36	8 53	8 40	9 35	10 5	10 5	10 34	10 58
Dirleton ,,	......	3 33	3 59	......	......	......	......	......	......	......	......	......	......	......	......	......
—Drem Jct. arr.	2 31	3 40	4 4	4 18	5 8	6 35	6 48	7‡37	7‡44	9 3	8 48	9 43	10 13	10 13	10 42	11 6
Arrives at ...	...	...	Edinburgh 4 53	Edinburgh 5 42	Edinburgh 7 11	Edinburgh 7 15	Edinburgh 8 3	Edinburgh 8 10	Edinburgh 9 42	Edinburgh 9 19	Edinburgh 10 12	Edinburgh 10 38	Edinburgh 10 49	Commences July 12.	...	...

No. 19.—‡ Until July 3, runs only when required to convey Passengers to join Up Pullman at Drem. Commencing July 5 runs unconditionally. A On Saturdays, commencing July 10, runs four minutes later.

Nos. 29 and 33.—‖ Does not run July 10 to September 11, inclusive.

Nos. 30 and 32.—‖ Runs July 10 to September 11, inclusive.

Nos. 32 and 33.—‡ Calls at Drem when required to set down Passengers for Newcastle and South thereof, for connection with 7.50 p.m. Express, Edinburgh to King's Cross.

No. 40.—‡ Runs during June, only if there are Sleeping Car Passengers.

GULLANE BRANCH—DOWN.

DOWN TRAINS.		Distance from Gullane.		1	2	3	4	5 Goods	6 Goods	7	8	9	10	11	12
WEEK-DAYS.															
CLASS				...	...	...	...	D	D	...	...	...	...	...	...
								SO	SX						
		M.	C.					p.m.	p.m.						
Gullane ... ...dep.		...	...	...	...	...	...	2 30	2 50	...	...	...	...	...	...
Aberlady ... ,,		3	18	......	......	......	......	2 51	3 30	......	......	......	......	......	......
—Aberlady Junction ... ,,		4	65	...	...	...	...	3 56	3 35	...	...	...	...	...	...
—Longniddry... ... arr.		6	25	......	......	......	......	3 1	3 40	......	......	......	......	......	......

NORTH BERWICK BRANCH

UP TRAINS   WEEKDAYS

	No.	529‡	203	204	205	211				
	Description		OP	OP	OP	OP				
	Class	C								
	Departs from	Portobello 4.28 a.m.								
	Previous Times on Page									

M.C.			529‡	203	204	205	211				
			am	am	am	am	am				
	Drem Junction ......(T)..	1	6 15	.....	7 32	8 8	.....	10 5	.....	11 16	.....
2 40	Dirleton	2	..	..	..	..	..	..	..	11 21	..
3 54	Gas Works Siding	3									
4 60	NORTH BERWICK (T)..	4	6 40	..	7 40	8 16	..	10 13	..	11 26	..

NORTH BERWICK BRANCH

DOWN TRAINS   WEEKDAYS

	No.	200	278	202		507‡	513		203		204	205		
	Description	OP	OP	EP		Live St'ck			OP		OP	OP		
	Class					A	D							
			am	am	am	TO am	TX am		am		PM	SO PM		
	NORTH BERWICK (T)..	1	7 13	7 50	8 20	.....	8 51	8 51	.....	10 40	..	12 4	1 38		
	Dirleton	2		7 55	..	.....	9 6	9 6	.....	10F45	..	..	..	..	..
	Drem Junction ......(T)..	3	7 21	8 0	8 28	.....	9 13	9 13	.....	10F48	.....	12 13	1 46	.....	.....
	Arrives at				Edinburgh 8.58 a.m.									
	Forward Times on Page													

No. **203**—F Two minutes later on Wednesdays.
F—Wednesdays only.

GULLANE BRANCH

UP TRAINS   WEEKDAYS

	No.	552‡	551‡	600‡	601‡							
	Description											
	Class	D	D	D	D							
	Departs from	Prestonpans 6.25 a.m.										

M.C.			552‡	551‡	600‡	601‡							
			TO am	am	SO PM	SX PM							
	Longniddry	1	7 0	9 0	1 15	1 31							
1 40	Aberlady Junction	2	7 5	9 5	1 20	1 35	..	..	..	..	..	..	..
3 7	Aberlady..................	3											
	Aberlady	4	7 25	9 25	1 40	..	..	..	..	..	..	..	..
6 25	Gullane	5	7 35	9 35	1 50	1 56	..						

Distance from Drem

Distance from Longniddry

NORTH BERWICK BRANCH

UP TRAINS — WEEKDAYS

	213	215	218	220	222	224	227	230	236
	OP	EP	OP	OP	EP	OP	OP	OP	OP
		Edinburgh 1.25 p.m.			Edinburgh 5.12 p.m.				Edinburgh 10.50 p.m.
	SO PM	SO PM	SO PM	PM	SX PM	PM	PM	PM	PM
1	12 44	2 0	2 48	4 38	5 38	6 20	7 17	8 58	11 24
2	..	..	2 53	4W043	..	6 25	..	..	..
3									
4	12 52	2 8	2 58	4F46	5 46	6 30	7 25	9 6	11 32

No. 220—F Arrives North Berwick 4.48 p.m. on Wednesdays.

NORTH BERWICK BRANCH

DOWN TRAINS — WEEKDAYS

	206	532	535	207	208	209	210
	OP			OP	EP	OP	OP
		D	D				
	SO PM	SX PM	SO PM	PM	PM	PM	PM
1	2 23	2 32	3 10	4 3	6 3	6 43	7 34
2	..	2 55	3 33	4S08	..	..	..
3	2 31	3 5	3 40	4 11	6 11	6 51	7 43
				Edinburgh 4F54 p.m.	Edinburgh 6.49 p.m.		

No. 207—F Two minutes later on Saturdays.

GULLANE BRANCH

DOWN TRAINS — WEEKDAYS

Distance from Gullane		No.	518	519
		Description		
		Class	D	D
M. C.			SX PM	SO PM
3 18	Gullane	1	2 10	2 30
4 65	Aberlady	2	2 30	2 51
6 25	Aberlady Junction	3	2 37	2 56
	Longniddry	4	2 42	3 1

The first post-war Working Timetable, October 1945.

(Worked by One Engine in Steam) GULLANE BRANCH
WEEKDAYS

UP TRAINS

Distance from Longniddry		No.	664	599
	Description			
	Class		K	K
	Departs from		Prestonpans Pilot	
M. C.			SO am	SX PM
1 40	Longniddry	1	9 45	2 10
3 7	Aberlady Junction	2	9 50	2 14
	Aberlady	3	...	...
	Aberlady	4	...	...
6 25	Gullane	5	10 0	2 30

DOWN TRAINS

Distance from Gullane		No.	664	599
	Description			
	Class		K	K
M. C.			SO am	SX PM
	Gullane	1	10 25	2 50
3 18	Aberlady	2	10 52	3 15
4 65	Aberlady Junction	3	...	...
6 25	Longniddry	4	11 5	3 28
	Arrives at		Prestonpans 11.48 a.m.	Haddington EBV 3.53p

AUTHORISED PILOT AND SHUNTING ENGINES—EDINBURGH DISTRICT—Continued

Station or Yard	Provided by	No. & Description	Period required at Station or Yard		Particulars of Work
Prestonpans ...	St. Margarets	1 GM	6.20 a.m. to 9.5 p.m.		S.T. L30 minutes each shift. Class J36 engine to be provided.

	arr. SX a.m.	dep. SX a.m.	
Longniddry Shed......	...	6 20	Detaches traffic off 6.55 a.m. OP ex Edinburgh. Conveys traffic off 4.25 a.m., Portobello to North Berwick and Parceis Van.
Prestonpans	6 5	7 35	
Haddington	8 5	9 30	
Longniddry	9 50	10 30	
Prestonpans	10 44	1 15p	Attaches Milk Van to 10.40 a.m. OP, Dunbar to Edinburgh. Works Seton Siding and Tranent Branch. Attaches Parcel Van to 4.18 p.m. OP, Newcastle to Edinburgh.
Longniddry Shed......	1 25p	2 15 L.E.	
Prestonpans	2 25	8 55	
Longniddry Sned......	9 5	...	

On Tuesdays, if necessary, runs to Gullane or Aberlady to work Live Stock to Prestonpans, after returning from Haddington.

	arr. SO a.m.	dep. SO a.m.	
Longniddry Shed......	...	6 20	Detach traffic off 6.55 a.m. OP ex Edinburgh. Conveys traffic off 4.25 a.m., Portobello to North Berwick and Parcels Van.
Prestonpans	6 30	7 35	
Haddington	8 0	9 15	
Longniddry	9 35	9 45	
Gullane..................	10 0	10 20	Lifts Gullane Branch traffic.
Aberlady	10 25	10 47	Attaches Milk Van to 10.40 a.m. OP, Dunbar to Edinburgh.
Prestonpans	11 9	1 15p	Lifts Haddington traffic detached from 7.50 a.m., Portobello to Dunbar.
Longniddry Shed......	1 25p	2 20	
Longniddry	...	2 30	
Haddington	2 50	3 40	Makes trip to Niddrie West with braked traffic from Prestonpans and Inveresk as required.
Longniddry	4 0	4 35	
Prestonpans	4 46	8 55	
Longniddry	9 5	...	

7.45 p.m. SX, Drem to High Street.—Conveys vegetable traffic from East Lothian Stations to High Street. Throughout single engine load must not be exceeded by the addition of mineral traffic and when amount of vegetable traffic exceeds throughout single engine it should not be augmented by attachment of mineral traffic, namely, mineral traffic should only be attached to train when throughout single engine load will not be exceeded. Trainmen change at Portobello.

From the BR Working Timetable for Winter 1950–1.

UP TRAINS — NORTH BERWICK BRANCH — WEEKDAYS

Distance from Drem M.C.		529½	202	203	204	205	215	208	209	210	211	213	216
No.		529½	202	203	204	205	215	208	209	210	211	213	216
Description													
Class		K	B	B	B	B	A	B	B	A	B	B	B
Departs from		Portobello 4.25 a.m.					Edinburgh 1.8 p.m.			Edinburgh 5.18 p.m.			Edinburgh 10.45 p.m.
Previous Times on Page		W5					W8			W10			W11
		am	am	am	am	SO PM	SO PM	PM	PM	SX PM	PM	PM	PM
—	Drem Junction ⊕ .....(1)	6 20	8 30	9 31	11 9	12 49	1 40	3 6	4 28	5 48	6 23	8 41	11 15
2 40	Dirleton ....(2)	...	...	...	11 14	...	1 45	...	...	5 53	...	...	...
3 54	Gas Works Siding .(3)	...	...	...	...	...	...	...	...	...	...	...	...
4 60	NORTH BERWICK ⊕ (4)	6 40	8 38	9 39	11 19	12 57	1 50	3 14	4 36	5 58	6 31	8 49	11 23

DOWN TRAINS — NORTH BERWICK BRANCH — WEEKDAYS

	201	202	507	203	204	205	532	207	207	532	208	210
No.	201	202	507	203	204	205	532	207	207	532	208	210
Description												
Class	B	A	K	B	B	A	K	B	B	K	A	B
		Edinburgh 8.57 a.m.				Edinburgh 1.45 p.m.		Edinburgh 4.51 p.m.	Edinburgh 4.53 p.m.		Edinburgh 6.52 p.m.	
	am	am	am	am	SO am	SO PM	SO PM	SX PM	SO PM	SX PM	PM	PM
NORTH BERWICK ⊕ (1)	7 53	8 17	8 52	10 45	11 56	1 8	3 27	4 3	4 8	5 0	6 13	8 10
Dirleton ....(2)	7 58	...	9 7	...	...	...	3 50	...	...	5 23	...	...
Drem Junction ⊕ (3)	8 3	8 25	9 15	10 53	12 4	1 16	3 57	4 11	4 13	5 30	6 21	8 18
Forward Times on Page		W 17				W 19		W 20	W 20		W 21	

From the BR Working Timetable for Winter 1950–1 (cont.).

Table 20   **Drem and North Berwick**

Mls	Leave	a.m	a.m	.	a.m	a.m	.	a.m	cash only a.m	p.m	p.m	Ex Sats p.m	p.m	p.m	p.m	.	p.m	p.m
	GLASGOW (Queen St.) —	—	—		6 30	9 10	—	10 0*	11 0	1 0	2 0	4 0	4 0	5 0	6 0	—		8 0
	EDINBURGH (Waverley)	6†55	.		8 50	1030		12†6*	1 T 8	2 30	3T45	5T18	5T38	6T35	7T40		—	104U
—	Drem — — — lev.	7 36	8 30	—	9 34	11 8	—	1249	1 41	5 0	4 30	—	6 23	7 19	8 12	—	8 45	1110
2¼	Dirleton . . .	.	.			1113		.	1 46	.	.	5 54	.	.	.		.	.
4¾	North Berwick — arr.	7 44	8 38	—	9 42	1118	—	1257	1 51	3 14	4 38	5 59	6 31	7 27	8 20	—	8 53	1118

	Leave	a.m	a.m	a.m	a.m	.	Sats only a.m	p.m	.	Sats only Ex cash Sats only p.m	p.m	p.m	p.m	.	p.m	.	p.m	.	p.m
	North Berwick — lev.	7 10	7 50	8 17	1042	—	1156	1 20	.	2 35	3 4	3 36	6 12	—	6 43	—	8 0	—	9 43
	Dirleton . . .	.	7 55	.	.		.	.		.	4 8	.	.		.		.		.
	Drem — — — arr.	7 18	8 0	—	1050	—	12 4	.	—	2 43	4 11	4 13	6 20	—	6 51	—	8 8	—	9 51
	EDINBURGH (Waverley)ar.	.	8 45	8T57	1142	T	1240	1T59	.	.	4T51	4T53	6T52	.	7*28	.	9 5	T	1017
	GLASGOW (Queen St.) ,,	—	10 5	10 5	1 0	—	2 3	4	—	6 22	6 22	9K49	—	9*49K	—	1132	—	—

* Saturdays only   † Except Saturdays
§ Mondays only   ‡ Except Mondays
B Via Berwick, extra charge
K Passengers can arrive Glasgow (Queen Street) 9-11 p.m by Pullman Car Express, Supplementary Charges

‡ Low Level
T Through Carriage between Edinburgh and North Berwick

The rivals – the winter of 1951 BR and SMT public timetables – in the bus table the letter 'Q' denotes services via Ballencrieff Cross Roads.

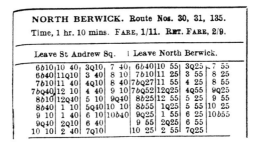

CHEAP DAY RETURN TICKETS

By Any Train—Any Day
(where train service permits)

NORTH BERWICK

WITH	Return Fares	
	1st Cl.	2nd Cl.
Corstorphine	10/3	6/10
Edinburgh (Waverley) ...	8/3	5/6
Haymarket	8/3	5/6
Pinkhill	10/3	6/10

DREM

WITH	Return Fares	
	1st Cl.	2nd Cl.
Corstorphine	8/-	5/4
Edinburgh (Waverley) ...	8/-	5/4
Haymarket	6/-	4/-
Pinkhill	8/-	5/4

The tickets are valid on the date for which issued
The above fares are liable to alteration without further notice.

WEEKLY SEASON TICKETS
(valid Monday to Saturday)

North Berwick WITH	Return Fares		Drem. WITH	Return Fares	
	1st Cl.	2nd Cl.		1st Cl.	2nd Cl.
Corstorphine	44/6	29/6	Edin. (Wav.)	31/6	21/-
Edin. (Wav.)	34/6	23/-	Haymarket	35/6	23/6
Haymarket	38/6	25/6			
Pinkhill	43/6	29/-			

OTHER SEASON TICKET RATES

NORTH BERWICK WITH	One Month		Three Months	
	1st Cl.	2nd Cl.	1st Cl.	2nd Cl.
	£ s. d.	£ s. d.	£ s. d.	£ s. d.
Corstorphine	8 2 0	5 8 0	21 18 0	14 12 0
Edin. (Wav.)	6 6 0	4 4 0	17 1 0	11 7 0
Haymarket	7 0 0	4 13 0	18 18 0	12 12 0
Pinkhill	7 19 0	5 6 0	21 11 0	14 7 0
DREM WITH				
Edin. (Wav.)	5 16 0	3 17 0	15 12 0	10 8 0
Haymarket	6 9 0	4 6 0	17 10 0	11 13 0

The above rates are liable to alteration without further notice.

Season Tickets are issued to young persons as follows:—
At one-half of above adult rates
* 14 and under 16 years of age.
* 16 and under 18 years of age where holder's weekly earnings do not exceed 25/-.
At two-thirds of above adult rates
* 16 and under 18 years of age where holder's weekly earnings exceed 25/-.
Note:—Tickets issued for age groups marked * are valid for travel only between place of residence and educational or other training establishment or place of employment.

B.R. 35033/72-RV/L-Sept., 1961   G. Outram & Co. Ltd., Perth

DIESEL TRAIN SERVICES

AND

CHEAP TRAVEL FACILITIES

FROM AND TO

NORTH BERWICK and DREM

11th September, 1961 to 17th June, 1962
(or until further notice)

Further information can be supplied on application to stations, accredited Rail Ticket Agencies or J. K. Cumming, District Commercial Manager, 23 Waterloo Place, Edinburgh, Telephone No. WAVerley 2477.

TRAVEL BY TRAIN

Notice as to Conditions:—Tickets are issued subject to the British Transport Commission's published Regulations and Conditions applicable to British Railways, exhibited at their Stations or obtainable free of charge at station ticket offices.

TRAIN SERVICE
NORTH BERWICK AND DREM TO
EDINBURGH (Waverley), HAYMARKET,
PINKHILL AND CORSTORPHINE
MONDAYS TO SATURDAYS

North Berwick	Drem	Edin. (Wav.)	Hay-market	Pinkhill	Corstor-phine
leave	leave	arrive	arrive	arrive	arrive
a.m.	a.m.	a.m.	a.m.	a.m.	a.m.
6b59	7 16	7 45	7d59	8d 5	8d 7
7 30	7 39	8 11	8 20	8 26	8 28
7 53	8 2	8 29	8 39	8 45	8 47
—	8 10	8 46	9d 2	9d 9	9d11
8 15	8 56	9 2	9 9	9 11	
—	8 32	9 5	—	—	—
9 30	9 39	10 12	10 19	10 25	10 27
10 30	10 39	11 12	11 19	11 25	11 27
—	10 59	11 32	—	—	—
11 30	11 39	12 14p	12 20p	12 26p	12 28p
—	11 59	12 28	12d41	12d49	12d49
12 43p	12 52p	1 22	1 29	1 35	1 37
1 30	1 39	2 14	2 22	2 28	2 30
—	2s 3	2s36	—	—	—
2 39	2 48	3 18	3 27	3 33	3 35
3 45	3 54	4 30	4d39	4d45	4d47
—	4 6	4 41	—	—	—
4 41	4 50	5 25	5 42	5 48	5 50
5 33	5 42	6 12	6 20	6 26	6 28
6 40	6 49	7 22	7 30	—	7 37
7 30	7 40	8 13	8 20	—	8 27
8 30	8 39	9 10	9 18	—	9 25
9 32	9 41	10 11	10 22	—	10 29
10 50	10 59	11 26	—	—	—

For notes see end of section.

TRAIN SERVICE
CORSTORPHINE, PINKHILL, HAYMARKET
AND EDINBURGH (Waverley)
TO
DREM AND NORTH BERWICK
MONDAYS TO SATURDAYS

Corstor-phine	Pinkhill	Hay-market	Edin. (Wav.)	Drem	North Berwick
leave	leave	leave	leave	arrive	arrive
a.m	a.m.	a.m.	a.m.	a.m.	a.m.
—	—	—	6 35	7 12	7 21
—	—	—	6 50	7 29	—
8 17	8 19	8 25	8 30	9 6	9 15
—	—	—	8 46	9 25	—
9 10	9 12	9 18	9 24	10 0	10 9
—	—	—	10 20	10 59	—
10 22	10 24	10 30	10 35	11 8	11 17
11 15	11 17	11 23	11 28	12 6p	12 15p
—	—	—	12s 6p	12s45	—
12 11p	12 13p	12 19p	12 30	1 7	1 16
1 25	1 27	1 33	1 38	2 13	2 22
2 10	2 12	2 19	2 28	3 2	3 11
—	—	—	3e30	4e 1	—
3 20	3 22	3 28	3 40	4 13	4 22
—	—	—	3s 4E	4s26	—
—	—	—	4s 5	4e45	—
4 11	4 13	4 19	4 30	5 6	5 15
5e 5	5e 7	5e13	5e18	—	5s56
—	—	—	5 38	6 16	6b28
5 57	5 59	6 5	6 16	6 51	7 0
—	—	—	6 39	7 17	—
7 12	—	7 19	7 30	—	8 11
—	—	—	8 5	8 28	—
8 12	—	8 19	8 30	9 3	9 12
9 35	—	9 42	9 49	10 25	10 34
10 42	—	10 49	10 55	11 36	11 45

For notes see end of section.

SUNDAY SERVICES
(Commencing 3rd June, 1962)
between
NORTH BERWICK and EDINBURGH (Waverley)
HAYMARKET and CORSTORPHINE

North Berwick	Edinburgh (Waverley)	Haymarket	Corstor-phine
leave	arrive	arrive	arrive
a.m.	p.m.	p.m.	p.m.
11 35	12 11	12 16	12 23
p.m.			
12 45	1 21	1 26	1 33
1 40	2 16	2 22	2 29
4 40	5 16	5 24	5 31
5 40	6 16	6 24	6 31
6 40	7 16	7 24	7 31
7 40	8 16	8 22	8 29
8 40	9 16	9 22	9 29

Corstorphine	Haymarket	Edinburgh (Waverley)	North Berwick
leave	leave	leave	arrive
a.m.	a.m.	a.m.	a.m.
10 12	10 19	10 30	11 5
11 52	11 59	12 5	12 40
p.m.	p.m.	p.m.	p.m.
12 40	12 47	12 55	1 30
1 15	1 22	1 30	2 5
2 15	2 22	2 30	3 5
3 15	3 22	3 30	4 5
6 15	6 22	6 30	7 5
7 15	7 22	7 30	8 5

d Change at Edinburgh (Wav.). b Change at Drem.
e Saturdays excepted. s Saturdays only.
p p.m.

The zenith of diesel power – a BR local timetable leaflet from September 1961.

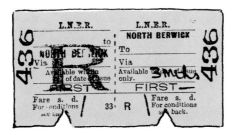

Table 16 **Weekd**

Edinburgh and North Berwick

Miles					SO	SO		SO	SX	SX	
—	EDINBURGH	d	07 22	08 08	12 10	13 20	14 15	15 15	17 26	18 20	20
9¼	PRESTONPANS	d	07 36	..	12 24	13 34	14 29	15 29	17 40	18 34	..
13¼	LONGNIDDRY	d	07 42	..	12 30	13 40	14 36	15 35	17 46	18 40	..
17¾	DREM	d	07 49	08 29	12 37	13 47	14 44	15 42	17 53	18 47	20
22¼	NORTH BERWICK	a	07 57	..	12 45	13 55	..	15 50	18 01	18 55	..

North Berwick and Edinburgh

Miles								SO	SO	SO	SX	S
—	NORTH BERWICK	d	07 31	..	08 07	..	..	12 50	14 30	16 05	18 13	19
4½	DREM	d	07 39	08 02	08 15	09 19	11 00	12 58	14 38	16 13	18 21	19
9½	LONGNIDDRY	d	07 47	08 10	08 23	..	..	13 06	14 46	16 21	18 29	19
13	PRESTONPANS	d	07 54	08 17	08 30	..	..	13 13	14 53	16 28	18 36	19
22¼	EDINBURGH	a	08 07	08 30	08 43	09 40	11 20	13 26	15 06	16 41	18 49	19

Heavy figures denote through carriages
Light figures denote connecting services
For general notes see page 2

The nadir of diesel power – the skeleton service operated from 4th January, 1970.

The first electric timetable, 8th July, 1991.

Table 238 **Mondays to Saturdays**

Edinburgh — North Berwick

For services to and from DUNBAR refer to Table 26

Miles														
0	**Haymarket** 225, 230, 241	d	07 40	08 35	and	16 35	17 05	17 35	18 08	19 35	21 05	23 05
1½	**Edinburgh 10** 225, 230, 241	d	07 45	08 40		16 40	17 10	17 40	18 13	19 40	21 10	23 10
6½	Musselburgh	d	07 51	08 46	every	16 46	17 17	17 47	18 19	19 46	21 16	23 16
11	Prestonpans	d	07 56	08 51		16 51	17 22	17 52	18 24	19 51	21 21	23 21
14½	Longniddry	d	08 01	08 56	hour until	16 56	17 28	17 58	18 29	19 56	21 26	23 26
19	Drem	d	08 07	09 02		17 02	17 33	18 03	18 35	20 02	21 32	23 32
23½	**North Berwick**	a	08 14	09 09		17 09	17 41	18 11	18 42	20 09	21 39	23 39

Sundays

Haymarket 225, 230, 241	d	10 35	12 35	14 35	16 35	18 35
Edinburgh 10 225, 230, 241	d	10 40	12 40	14 40	16 40	18 40
Musselburgh	d	10 46	12 46	14 46	16 46	18 46
Prestonpans	d	10 51	12 51	14 51	16 51	18 51
Longniddry	d	10 56	12 56	14 56	16 56	18 56
Drem	d	11 02	13 02	15 02	17 02	19 02
North Berwick	a	11 09	13 09	15 09	17 09	19 09

Mondays to Saturdays

Miles			SX A							SX	SO		
0	**North Berwick**	d	07 07	07 38	08 23		16 23	17 18	18 23	19 23	19 33	20 23	22 23
4½	Drem	d	07 14	07 45	08 30	and	16 30	17 25	18 30	19 30	19 40	20 30	22 30
9	Longniddry	d	07 21	07 52	08 36	every	16 36	17 31	18 36	19 36	19 46	20 36	22 36
12½	Prestonpans	d	07 26	07 57	08 41	hour until	16 41	17 36	18 41	19 41	19 51	20 41	22 41
17	Musselburgh	d	07 32	08 03	08 47		16 47	17 42	18 47	19 47	19 57	20 47	22 47
22½	**Edinburgh 10** 225, 230, 241	d	07 45	08 12	08 55		16 55	17 50	18 55	19 55	20 05	20 55	22a54
23½	**Haymarket** 225, 230, 241	a	07 48	08 16	08 59		16 59	17 54	18 59	19 59	20 09	20 59	

Sundays

North Berwick	d	11 23	13 23	15 23	17 23	19 23
Drem	d	11 30	13 30	15 30	17 30	19 30
Longniddry	d	11 36	13 36	15 36	17 36	19 36
Prestonpans	d	11 41	13 41	15 41	17 41	19 41
Musselburgh	d	11 47	13 47	15 47	17 47	19 47
Edinburgh 10 225, 230, 241	d	11 55	13 55	15 55	17 55	19 55
Haymarket 225, 230, 241	a	11 59	13 59	15 59	17 59	19 59

For general notes see front of timetable

A To Glasgow Queen Street (Table 228)

Appendix Seven

Statistics, Facts and Figures

(i) Returns from North Berwick Branch Stations for Half-Year Ending 31st January, 1856.

North Berwick

	Outwards (tons)	Inwards (tons)	Total (tons)	Receipts £	s.	d.
Goods:						
Merchandise	1,274	1,749	3,023	838	6	0
Minerals	44	880	924	126	4	1
Livestock				13	19	11
	1,318	2,629	3,947	978	10	0
Average per week:	50	101	152	37	8	10
Passengers:						
Total:	4,912			614	16	0
Average per week:	189			23	2	11

Dirleton

	Outwards (tons)	Inwards (tons)	Total (tons)	Receipts £	s.	d.
Goods:						
Merchandise	876	378	1,254	312	4	10
Minerals	Nil	496	496	76	4	1
Livestock				13	19	7
	876	874	1,750	401	18	6
Average per week:	34	34	67	15	9	2
Passengers:						
Total:	1,306			123	11	9
Average per week:	50			4	15	1

Drem

	Outwards (tons)	Inwards (tons)	Total (tons)	Receipts £	s.	d.
Goods:						
Merchandise	2,926	1,072	3,998	846	16	9
Minerals	Nil	147	147	23	18	8
Livestock				48	2	4
	2,926	1,219	4,145	918	17	9
Average per week:	112	46	158	34	9	6
Passengers:						
Total:	5,450			465	9	4
Average per week:	209			17	18	10

(ii) Traffic Statistics in selected years from 1900 to 1932.

Year	Station	Passrs	Revenue £	(1)	(2)	(3)	(4)	(5)	(6)
1900	ABERLADY	14,650	711	2,658	2,577	1,222	310	2,010	12
1910	,,	12,588	789	3,737	3,185	1,516	858	5,637	3
1925	,,	15,711	1,121	2,933	2,528	2,886	861	3,851	158
1900	DREM	17,368	1,260	8,511	2,181	2,056	2,009	8,763	38
1910	,,	12,405	1,408	13,127	3,722	1,743	2,024	11,474	6
1925	,,	20,033	2,199	6,387	6,316	1,736	2,143	19,040	251
1932	,,	15,414	2,001	3,063	397	722	–	9,408	–
1900	DIRLETON	7,825	342	4,370	1,224	963	1,223	6,675	5
1910	,,	7,275	360	5,567	1,305	732	1,516	7,616	72
1925	,,	6,452	359	3,884	707	1,087	1,468	5,904	36
1932	,,	1,559	97	1,673	145	1,855	–	6,981	–
1900	GULLANE	20,930	1,542	2,814	4,989	2,450	340	1,367	17
1910	,,	25,652	2,129	4,293	3,233	2,936	753	5,537	16
1925	,,	28,231	2,760	2,954	2,869	3,260	656	2,991	56
1932	,,	2,071	235	3,467	1,254	4,584	–	4,628	–
1900	L'NIDDRY	34,230	1,419	6,125	6,093	19,361	2,661	12,317	3
1910	,,	27,247	1,401	8,608	8,103	21,290	2,650	10,810	33
1900	N. BERWICK	58,278	6,024	9,734	10,483	10,723	750	1,991	111
1910	,,	52,613	7,673	9,868	7,706	12,676	941	2,563	416
1925	,,	93,965	13,754	6,052	5,259	13,454	1,069	3,243	293
1932	,,	55,829	7,713	3,029	2,303	107054	–	2,688	–

Notes:
(1) General goods (tons); (2) Minerals (tons); (3) Coal (tons); (4) Cattle (head);
(5) Sheep (head); (6) Pigs (head).

(iii) Train Passengers to/from Aberlady and Gullane 1924–1932.

Half Year Ending	ABERLADY	GULLANE
Dec. 1924	10,351	18,289
Jun. 1925	8.121	14,302
Dec. 1925	7,590	13,929
Jun. 1926	2,295	4,164
Dec. 1926	2,104	4,504
Jun. 1927	1,527	3,151
Dec. 1927	1,999	4,205
Jun. 1928	1,382	3,299
Dec. 1928	1,225	3,142
Jun. 1929	635	1,723
Dec. 1929	533	2,409
Jun. 1930	276	1,612
Dec. 1930	386	2,608
Jun. 1931	420	1,815
Dec. 1931	522	2,514
Jun. 1932	285	2,071

(iv) Traffic and Receipts, Gullane Branch, 1959.

The following come from the BR report on the possible closure of the branch and all figures relate to the year ending 31st May, 1959.

Aberlady Station

Goods forwarded and received:

	Forwarded		Received		Total	
	Tons	£	Tons	£	Tons	£
Goods	43	156	37	153	80	309
Minerals	1,457	1,565	216	147	1,673	1,712
Livestock	–	–	–	–	–	–
Coal	–	–	–	–	–	–
	1,500	1,721	253	300	1,753	2,021

Details:

	Forwarded			Received	
	Wagons	Tons		Wagons	Tons
Potatoes	7	43	Empty Boxes & Bags	7	13
Tar in O.T.W. (a)	3 (b)	30	Beet Pulp	12	79
Sugar Beet	141	1,419	Seed Wheat	1	12
Fertilisers	1 (c)	8	Fertilisers	14	147
			Various	2	2
	152	1,500		36	253

Notes:
(a) Own trader's wagon; (b) Not now passing – gas works closed; (c) Reconsigned.

Other income:

Camping Apartments	£141 10s. 0d.	
Pass. Fares from above	£149 8s. 6d.	
Pass. luggage in advance	£ 3 4s. 6d.	
		£294 3s. 0d.
Hire of Sacks		£110 8s. 11d.
		£404 11s. 11d.

Staff Costs:

Leading Porter at 162s. p.w.	£421 2s. 3d.
Payments to wife for cleaning camping accommodation	£ 3 4s. 0d.
NHI Contributions at 8s. 3d. p.w.	£ 21 9s. 0d.
	£445 15s. 0d.

Gullane Station

Goods forwarded and received:

	Forwarded		Received		Total	
	Tons	£	Tons	£	Tons	£
Goods	299	1,084	2	22	301	1,106
Minerals	2,815	2,541	18	79	2,393	2,620
Livestock	–	–	12	29	12	29
Coal	–	–	2,507	1,703	2,507	1,703
	2,614	3,625	2,599	1,833	5,213	5,458

Details:

	Forwarded		Received		
	Wagons	Tons		Wagons	Tons
Potatoes	48	299	Furniture	17	1
Sugar Beet	214	2,305	Agricultural Implements	1	1
Beet Pulp	1	10	Beet Pulp	9	50
			Fertilisers	3	28
			Livestock (61 cattle)	4	12
			Coal	219	2,507
	263	2,614		237	2,599

Other income:

Camping Apartments	£150 10s.	0d.
Pass. Fares from above	£129 4s.	0d.
Pass. luggage in advance	£ 3 11s.	6d.
	£283 5s.	6d.
	£204 10s.	0d.
Camping Coach		
Pass. Fares from above	£186 14s.	5d.
Pass. luggage in advance	£ 1 13s.	0d.
	£392 17s.	5d.
Hire of sacks	£146 1s.	7d.
Rents from coal merchants	£ 31 10s.	6d.
	£853 13s.	0d.

Staff Costs:

Leading Porter at 162s. p.w. plus enhancement	£426 19s.	9d.
Overtime	£ 3 6s.	3d.
Payments to wife for cleaning camping accommodation	£ 4 2s.	0d.
NHI Employer's contributions at 8s. 3d. p.w.	£ 21 9s.	0d.
	£455 16s.	0d.

Sources, Bibliography and Acknowledgements

Wherever possible the author has used primary and contemporary sources from the Scottish Record Office in Edinburgh, the National Railway Museum archives in York and from various other public and private collections. These have included the following: the Minute Books, correspondence, General Manager's files, miscellaneous documentation, public and working timetables, special traffic and signalling notices, general and sectional appendices and rule books of the North British Railway, the Aberlady, Gullane and North Berwick Railway, the LNER Southern Scottish Area and British Railways Scottish Region, Bradshaw's Guide, SMT timetables, the Session Papers, Minutes of Evidence in the Parliamentary Hearing on the AG&NBR Bill, Local Acts of Parliament, Railway Clearing House maps and handbooks, Board of Trade accident reports, Ordnance Survey maps, photographs, reminiscences of several members of the Gullane and Dirleton local history societies and reports in *The Scotsman, Haddingtonshire/East Lothian Courier, Haddingtonshire Advertiser, East Lothian News, LNER Magazine, Railway Magazine, Railways/Railway World, Modern Railways, Rail, Stephenson Locomotive Society Journal* and *The Railway Observer.*

The following bibliography relates to secondary sources which the author found useful and it should be emphasised that where these conflicted with primary sources, the latter have been preferred unless there was convincing evidence to the contrary.

Local History and Topography

New Statistical Account of Scotland: Haddingtonshire, (1839)
Prehistoric Annals of Scotland, Wilson, (1863)
North Berwick and its Vicinity, George Ferrier, (1875)
Sketch of the Life of George Hope, Hope, (1878)
Adventures at North Berwick, Aitken, (1880)
Thorough Guide to Scotland: The Lowlands, Baddeley, (1894)
Ordnance Gazetter of Scotland, (1895)
Guide to North Berwick, Wilson, (1907)
The Berwick and Lothian Coasts, Hannah, (1913)
Historical Guide to Aberlady, Reid, (1926)
Third Statistical Account of Scotland: East Lothian, (1953)
Portrait of the Lothians, Tranter, (1979)
The North Berwick Story, Walter Ferrier, (1980, 2nd ed. 1991)
Edwardian East Lothian: The Journeys of W.F. Jackson, (1989)

Railway Guides

Account of the North British Railway, Thompson, (1848)
Handbook of the Trip to Dirleton and North Berwick, (1850)
Through the Lothians, NBR, (1907)
North British Railway Official Tourist Guide, (1914)

Railway History

The North British Railway, Hamilton Ellis, (1955)
The North British Railway, Thomas, 2 vols. (1969, 1975)
Locomotives of the NBR 1846–1882, SLS, (1970)
Locomotives of the LNER, RCTS, various dates.
Coaching and Wagon Stock of the NBR, Watson, HMRS Journal.
The Romantic Rationalist, McAra, (1975) [James Gowans]

Other Transport

Steamers of the Forth, Brodie, (1976)
Railway Motor Buses and Bus Services in the British Isles, 1902–1933,
    Vol. I, Cummings, (1978)
From SMT to Eastern Scottish, Hunter, (1985)

Periodicals

The NBR in Haddingtonshire, Moffat, Railway Magazine, July 1912.
Scottish Coastal Lines of the LNER, Gairns, Railway Magazine, January 1926
Town Development and Transport: North Berwick and Haddington, Mac-
    gregor, Scottish Geographical Magazine, September 1949
Incidents in the Life of the Aberlady, Gullane and North Berwick Railway,
    Furley, Transactions of the East Lothian Antiquarian and Field Natu-
    ralists' Society, 1979
The Lothian Coast Express, Rankin, Railway World, May 1983
Two Scottish Railways, Marshall, HMRS Journal, October 1985

Maps

The course of both lines can be clearly traced on the Ordnance Survey
1:25,000 sheets NT 45/57 Haddington and NT 48/58/68 North Berwick.

Finally the author would like to thank all of those who have assisted him
in the research and writing of this book and those include the staff of the
Scottish Record Office, the staff of the National Library of Scotland and its
Map Library, the Edinburgh, North Berwick and Haddington public
libraries, the Royal Commission on Ancient and Historical Monuments of
Scotland, the National Railway Museum archives, Glasgow University
Archives, the Northern Lighthouse Board, the East Lothian Courier, the
British Railways Board and his publishers. In particular mention must be
made of the following individuals, the help of whom was invaluable: George
Barbour at the SRO; Michael Cox, Allan Campbell, Robert Hunter, James
Harrold and D. Marston of the Gullane and Dirleton Local History Groups;
Stewart Black, Bill Lynn, Marshall Shaw and Francis Voisey – all fellow
members of the North British Railway Study Group (membership of which is
a prerequisite for any serious study of the NBR and its constituents);
Margaret Furley; Mrs J. Carolan; Douglas Blades; John Beskow; the Earl of
Wemyss and March; Ed Nicoll and David Stirling for information on signal-

ling; Hamish Stevenson; George McLeod of Wilson S. Groat, photographers, Edinburgh; Stuart Sellar; Norman Turnbull; James McEwan; David Bayes; A.M. Jervis; Bruce Ellis for locating and allowing me to reproduce items from his late father's magnificent collection; Peter Marshall and David Neilson for providing the photographs from the AG&NBR shareholders' album of the Gullane line under construction; John Wilkie, photographer, Edinburgh for the Fidra Island picture; and to all the photographers or owners of collections who are individually credited, with apologies to any whose photographs or collections have been inadvertantly misdescribed. Uncredited items are from prints in the author's collection the provenance of which are, to him, unknown. He would be pleased to receive any additional information, corrections, criticisms or photographs via his publisher and would issue the usual caveat that, despite all the above help, all mistakes remain his. The author, however, undoubtedly owes his greatest debt to his son David whose enthusiasm for North Berwick, its beach and railway, provided the initial impetus for writing this book and whose company enlivened the many Saturday afternoons spent exploring the North Berwick and Gullane lines and the country through which they run.

Index